Big Questions and Where to Find

PURSUING THE

BEST

Forewords

When Carey Waldie first told me about his book *Pursuing the Best*, I was thrilled! I've spent years of ministry traveling around the country, speaking to young people about how to make right moral choices. And any resource that will help them in this process is a welcome sight!

Carey has such a heart for youth! I've seen his passion for ministry, for seeing young people come to Christ, and for helping them to deepen their faith. *Pursuing the Best* accomplishes just that. It's a well-organized, topical resource that deals with the tough issues facing today's youth. Whether a young person is asking the big questions about faith and religion, or just dealing with the daily struggles of relationships, school, and decisions for the future, they will find practical wisdom in the pages of this book.

In over 35 years of ministry, I've spoken to more than 7 million young people in at least 84 countries, including 700 university and college campuses. One of my greatest concerns about this generation of youth is that so many hold beliefs but not convictions. They may believe that certain things are right and certain things are wrong, but very few can tell you *why* it's right or wrong. And this leaves them open to changing their beliefs with every reasonable sounding argument that comes along.

In Ephesians 4:14-15, the apostle Paul wrote, "As a result, we are no longer to be children, tossed here and there by waves, and carried about by every wind of doctrine, by the trickery of men, by craftiness in deceitful scheming; but speaking the truth in love, we are to grow up in all aspects into Him, who is the head, even Christ" (NASB). Carey Waldie has put together a resource that speaks the truth in love, and will help young people "grow up" in their relationship with Christ to become wise, confident, and fruitful children of the King!

I pray this book will be an encouragement to you and your family as you seek His will in every area of your life.

Until the whole world hears,

Josh McDowell

Foreword by Josh McDowell

PURSUING THE BEST

The how's and why's of living life to the fullest

By Carey Waldie

The information in this book is protected material. However, there is nothing new under the sun. Any person may use any portion of this book that is not already copyrighted for non-profit use only. Don't bother writing for permission, go ahead and use it. It would be ethical to give credit however, so as to avoid plagiarism. Also remember, the more you copy from someone else, the less your own creativity can be developed. If you would like to use portions of this book for use in profit making materials such as books and periodicals, you must write for permission.

Scripture taken from Holy Bible New International Version. Copyright 1973, 1978,1984 By International Bible Society, used by permission Zondervan Publishing.

ISBN 0-9706478-0-8

Library of Congress Control Number: 2001126153

Printed in U.S.A. by Morris Publishing
3212 E. Hwy 30
Kearney, NE 68847
1-800-650-7888

For current information about all releases from Daniel Communications see the web site at: www.PursuingtheBest.com

A decade ago, one of God's choice prophetic leaders was given this astonishing word of the Lord for the time in which we now find ourselves: "I will change the expression of the Church in a single generation." In every area we do indeed see such changes for the honor of God taking place; in worship, in ministry, in approaches to outreach in missions and evangelism, church growth, fields of reconciliation and now the discipling of the emerging harvest.

This is a great example of a new breed of training manual designed for a whole new era of involvement by the followers of Jesus - aware, comprehensive and decidedly practical. At the edge of a new Millennium, *Pursuing the Best* aims at helping today's young leadership do just that - seek first the Kingdom in all that they do and bring honor to God in every area of life.

Winkie Pratney

What others are saying about this book.

"Pursuing the Best is a fantastic book on the basic issues of life. Parents, students, and leaders can all glean spiritual and practical insight into everyday questions. Carey has been able to combine into one book a wealth of resources. I give it my highest recommendations and know it will help you."

Rick Pasquale
Former Youth Director for the State of Michigan
Pastor of Jordan Assembly of God

"Great body of info! Very thorough and well presented, good detail."

Ron Heitman
Illinois State Youth Director

"As an editor and author of youth ministry materials as well as a former youth pastor, I have read hundreds of books ON youth ministry, but few geared to students themselves with the excellence of Pursuing the Best. Today's Christian students are needing help developing a holistic worldview.

Carey Waldie writes from experience, challenging young adults to come to their own conclusions about integrating their faith in Christ into their every day lives. Carey's thorough, Biblical approach to subjects as wide ranging as sex, attitude, work and adversity is refreshing."

Clint Bryan,
Pastor to singles and young couples, First Assembly of God
Rockford Illinois
Former editor, National Youth Department

PURSUING THE

BEST

PursuingtheBest.com

CONTENTS

READ THIS FIRST!

How to Use This Book

This book contains over 300 pages of the best wisdom for living that exists. We divide it into seven sections for seven important life categories. You can use this book in a number of ways:

- Go through the table of contents and pick out what interests you. Each section stands on its own. After the first section on faith, we use Biblical principles as our foundation. If you do not agree with these principles, read section one first.

- You can read the book straight through from cover to cover. Some sections contain technical and philosophical material. I wanted to include it because many of life's questions need deep technical answers. If you get bogged down in it, don't worry. When you need it, you will find the will to digest it.

- Keep this book as a reference. You will not need all of this wisdom at one time. As you grow, you will face decisions that will challenge you in all the areas we discuss. If you want to pursue the best life has to offer, read the book again - especially those sections that pertain to your situation.

- This book also lends itself to youth group study, young adult mentoring and sermon preparation. It has worked great for me in my ministry.

I did not invent the principles of this book. They existed long before me and will exist long after me. I merely collected, categorized and communicated them. I tried to give credit and gain permission wherever I could.

During an age where books written for young people drift toward the comic book style, I wanted to bring the reader up a notch. Some of these concepts will take thought and meditation and perhaps some extra study. I wrote it at a senior high level. If you don't understand a word, look it up and write the definition in the margin. If you dig, you will find treasure.

I owe a great debt to the people that have influenced me: Josh McDowell, Winkey Pratney, Ravi Zacharias, Rick Pasquale and others. You would do well to read their material. I recommend specific titles throughout this book.

My great thanks to my wife Kimberly, your contributions are numerous and often unnoticed. And thank you to my two really cool children, Callen and Madison. This book is really for you and for your generation.

God bless you in your Pursuit of the Best.

"We do however speak a message of wisdom among the mature, but not the wisdom of this age or of the rulers of this age, who are coming to nothing. No, we speak of God's secret wisdom, or a wisdom that has been hidden and that God destined for our glory before time began."
I Corinthians 2:6-7

"And this is my prayer; that your love may abound more and more in knowledge and depth of insight, so that you may be able to discern what is best and may be pure and blameless until the day of Christ."
Philippians 1:9-10

"And Jesus grew in wisdom and stature and in favor with God and man."
Luke 2:52

Thank you, God. I present this to you as an offering.

Sincerely,
Carey Waldie

WELCOME

Welcome to life. Is it what you expected? I'm excited and scared for you at the same time. Excited because life is thrilling. It's great to be able to make decisions, build relationships, earn and spend money, soak in the good times and persevere through the tough ones. But I'm scared for you because our culture has not prepared you well enough to experience life to its fullest. Before your conscience was fully formed, our culture bombarded you with a steady diet of fantasy and falsehood. Many of the decisions you will make (or already have made) will be based on these fallacies. What scares me is that fantasy has no power to sustain you in the real world.

You see, life doesn't care if your ready. Life doesn't care if you 'didn't know.' Life doesn't feel sorry for you if you've blown it and it doesn't rejoice with you if you've made it. What life does offer you, though, are a set of eternal principles, principles which govern the earth and everyone in it. Laws that you cannot break, you can only break yourself against them or better, use them as your life's foundation. These principles don't care about your skin color. They don't care about your stature, family history or ethnic background. They are for everyone.

These principles enable you to experience life at its ultimate. They make wise the simple and give joy to the heart. They keep you from the world's pitfalls and from unnecessary grief.

They are wisdom. Wisdom is more precious then gold, nothing you desire can compare with it. Wisdom is a tree of life to those who embrace her and those who lay hold of her will be blessed. Wisdom enables you to *live life skillfully*.

Wisdom has but one requirement before she will allow you to use her. *She must be pursued and attained.* You will not become skilled at living by accident. These concepts will not seek you out. Most people find too late that they missed out on some of life's potential. Study, watch, listen and work at sharpening your life skills. Wisdom will reward you - for she will allow you to use her.

There are seven crucial areas of life. The decisions you make while you are young in these areas will definitely affect your future. In this book, we have attempted to summarize for you the *best wisdom* available in these crucial areas. They are:

- Faith
- Attitude
- Authority
- How you handle Pleasure
- Relationships and Sex
- How you handle Adversity
- Production (education, work, time and money management)

Because the *best* is not normal, some of these concepts may seem a little different to you. None of them are easy. We did not want to place in front of you a mediocre standard. For if you secure it, you have only secured mediocrity. The world is never changed by mediocrity and it offers you no promise for living life to its fullest.

We have been thorough because you may follow the principles in six of the seven areas but if you blow it in just one of them, you will miss out on the best life has to offer. A little folly outweighs a lot of honor.

This book is for those who dare to pursue the best, for those who wish to leave average behind and soar to the heights they were created for. It is for those who are willing to pay the ultimate price for reaching the it - themselves. Life's definitive paradox is that we must give to get, forsake all to find all.

Both wisdom and folly call out to you in the streets. Which will you pursue?

I love you,
CW

FAITH

Of all the areas in your life, the area of your faith is by far the most important. It is the cornerstone of all other categories in your life. It answers life's biggest questions and provides a framework for your decisions. What you believe about where you came from, where you are going, what gives life meaning and how we should live will determine the course of your life.

The questions humanity must answer are these:

Is there a God?

Has he communicated with us?

Has he made a way for us to know him?

The answers to these questions are all "yes."

There is a God, a Heavenly Father, a Creator of all there is. He knows you, everything about you. He knows your thoughts and everything you have ever done in public and in private; and he *loves* you. His desire is that you would know him, that you would fulfill the destiny for which you were created - to have a love relationship with the living God.

In the next six chapters, you will discover:

- That it is impossible for the worlds to have come into existence without an intelligent designer.

- That this intelligent designer has communicated with the human race through the Bible.

- That a good God made a way for sinful man to have a relationship with him through the person of Jesus Christ.

When we read, study and think about God, it humbles the mind, while at the same time expanding it. He who often thinks of God, will have a larger mind than the man who simply plods around this narrow globe thinking only of himself.

CW

"SOME PEOPLE SAY THAT SCIENCE HAS BEEN
UNABLE TO PROVE THE EXISTENCE OF A DESIGNER.
THEY CHALLENGE SCIENCE TO PROVE THE
EXISTENCE OF GOD. BUT MUST WE LIGHT A CANDLE
TO SEE THE SUN?"
WERNER VON BRAUN

IS THERE A GOD?

A Fatherless World?

Bobby was a little boy who was born not knowing his father. He was two years old when he first started talking about him. He would cry out for him during times of distress. He asserted over and over that his daddy was real. He would stop in the middle of a game and shout, "Yes, I do have a daddy! I do have a daddy!" although no one had disputed it. [1] The world becomes a lonely place when children grow up without their fathers. How much more desolate an existence it would be if the world itself was fatherless.

Fathers do so many important things for their children. They offer fatherly protection, fatherly provision and nurturing. But one of the greatest things fathers offer their children is a sense of identity. Knowing your father answers the questions "Who am I?" and "From where have I come?" As human beings, we must answer these questions. But if we have no heavenly Father our sense of identity is lost even though our hearts may instinctively cry, "I do have a daddy! I do have a daddy!"

As you read this chapter, remember that God has placed enough evidence in the world around us to make it logical to believe in Him. He has, however, left out enough to keep us from believing in Him by logic alone. For without faith, it is impossible to please God and those who come to Him must believe that He exists and that He rewards those who diligently seek Him.

Lots of people say they will not believe in something unless it can be scientifically proven, that they don't have room for faith in their life. But that can never be true. Not only is it impossible to please God without faith, it is impossible to live without it. You don't wake up in the morning and verify the time on the alarm clock by three different sources. (While I was in college I snuck into my suite-mates' room and set all their clocks ahead one hour. They were sitting in their eight o'clock class at seven.) You don't test the chemical composition of the water in your shower to assure no harmful bacteria are present. (I also have had Montezuma's revenge while in Mexico.) You don't scientifically determine your toothpaste and

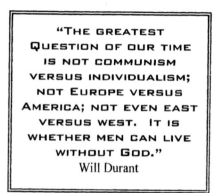

"THE GREATEST QUESTION OF OUR TIME IS NOT COMMUNISM VERSUS INDIVIDUALISM; NOT EUROPE VERSUS AMERICA; NOT EVEN EAST VERSUS WEST. IT IS WHETHER MEN CAN LIVE WITHOUT GOD."
Will Durant

mouthwash is safe and free from toxins, or that your little sister didn't put soap on your toothbrush.

If you didn't trust anything you would go insane from a chronic case of paranoia. Why don't we test everything? Because most things have proven themselves over time. God is the same way. He has placed enough in the world to make believing in Him reasonable, but left enough out to keep us from believing in Him by reason alone.

In this chapter we will discuss five reasons why God must exist:

- There is a creation, there must be a Creator
- The universe is fine-tuned for life
- Life is incredibly informed, organized and complex
- The failure of the theory of evolution
- An existence of an objective moral law

There is a Creation

Have you ever stopped to look at the universe on a cloudless night? What is more awe inspiring than that? Where did it all come from? Where did all the matter and energy in the universe originate? Did it come from nothing? Did it create itself from nothing? Where did your mind come from? The fact that you can read this and ponder it tells us there must be an intelligent mind above ours. If our minds are just products of random chance, then how do you know your thoughts aren't random? How do you know your thoughts inform you about reality? Nobody has ever observed a mind coming from mindlessness. The fact you have a mind is evidence that there must be an ultimate mind to give rise to the first human mind.

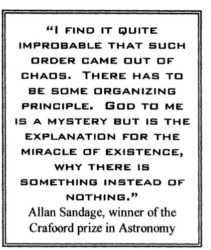

"I FIND IT QUITE IMPROBABLE THAT SUCH ORDER CAME OUT OF CHAOS. THERE HAS TO BE SOME ORGANIZING PRINCIPLE. GOD TO ME IS A MYSTERY BUT IS THE EXPLANATION FOR THE MIRACLE OF EXISTENCE, WHY THERE IS SOMETHING INSTEAD OF NOTHING."
Allan Sandage, winner of the Crafoord prize in Astronomy

How is it that we determine if something had a creator or not? What characteristics of an object point to it existing by virtue of an intelligent designer or simply by natural processes? How is it that we can tell a log jam from a beaver dam? What do we see that allows us to distinguish between a rock and an arrow-head, between a cliff and Mt. Rushmore? When we look at something and conclude that an intelligent designer created it we usually see at least two of four things:

- Complexity: The object is made of many different parts.
- Organization: Parts are placed in an order to benefit the whole.
- Information: The communication of data, knowledge or intelligence by the object or parts of the object.
- Purpose: The object serves a purpose (this is not always known).

When we look at life, do we find organized complexity? Of course we do. When we study natural processes, do we find that they can account for the organized, complex and purposeful variations of life? I'm afraid not.

The fact that there is an information packed, organized, complex creation points to an incredible, creative Designer.

> IT TURNS OUT THAT IF THE CONSTANTS OF NATURE-UNCHANGING NUMBERS LIKE THE STRENGTH OF GRAVITY, THE CHARGE OF AN ELECTRON AND THE MASS OF A PROTON- WERE THE TINIEST BIT DIFFERENT, THEN ATOMS WOULD NOT HOLD TOGETHER, STARS WOULD NOT BURN AND LIFE WOULD NEVER HAVE MADE AN APPEARANCE.
> "Science Finds God," *Newsweek* Magazine, July, 20 1998

The Universe is Fine-Tuned for Life

Scientific discoveries over the past century have shown us that the universe and our solar system were put together with such precision as to leave no doubt that only God could have done it.

Astrophysicist Hugh Ross lays out in his book *The Creator and the Cosmos* a number of examples of the precision required in order to have a universe that will support life.

Getting the Right Molecules

For life to be possible, more than forty different elements must be able to bond together to form molecules. Molecular bonding depends on two factors: the strength of the force of electromagnetism and the ratio of the mass of the electron to the mass of the proton.

If the electromagnetic force were significantly larger, atoms would hang on to electrons so tightly that no sharing of electrons with other atoms would be possible. But if the electromagnetic force were significantly weaker, atoms would not hang on to electrons at all, and molecules could not form.

If more than a few kinds of molecules are to exist, the electromagnetic force must be even more delicately balanced. The size and stability of electron shells around the nuclei of atoms depends on the ratio of the electron mass to proton mass. Unless this ratio is delicately balanced, the chemical bondings essential for life chemistry could never take place.

**If you slept through or have never taken physics or chemistry, it will serve you well to study or re-study these subjects. Just like a painting reveals much about an artist and a machine reveals much about its inventor, the sciences reveal much about the Creator. James Joule (known for Joules law) put it this way:

> "After the knowledge of, and obedience to, the will of God, the next aim must be to know something of his attributes of wisdom, power and goodness as evidenced by his handiwork. It is evident that an acquaintance with natural laws means no less than an acquaintanceship with the mind of God therein expressed."

Getting the Right Electrons

Not only must the forces inside the atom be perfectly balanced but the number of electrons that exist in the universe must be perfectly balanced. Unless the number of electrons is equivalent to the number of protons to an accuracy of one part in 10^{37} or better, electromagnetic forces in the universe would have so overcome the gravitational forces that galaxies, stars, and planets would never have formed.

Ross gives an idea of what the odds of one in 10^{37} looks like.

> "Cover the entire North American continent in dimes all the way up to the moon, a height of 239,000 miles. Next, pile dimes from here to the moon on a billion other continents the same size as North America.
>
> Paint one dime red and mix it into the billion piles of dimes. Blindfold a friend and ask him to pick out one dime. The odds that he will pick the red dime are one in

$10^{37}.$"[2]

The Expansion of the Universe

The first parameter of the universe to be measured was the universe's expansion rate. If the universe expanded too rapidly, matter would disperse so efficiently that none of it would clump enough to form galaxies. If no galaxies form, no stars will form. If no stars form, no planets form. You get the picture. On the other hand, if the universe expanded too slowly, matter would clump together too easily that all of it, the whole universe, would collapse on itself.

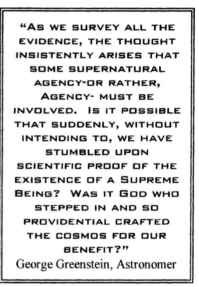

"AS WE SURVEY ALL THE EVIDENCE, THE THOUGHT INSISTENTLY ARISES THAT SOME SUPERNATURAL AGENCY-OR RATHER, AGENCY- MUST BE INVOLVED. IS IT POSSIBLE THAT SUDDENLY, WITHOUT INTENDING TO, WE HAVE STUMBLED UPON SCIENTIFIC PROOF OF THE EXISTENCE OF A SUPREME BEING? WAS IT GOD WHO STEPPED IN AND SO PROVIDENTIAL CRAFTED THE COSMOS FOR OUR BENEFIT?"
George Greenstein, Astronomer

What is truly amazing is how delicately balanced that expansion rate must be for life to exist. It cannot differ by more than one part in 10^{55} from the actual rate!

An analogy that still does not come close to describing the precarious nature of this balance would be a million pencils all simultaneously positioned upright on their points on a smooth glass surface with no external supports!

The Right Galaxy

Not all galaxies can foster life. It takes a spiral galaxy like our Milky Way to support life. Only 5% of the galaxies out there are spiral galaxies. The other 95% are either elliptical or irregular.

Elliptical galaxies do not allow for the formation of enough heavy elements. Large irregular galaxies have nuclei that spew out life-destroying radiation and material. Small irregular galaxies also do not have enough heavy elements to form life.

The Right Planet

For life molecules to exist and operate to sustain life an environment must exist where liquid water is stable. This means a planet cannot be too close or too far away from a star. In the case of earth, a change in the distance from the sun as small as 2% would rid the planet of all life.

The temperature of a planet and its surface gravity determine the escape velocity, a measure of which atmospheric gases dissipate to outer space and which are retained. For a planet to support life it must retain water vapor (molecular weight 18) while allowing molecules as heavy as methane (molecular weight 16) and ammonia (molecular weight 17) to dissipate. Therefore, a change in surface gravity or temperature of just a few percent will make the difference of life or death.

Any appreciable change in the rate of rotation of the earth would make life impossible. If the earth were to rotate at 1/10 its present rate, all plant life would either be burned during the day or be frozen at night.[3] If the planet were to speed up its rotation wind velocities would speed up to catastrophic levels. Jupiter rotates in about 10 hours and on a quiet day generates one thousand mile per hour winds.

The thickness of the earth's crust and depth of the oceans appear to be carefully designed. Increases in thickness or depth of only a few feet would so drastically alter the absorption of free oxygen and carbon dioxide that plant and animal life could not exist.

The Right Moon

The moon plays a critical role in our survival. Our moon stands unique in our solar system in that it is so large in relation to its host planet. Because it is large, it exerts a powerful gravitational pull on earth. Thanks to its gravity, the earth's coastal sea waters are cleansed and its nutrients are replenished. The moon is also the right distance from our planet, about 240,000 miles. If it orbited 20% closer, the continents would be flooded twice a day.

The scientific literature now includes discussion on over forty different characteristics that must be precisely tuned for life to exist. In 1966, the scientists studied only two; by the end of the '60s the list grew to eight. By the end of the '70s the list grew to twenty three; by the end of the '80s to thirty; up to the current list of more than forty and the list is growing.

With so many parameters finely tuned to support life, to believe that it all just happened without the aid of an incredible Designer is absurd. In light of this scientific research, Hugh Ross has calculated the probability of life forming naturally (without the aid of an intelligent Designer) on any planet; he concludes:

> "If past research is any indication, the number of parameters should increase and the probabilities decrease. Thus with considerable security, we can draw the conclusion that much fewer than a trillionth, of a trillionth, of a trillionth, of a trillionth of a percent of all stars could possibly possess, without divine intervention, a planet capable of sustaining advanced life. Considering that the observable universe contains less than a trillion galaxies, each averaging a hundred-billion stars, we can see that not even one planet would be expected, by natural processes alone, to possess the necessary conditions to sustain life."[4]

The Complexity of Life

To explain how we arrived here in this universe and on this planet as a result of purely unguided, natural processes, one would have to discount not only the probabilities against a just right universe and solar system but the probabilities of life just "happening." One hundred years ago, we had no idea of the complexity of life at its smallest level; so it was easy to dismiss it as just being "possible." Today, science has peered into the smallest workings of the cell and as life gave up her secrets, we discovered a staggering complexity with dozens, even hundreds of precisely tailored parts. As the number of required parts increases, the difficulty of gradually putting the system together skyrockets and the likelihood plummets.

Life is built upon information and a number of different building blocks. Much like a house, life has a blueprint (DNA), building materials (proteins-made of chains of amino acids) and machines like ribosomes that help put everything together. These molecular machines with thousands of interwoven components play together like a symphony. Let's look at some of these basic parts of life to give you an idea of why non-living chemicals could not become living just by chance, natural (unaided) processes.

A **protein** is a biological chain constructed of links of **amino acids**. Every one of us has tens of thousands of different kinds of proteins, each with a different type of three dimensional structure. There are seven major classes of proteins, some of which include structural proteins, storage proteins, defensive proteins, messenger proteins and transport proteins. Enzymes are also proteins that serve as chemical catalysts.

Amino acids do not just spontaneously join together to make proteins. The major problem in hooking amino acids together is that chemically, it involves the removal of a molecule of water for each amino acid joined together to the growing protein chain. Problem: the presence of water strongly inhibits amino acids from forming proteins. Because water is abundant on the earth, and amino acids dissolve readily in water, origin of life scientists are forced to propose some really unusual scenarios to get around the water problem. Also, many of the forces needed to put together some proteins (heat, electricity, or ultraviolet rays) destroy others. When amino acids are generated in experiments, many other destructive chemicals are also generated.

Each amino acid is made up of different atoms attached to one side of another atom. Depending on the side of the attachment, we call them left or right handed. One puzzling item to the naturalist is that when these amino acids are made in a lab there appears an equal distribution of left and right handed molecules. However, in life molecules all the acids (20) are left handed. If random chance produced them then why are they all left handed? Why not half left and half right? Try flipping a coin and getting all heads 20 times in a row to understand a small portion of this problem for those who wish to believe life generated itself. Is God left handed? My wife is. I wonder if left handed amino acids write funny? I wonder if they have to use those special made desks and if they have a hard time sitting next to people when they eat? I wonder if I have been writing too long? :)

Mathematicians work out what is called probability theory. We talked a little about this earlier when discussing the universe. Using probability theory, it is possible to tell just how likely it is for something to happen. Whenever we have a number of things that need to happen at the same time, we can use probability to find out how likely it is they will happen together by chance.

Scientists say that anything with a probability of 10^{50th} power is considered impossible. The average protein in the smallest known living thing has about 400 amino acid links. And for the most part, each amino acid link must be in the right order for that protein to function correctly. It is something like the alphabet. To make words, the letters must be in a particular order. What is the probability of just one protein, 400 units long happening by chance? The probability is one chance in 10 followed by 240 zeros or just plain impossible. But life is made up of much more than just proteins. It also contains...

DNA, the blueprint of life, stands as nothing short of a miracle. The information needed for building any life form is programmed in this molecule. In the human body, DNA contains the blueprint for all of our characteristics such as hair, skin, eyes, and height. DNA determines the arrangement for 206 bones, 600 muscles, 10,000 auditory nerve fibers, two million optic nerve fibers, 100 billion nerve cells, 400 billion feet of blood vessels and capillaries and much more.

In 1952, James Watson and Francis Crick discovered the shape of this molecule. They found that DNA is shaped like a twisted ladder with the rungs on the ladder consisting of groups of molecules called nucleotides because they are made of nucleic acids. The acids link together. One side of the ladder meets in the middle with the other much like a zipper. The scientific term for these rungs is "base pair." The sequence and order of the base pairs gives us the blue print for life.

The problem for those who think that only natural processes can account for life (naturalists) is that no processes can account for the enormous probabilities against nucleotides naturally coming together *in the right order*. Michael Behe, professor of micro-biology at Lehigh University, writes in his book *Darwin's Black Box*,

> "Imagining realistic scenarios by which natural processes may have made proteins on an early earth somewhere are extremely difficult. However, they are a walk in the park when compared to imagining the formation of nucleic acids such as DNA and RNA. The problem is that each nuecleotide "building block" is itself built up from several components, and the processes that form the components are chemically incompatible. If you put them in a bowl together in some soup arrangement, the natural forces that govern them cause them to destroy each other rather than build something."[5]

Chemistry, it seems, is not our ancestor but our problem. **There are no known natural forces that bring life chemicals together**. Years ago, molecular biophysicist Harold Morowitz calculated the odds of the simplest living cell reassembling itself under ideal natural conditions after breaking all the chemical bonds within it. He calculated the odds to be one chance in $10^{100,000,000,000}$.[6] Most of us cannot even begin to picture the speck of a chance so remote. With this the case, the myth of life coming together via natural processes persists in our textbooks and "scientific" documentaries. The PBS program NOVA started its *Miracle of Life* documentary with this script:

> "Four and a half billion years ago, the young planet Earth was a mass of cosmic dust and particles. It was almost completely engulfed by the shallow primordial seas. Powerful winds gathered random molecules from the atmosphere. Some were deposited in the seas. Tides and currents swept the molecules together. And somewhere in this ancient ocean the miracle of life began..."

That was as much of a fairy tale as you will ever read, yet you will find similar stories in practically all high school biology textbooks. Not only is life incredibly complex, but...

Life Contains Information

Imagine you and a friend were walking along a beach and you spotted a big heart scraped in the sand. Inside the heart you read the words, "I love Lucy." Your common sense tells you that someone who loves Lucy took the time to inscribe this information into the sand. You don't comment to your friend, "Wow, isn't that cool how the wind and the waves randomly ordered the sand to send us this message!" Whenever you find ordered information, **you assume an author**. Life is more than just matter. It is also information. The discovery of DNA and its written code has provided us with logical, empirical, irrefutable evidence for the divine authorship of life.

The amount of information programmed into a common bacteria cell would fill eight, 200 page books. The amount of information contained in the DNA of a small worm is about 168, 200 page books. The amount of material coded in the DNA of a human being would fill 10,000, 200 page books![7] Further, the capacity of DNA to store information vastly exceeds that of modern technology. Using DNA, the information needed to specify the design of all the species of organisms that have ever lived could be held in a teaspoon and there would still be room left over to hold all the information in every book ever written!

Scientists and astronomers have searched the universe for other signs of intelligence. This is formally called the SETI program or Search for Extra Terrestrial Intelligence. They have their receptors pointed to the heavens constantly listening. How will they know if they hear another form of intelligence communicating with them? They will tell you that if their sensors detect consistent non-random impulses or ordered information of some type, they can be sure that another intelligence is trying to communicate with them. Well, God has allowed us to crack the very code of life and we have 10,000, 200 page books staring us in the face but some people still conclude that there was no intelligence required to create us! This is blatant hypocrisy.

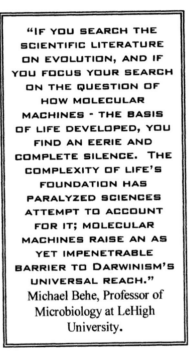

"IF YOU SEARCH THE SCIENTIFIC LITERATURE ON EVOLUTION, AND IF YOU FOCUS YOUR SEARCH ON THE QUESTION OF HOW MOLECULAR MACHINES - THE BASIS OF LIFE DEVELOPED, YOU FIND AN EERIE AND COMPLETE SILENCE. THE COMPLEXITY OF LIFE'S FOUNDATION HAS PARALYZED SCIENCES ATTEMPT TO ACCOUNT FOR IT; MOLECULAR MACHINES RAISE AN AS YET IMPENETRABLE BARRIER TO DARWINISM'S UNIVERSAL REACH."
Michael Behe, Professor of Microbiology at LeHigh University.

"SOME IDEAS ARE SO ABSURD, THAT ONLY AN
INTELLECTUAL WOULD BELIEVE THEM."
C.S. LEWIS

EVOLUTION AND EVIL

The Creation Myth of Evolution

A century and a half ago, Charles Darwin popularized a theory which proposed that all life evolved from simple to more and more complex beings. Long after his death, the theory of evolution has permeated almost every academic discipline, and even fostered its own religious philosophies. In reality, evolution is just a theory, and in light of scientific discoveries made during the past 50 years, it has proven to be a poor one at that. Nevertheless, people still cling to the faint hope that there needn't be a creator to explain the complexity and diversity of life, and evolution still has a stranglehold on academia.

There are many fatal flaws in the theory of evolution; however, we only have room to discuss a few. A good working knowledge of the theory of evolution and basic biology will help you understand these nuggets of truth. Your local biology textbook or most encyclopedia's will give you the foundation from which we will spring.

We will discuss the fatal flaws in two groups:
- Lack of a working mechanism
- The fossil record

Remember, the underlying question as we examine these areas is: "Can natural processes (wind, erosion, gravity, etc.)account for what we see or does the evidence point to an intelligent designer?"

Word-games

Before you start any discussion, it is best if you define your terms. Most evolutionists will mix the term "evolution" with the word "change." This may not seem so bad since one definition of evolution means change. But just because a species has undergone a change does not mean it evolved in the broader sense of the term.

It is commonly understood that animals have undergone change. Let's take the dog family. Through selective breeding dog enthusiasts have created new breeds, new types of dogs; change. This is through emphasizing (breeding for) certain traits already programmed in the genetic code (spots for a dalmation, speed for a greyhound, etc.) This is known as **variation within a type**. Some call this evolution. If you will listen closely, any time someone uses the term "observed evolution" they most always mean variation within a type. The dog is still a dog. The technical term for such a thing is micro-evolution. Micro-evolution or variation within families of plants and animals happens. It is observable. But it happens within strict, fixed limits. You can change the way a dog looks but you cannot change him into a bear. That would be called macro-evolution, change from one family type to another, reptile to bird for example.

In short, micro-evolution happens (Darwin's famous finches), macro-evolution doesn't.

The Missing Mechanism

We have already discussed some of the problems the naturalist must hurdle in order to reasonably believe that life arose from non-living chemicals without the aid of an intelligent designer. These problems are only the start of the biological mangling irrational science must do to prove simple life evolved into more complex life over time. There is no proven mechanism that changes one type of life form into another type of life form - no matter how much time you give it.

A high school textbook says this about how animals changed from simple to complex:

"...the theory of evolution accounts for the present variety of organisms and explains how changes have occurred in populations over time.... Natural selection appears to be the chief mechanism of evolutionary change."

Most texts define natural selection as: changes by mutation and genetic variation are selected by the environment. Over long periods of time these small changes add up to big changes.

The books give examples of birds with different kinds of beaks, dark and light moths (the famous peppered moth argument), fish, fruit flies and so on. All these examples have one thing in common: they are all variations *within* a type of animal. Change occurs, but within strict and fixed limits (micro-evolution). You can change a way a fruit fly looks but you can never change it into a grasshopper, and grasshoppers have always been grasshoppers.

I must admit there is a potential connection between observed natural selection within types and hypothetical evolution from one type to another. That connection is called **extrapolation** or following a trend to its conclusion. Scientists extrapolate from population records, for example, to predict changes in the world population. If world population growth continues at the rate observed in the '60s, statisticians say the world population by 2010 AD would be over 6.2 billion. Similarly, if natural selection continues over long periods of time, evolutionist say the same process that changes moths from dark to light variations will gradually change fish into a salamander or single celled bacteria into a jelly-fish.

Now, there is nothing wrong with the extrapolation principle, but there are things to watch for in practice. For example, simple extrapolation would suggest a population of a quadrillion people by 3000 AD. But of course, there will come a point when the earth is simply not big enough to support any more people. In other words, **there are limits, or boundary conditions, to logical extrapolation.**

Consider my running times. Starting at an embarrassing 12 minutes per mile, I knocked of a minute each week. I ran a mile in 11 minutes, then 10, then 9, 8, 7, 6, 5, 4, 3, 2, then on my twelfth week I broke the one minute barrier for the mile! Hooray for me! Now, as you well know, I would reach my limit long before the one-minute mile. This example raises an important point: No scientist would consider extrapolation without also considering the logical limits or boundary conditions of that extrapolation.

So what does the evidence suggest? Can natural selection form molecules to men or are there boundary conditions and logical limits to the amount of change that time, chance mutations, and natural selection produce?

The answer is: Natural selection *does* produce micro variations in living things. It *does not,* however, produce enough change to cause one type of animal to evolve into another because there are several factors which limit the amount of change that time, chance mutations, and natural selection can yield.[8]

- There is no known mechanism that adds genetic information
- Mutations are moving the wrong way

My Kingdom for a Mechanic!

Once a life form is established (impossible by natural processes), it must not only live but find a way to reproduce. After it has attained reproductive capability (no simple feat), if it plans to grow more complex it must find a way to add genetic information. To go from a molecule to man, you must move from 1600 pages of information to approximately 200,000 pages of information.

There is no known mechanism that can add that much genetic information. Some single celled life forms combine together to double their genetic information. This however, does not change the organisms. Mutations may add an extra base pair or two, but they mainly scramble existing information. Nobody has ever observed genetic information spontaneously generating. A theory of life must not only explain the origin of life chemicals but the origin of the information. Naturalism fails miserably here.

Lynn Margulis, professor of biology at the University of Massachusetts, during many of her public talks, asks molecular biologists in the audience to name a single, unambiguous example of the formation of a new species by the accumulation of mutations. Her challenge goes unmet.[9]

An award winning biochemist from Australia said in an interview with *Creation* magazine,

> "All you see in the lab is either gene duplications reshuffling existing genes, or defective genes with loss of information. That might help a bug to survive - say by not being able to bind to the drug as effectively. But you never see any new information arising in a cell.
>
> It's hard to see how any real scientist could believe that real information can arise just by itself, from nothing."[10]

Drive, Neutral, or Reverse?

A mutation is a genetic mistake. When DNA replicates itself, sometimes a mistake occurs and there is a change in the nucleotide sequence. This change in the genetic blueprint causes change in the structure itself. But mutations don't create, they corrupt. It's hard to explain evolution on the basis of mutations that are harmful at least 1000 times more often than they are helpful. It's not that beneficial mutations are theoretically impossible. Bacteria that lose the ability to digest certain sugars, for example, can regain that ability by mutation. That is no help to evolution since the bacterium is only back where it started - not forging ahead.

While giving a talk on creation vs. evolution in a local public high school, I pointed out something to them their textbook failed to show. Their biology book tried to justify mutation and natural selection as a valid mechanism for evolutionary change. They pointed out that over the "evolutionary life" of a species, there could conceivably be ten million beneficial mutations to help it climb out of the slime. What they failed to point out (and I did the math) was that for every theoretically beneficial mutation, according to their own figures, there would be 99,900 harmful or neutral mutations. That would be one step forward and 99,900 steps back, not out of the slime, but into extinction. This is not exactly a recipe for the upwardly mobile world of evolution.

> "...THERE HAS NEVER BEEN A CASE ESTABLISHED WHERE A LIVING ORGANISM WAS OBSERVED TO CHANGE INTO A BASICALLY DIFFERENT ORGANISM WITH DIFFERENT STRUCTURES. NO OBSERVED MUTATION HAS EVER BEEN DEMONSTRATED TO BE MORE BENEFICIAL TO THE OVERALL POPULATION OUT IN NATURE."
> Luther Sutherland
> *Darwin's Enigma*

Scientists have bred fruit flies in the laboratory for over 1000 generations. They subjected the flies to continual radiation bombardment to induce mutations. One would suppose that after these experiments some kind of evolutionary development would arise. Yet, while it has managed to produce a great variety of mutational disorders and deformities, no new evolutionary life forms have been produced; it is still a fruit fly.

R.B. Goldschmidt, after observing fruit flies for many years commented, "The changes were so hopelessly micro that if a thousand mutations were combined in one specimen, there would still be no new species."[11]

The fact is that mutations are mostly harmful and as time goes on, they impose an increasingly heavy genetic burden on a species. Nobody hopes to have a mutated child so that it will be on the cutting edge of human evolution. We have another name for mutations - birth defects. Human beings are subject to over 1500 mutational disorders. Genetic engineers are trying to fix our genetic code to keep us from the maladies that genetic mutations place on us.

The Fossil Record

Many say that we can't see evolution happen because it happens too slowly. If we can't observe evolution occurring now, it must have happened in the past. After all, that is what the fossil record shows us, right? Actually, the fossil record is one of evolution's great embarrassments. What we have found actually fits the creation model better than the evolutionary model.

If the evolution model is true, the fossil record would show a continuous, unbroken line of transitional forms from single celled life to mankind. If the creation model proves correct, we would find three things:

- sudden appearance of animal and plant life in the fossil record
- stasis: life forms appear in the fossil record similar to what we have today
- gaps between types of animals

We find exactly the above three clues in our fossil research.

Sudden Appearance

Scientists classify fossils into eras or time spans (however, they assume evolution to be true when they assemble the geologic column). When they look at the geologic column, they find nothing or one celled organisms for supposed eons of time. Then, in the Cambrian rock they find an explosion of very complicated life like fish, worms, snails, mollusks, and brachiopods. Scientist appropriately call this, "The Cambrian Explosion." It's as if life wasn't there and then it exploded on the scene. This fits the creation model perfectly. The Cambrian Explosion even made the cover of *Time* magazine in December of 1995 when they entitled the article, "When life exploded."

Walter Brown, PhD from Massachusetts Institute of Technology, says in his book *In the Beginning*,

> "There is a sudden explosion of complex species at the bottom of the fossil record. Complex species such as fish, worms, snails, corals, trilobites, jelly fish, sponges, mollusks, and brachiopods appear suddenly in the lowest (Cambrian) layers that contain multicellular life. These layers contain representatives of all plant and animal phyla, including flowering plants, vascular plants, and animals with backbones. Insects, a class comprising of four-fifths of all known animals (living and extinct), have no evolutionary ancestors. The fossil record does not support evolution."[12]

What is he saying? When we look in the fossil record for the ancestors of fish, we find fish fully formed. When we look in the fossil record for the ancestors of four-fifths of the living animals on earth, we find insects fully formed. Shrimp, squid, worms, snails and more, we find fully formed; just what the creation model would predict.

Stay Boy Stay

Many fossils of plants and animals found in the supposed oldest of rocks, when compared to their living counterparts, are found to be essentially the same. In fact, if there is a difference, most of the time the fossils show us larger and more advanced creatures than we see today!

In spite of presumed millions of years of evolution, the present animal and plant groups are essentially still the same as when they first appeared in the fossil record. This is called stasis.

True to this day are the words of Charles Darwin who conceded in his writings that, "Not one change of species into another is on record....we cannot prove that a single species has been changed."[13]

Animals have reproduced as what they were intended to be since they appeared on this planet - just as the creation model would predict.

In Search of the Missing Link

Charles Darwin claimed that if evolution is true the fossil record would show a continuum with no gaps but a continual evolution from one type of animal to another. That is not what he found, however. In fact, he found huge gaps in the fossil record. He blamed this on the incompleteness of the fossil record at the time. Surely, he thought, when we find more fossils we will find the links to fill in the gaps. He said,

> "The geological record is extremely imperfect and this fact
> will to a large extent explain why we do not find intermediate
> varieties connecting together all the extinct and existing
> forms of life by the finest graduated steps. He who rejects
> these views on the nature of the geological record will rightly
> reject my whole theory."[14]

Some say the fossil record is still incomplete. We are waiting for a more thorough catalog of fossils before we can say there are missing links between life forms. This is far from the case. During the 1970's, scientists started to realize that even after years of research all over the globe, the transitions did not exist.

A leading evolutionary geologist named David Raup wrote in the *Field Museum of Natural History Bulletin* in January of 1979 an article entitled *Conflicts Between Darwin and Paleontology*. In it he said,

> "We are now about 120 years after Darwin and the knowledge
> of the fossil record has been greatly expanded. We now have
> a quarter of a million fossil species but the situation hasn't
> changed much. The record of evolution is still surprisingly
> jerky and ironically, we have even fewer examples of
> evolutionary transition than we had in Darwin's day."

Steven J. Gould, a prominent paleontologist (fossil digger) at Harvard University said,

> "The extreme rarity of transitional forms in the fossil record persists as the trade secret of paleontology. The evolutionary trees that adorn our textbooks have data only at the tips and nodes of their branches, the rest is inference, however reasonable, not the evidence of fossils."[15]

The links between...

- dead matter to living matter
- one celled micro-organisms and complex invertebrates
- invertebrates and vertebrates
- fish to amphibians
- amphibians and reptiles
- reptiles and mammals

are still missing.

The gaps in the fossil record are absolutely incredible since evolutionists propose hundreds of millions of years of developmental time which would have involved billions perhaps trillions of transitional forms. Yet paleontologists have yet to find one undisputed transitional fossil. Each year a scientist or two puts forth evidence of a transitional form newly discovered. Keep in mind when you hear of these findings that one find of a transitional looking fossil by a paleontologist instantly makes him or her a celebrity. They find themselves in the news, on the cover of major magazines and a lifetime of funding for their excavations. So the pressure is intense to make some doubtful fossil into an ancestor or transitional fossil.

This happened in November of 1999. The headline in *National Geographic* read, "Feathers for T. Rex? New birdlike fossils are missing links in dinosaur evolution." Paleontologists reportedly found a conclusive link between birds and dinosaurs in the Liaoning Province of China. They named it Archaeoraptor liaoningensis. They hyped it to the max, complete with color pictures and models. They fooled some of the best fossil diggers in the world only to find that it was a hoax. Somebody put two fossils together.[16]

In his book *Defeating Darwinism by Opening Minds*, Philip Johnson makes an interesting point:

> "Human evolution is also an area where the evidence is most subject to subjective interpretation, because ape and human bones are relatively similar. If you find an ape or human bone that's a bit unusual, can you construe it as a piece of pre-human ancestor? If you can, and if the other experts will support you, your future may be a glorious one."[17]

Space does not permit me to go into much depth regarding specific fossils such as Archeopteryx or Neanderthal. For answers to specific challenges of the fossil record, I would recommend two books: *Bones of Contention* by Marvin Lubenow and *Evolution: The Fossils Still Say No* by Duane Gish.

Similarities Prove What?

One common argument for evolution is that organisms have similar structures and chemical compositions and that proves they must have a common ancestry. Books and documentaries show different animals and the similarities of their various body parts. But is similarity proof for a common ancestor? Not necessarily.

We can explain similarities just as easily - perhaps more logically - by using the creation model. We look at different houses and we find that they have amazing similarities. But these similarities are driven by similar needs. People have needs for preparing food so houses have kitchens. People need to sleep so houses have bedrooms. People need to stay dry and warm so houses have roofs and walls and heating systems.

Houses, and all created things for that matter, have **similar structures for similar functions.**

Living things have similar parts for similar purposes, similar chemical compounds to accomplish similar reactions needed for life functions. The Creator designed them to have similar structures for similar functions.

Jurassic Science

As people begin to think honestly about the theory of evolution they will see that new scientific discoveries are piling a mountain of evidence against it. Hopefully, those with an evolutionary bias, despite the evidence, will be seen for what they are: dinosaurs. For the science of the '50s cannot explain what we know of life into the new millennium.

If there is a God, why is there all of this evil?

On a trip to Poland, I visited the twin concentration camps of Auschwitz and Birkenau. The evils done there have defined the word since the 1940s. A common argument against the existence of God is if God existed, we wouldn't have all this evil. Because evil exists, God must not exist. The opposite is true, however. Because we can know what evil is, there must be a God. When I talk with people using this argument to disprove the existence of God the conversation usually goes similar to this.

"With all this evil in the world, there must not be a God."

"If you say evil exists than there must be such a thing as good, right?"

"Well, yeah."

"If good exists and evil exists then there must be an objective moral law by which we differentiate between good and evil, right?"

"Well, yeah."

"If a moral law exists so that we can tell the difference between good and evil, than logically it would follow that somewhere out there is a moral law-giver. That moral law-giver is God. He tells us what is right and what is wrong in accordance with his character and nature."

So you see that because evil exists and we can point to it and say "That is wrong" or "That is bad" actually supports the existence of God. For if there was no God then there would be no moral law-giver and no moral law for us to measure good and evil by. Actions would be mere actions devoid of any label. Torturing a baby would be just as valid as nurturing it. Killing somebody might actually improve my survival or position. We forget that natural selection inherently involves natural rejection, and the domination of the strong over the weak is at the heart of evolution. If no God exists and we arrived here by clawing our way to the top of the food chain then there is no rule of conduct that goes beyond the individual. Without a moral law-giver, right and wrong are self determined. Some individuals like to rape and murder some like to plant gardens. How can we say that one is wrong and one is right? Because we have a moral law to tell us the difference between right and wrong. A moral law must have its origination in a law-giver. There must be a God, something outside of ourselves to tell us right from wrong.

So the next time someone tries to point to the evil in the world and concludes that God does not exist because of it, make sure you help them. Point out that the fact that we can distinguish between good and evil logically points to a divine moral law-giver.

We will discuss more of the how's and why's of evil in the section on adversity.

Heavy Thinking

Just the thought of the existence of an eternal, all powerful being can be daunting. Finite minds cannot "hold" the infinite and not every question will be answered. But is it any less daunting to conceive of a universe that created itself out of hydrogen with the capacity to create man than it is to accept a Creator created man?

The only way human beings can be reasonably sure God exists is if He has revealed himself to us. And he has. He has revealed himself in our ability to think, an objective moral law, and a fine-tuned creation. But what 'god' has revealed himself? We narrow down the choices as God has also revealed himself via *revelation*. We will explore this in the next chapter.

For more on any of this, I highly recommend: *It Just Couldn't Happen by Chance*, by Lawrence Richards, *What is Creation Science*, from the Institute for Creation Research, *The Collapse of Evolution*, by Scott Huse, and *Darwin's Black Box* by Micheal Behe.

1. Freud, Anna and Burlingham, Dorothy. *Infants Without Families and Reports on the Hamstead Health Nurseries* 1939-1945. Hogarth Press. 1974, pg 635

2. Ross, Hugh, *The Creator and the Cosmos*, NavPress 1993, pg 115

3. Riegle, D.D., *Creation or Evolution*, Zondervan Publishing House, Grand Rapids, MI, 1971, pg 18

4. Ross, Hugh, *The Creator and the Cosmos*, Nav Press 1993, pg 143

5. Michael Behe, *Darwin's Black Box : A Biochemical Challenge to Evolution*, New York : Free Press, 1996, pg 171

6. Robert Shapiro, *Origins: A Skeptics Guide to the Creation of Life on Earth,* New York Summit Books, 1986, Pg 128

7. David Suzuki, *The Secret of Life,* pg 32

8. Morris and Parker, *What is Creation Science,* 1987, Institute for Creation Research, pg 84

9. Micheal Behe, *Darwin's Black Box : A Biochemical Challenge to Evolution*, New York: Free Press, 1996, pg 26

10. Answers in Genesis, *Creation Magazine*, posted on the web-site, October '99

11. Norman Macbeth, *Darwin Retried,* Boston: Gambit, 1971, pg 33

12. Walter Brown, *In the Beginning*, Center for Scientific Creation, 1986, pg 3

13. Francis Darwin, *The Life and Letters of Charles Darwin*, vol. 1 pg 210

14. Charles Darwin, *Origin of the Species*, pg 341-342

15. Steven J. Gould, "Evolutions Erratic Pace," *Natural History*, vol. 86, May 1977, pg 14

16. See Institute for Creation Research, *Impact* article, April 2000 and November, 1999 *National Geographic.* pg 99

17. Philip Johnson, Defeating Darwinism by Opening Minds, Intervarsity Press, 1997, pg 61

> **"MAN SHALL NOT LIVE BY BREAD ALONE, BUT BY EVERY WORD THAT COMES OUT OF THE MOUTH OF THE FATHER."**
> **JESUS CHRIST**

> **"MOST PEOPLE ARE BOTHERED BY THOSE PASSAGES OF SCRIPTURE THEY DO NOT UNDERSTAND, BUT THE PASSAGES THAT BOTHER ME ARE THOSE I _DO_ UNDERSTAND."**
> **MARK TWAIN**

THE LIGHTHOUSE

God has shown us himself, his character and his nature. He has given us the answers to life's largest and most important questions. He has shown us the big picture and pulled back the curtain a little to help us through hard times. Where has he done this? In the Bible.

What is the Bible? Is it just another ancient book? Some think it is the Word of God. Some think it *contains* the Word of God; that certain parts of the Bible are divine and true, but other parts are clearly human and error. They feel the Bible is a victim of the times. They say that many of the legends, myths, and false beliefs about science were incorporated into the Bible. They argue that since these are not inspired of God they must be rejected by *enlightened* men as remnants of a primitive mentality unworthy of Christian belief.

Don't be fooled, the Bible is a supernatural book. It is a book from God, about God, with one particular purpose: to define and communicate himself and his purpose to humanity. It is the story of his love for people. Its central figure is Jesus Christ, God in the robe of man. It is the record of his eternal existence, birth, life, death, and resurrection.

The Bible message is stranger than science fiction: The God who spun worlds into existence has visited our earth to show us the way to heaven.

Frank Koch gave us his account of a near disaster at sea in

Proceedings magazine:

> Two battleships assigned to the training squadron had been at sea on maneuvers in heavy weather for several days. I was serving on the lead battleship and was on watch on the bridge as night fell. The visibility was poor with patchy fog, so the captain remained on the bridge keeping and eye on all activities. Shortly after dark, the lookout on the wing of the bridge reported, "Light, bearing on the starboard bow."
>
> "Is it steady or moving astern?" the captain called out. The lookout replied, "Steady, captain," which meant we were on a dangerous collision course with that ship.
>
> The captain then called to the signalman, "Signal that ship: We are on a collision course, advise you change course 20 degrees." Back came a signal, "Advisable for you to change course 20 degrees." The captain said, "Send, I'm a captain, change course 20 degrees." "I'm a seaman second class," came the reply. "You had better change course 20 degrees."
>
> By that time the captain was furious. He spat out, "Send, I'm a U.S. Naval battleship. Change course 20 degrees." Back came the flashing light, "I'm a lighthouse."
>
> We changed course.

Many people, Christians included, want to chart their own course in life. They do so neglecting the principles taught in God's Word. I don't care how big you think your ship is, if you navigate your life contrary to the Word of God you should not be surprised at the wreckage. Henry Ward Beecher (brother of Harriet Beecher Stowe, author of *Uncle Tom's Cabin*) put it this way:

> "Sink the Bible to the bottom of the ocean, and still man's obligations to God would be unchanged. He would have the same path to tread, only his lamp and his guide would be gone; the same voyage to make, but his chart and

compass would be overboard."

The Bible is no ordinary book. It is strangely different because it was written by men who listened to the voice of God. The words they wrote were more than human. They live like a fire for each new generation, your generation. If you dare to become the person God has called you to be, you must lay hold of it and let it chart your destiny.

How on Earth?

The Bible is your absolute foundation life itself. It gives you the answers to the big questions in life. It tells you where you came from and where your going. But where did the Bible come from? How did we get our Bible? Who put the Bible together and how did they decide what to let in and what to leave out? Most people are clueless about how we got our Bible. The next few paragraphs are a brief, (very brief*), overview of how the Bible came to be.

The Bible did not originate with any man; it started within the heart of God. The Bible was *inspired* by God. The writers of scripture continuously claim their message was not human opinion, but divine revelation. Genesis opens with the words, "And God said..." nine times in the first chapter. "The Lord spoke..." appears 560 times in the first five Bible books. At least 3800 times in scripture, writers declared their message divine in origin.

The process by which God communicates his authoritative message to man is described in many ways. Paul wrote to Timothy, "All scripture is inspired by God and is profitable for teaching, for reproof, for correction, and for training in righteousness" (2 Timothy 3:16). The word used for our English word *inspired* here literally means "God breathed" (Gk. theopneustos). A kindred passage in 1 Corinthians 2:13 stresses the same point. "And we impart this," wrote Paul, "in words not taught by human wisdom but taught by the Spirit, expressing spiritual truths in spiritual words."

The second great passage in the New Testament on the inspiration of the Bible is 2 Peter 1:21. "No prophecy ever came by the impulse of man, but men moved by the Holy Spirit spoke from God." In other words, the prophets were men whose messages did not originate with their own desires or inspiration but were "Spirit-moved."

I think it's important to point out that the people who wrote the Bible were more than recording secretaries or dictation machines. They wrote within their own personalities, styles and vocabularies. God used their personalities to convey His ideas.

I also think it's important to point out that the inspiration and authority of the Bible does not automatically extend to every copy and translation of the Bible. Only the original manuscripts, called *autographs*, were inspired. Mistakes and changes made in copy and translation cannot claim this original inspiration. Second Kings 8:26, for example, says that Ahaziah was twenty-two years old at his coronation, whereas 2 Chronicles 22:2 says he was forty-two years old. Both cannot be correct. Only the original and not the scribal error is authoritative.

Some say because of human error in transcribing the Bible from one document to another, the Bible we have today is unreliable. While there are some minor transcription errors and parts of the Bible where translation is ambiguous, history has given us plenty of evidence to show that the Bible we have in our hands today is still, in essence, what God intended us to have.

Who Was That Masked Man?

So who were these guys that God picked and how do we know they *really* heard from God? After all, haven't many men said, "God told me to tell you...." How did the people of the day know that these men had the real deal? God had his criteria by which people could know who was real and who was counterfeit.

The men who penned the **Old Testament** were designated prophet by either title or function. A prophet is someone who hears from God and speaks to man.

The people detected false prophets by their false prophecies and by the lack of miraculous confirmation. Deuteronomy declares, "When a prophet speaks in the name of the Lord, if the word does not come true, that is a word which the Lord has not spoken" (18:22). Whenever there was any other question of a prophet's validity, God seemed to have a knack for designing his own supernatural tests to show who was money and who was not.

- The earth opened up and swallowed Korah and those with him who contested Moses' call (Numbers 26:10).
- God vindicated Elijah over the prophets of Baal by fire from heaven (1Kings 18:38).
- The Egyptian magicians finally conceded of Moses' miracles, "This is the finger of God" (Exodus 8:19).

Not all of the writers were prophets by training, but all possessed a prophetic gift. Amos confessed, " I am no prophet, nor a prophet's son....And the Lord said to me, 'Go prophesy to my people Israel.' David was a king by profession, but he said 'The Spirit of the Lord speaks to me, his word is upon my tongue' (2 Samuel 23:2).

According to Ezekiel 13:9, there was an official register of the true prophets of God. Anyone who uttered false prophecies was excluded from the official roll. The people sanctioned only these true prophets of God and the writings of these prophets were kept among the inspired books.

As these men of God heard from God and wrote God's words, they compiled them into books and kept them as "The sacred writings." Starting with Moses there was a prophetic lineage, each adding his book to the prophetic predecessors. By the time Babylon invaded Judah in 605 B.C. (see your history books), Daniel referred to this collection of prophetic writings as the "books" or "scriptures" (Daniel 9:2). From the earliest known times, all thirty-nine books of the Old Testament constituted these prophetic writings.

People had five basic criteria for determining if a book was divinely inspired and thus should be included in the sacred writings:

- Is the book *authoritative* - does it claim to be of God?

- Is it *prophetic* - was it written by a prophet of God?
- Is it *authentic* - does it tell the truth about God and man?
- Is the book *dynamic* - does it possess life transforming power?
- Is the book *received* - accepted by the people of God?

The apostles and prophets of the **New Testament** did not hesitate to classify their writings as inspired along with the Old Testament. Their books were revered, collected, and circulated in the early church as sacred scripture. The early church fathers - guys like Paul, Peter, Luke, Ignatius, and Polycarp considered the New Testament books divinely inspired.

Where the rubber meets the road.

After studying where the Bible originated, all great men of God conclude that Spirit-moved men wrote God breathed words which are divinely authoritative for the human race. God's people scrutinized collected and preserved these books through history to give us our Bible.

*For much more on this all-important topic I would recommend "*From God to Us*" by Norm Geisler and William Nix.*

> ### "I WILL GO THROUGH THE FOREST OF THE SCRIPTURES AND GIRDLE ALL THE TREES, SO THAT IN 100 YEARS CHRISTIANITY WILL BE BUT A VANISHING MEMORY."
> #### VOLTAIRE

(Fifty years after Voltaire's death in 1778 the British and foreign Bible society used his house and his printing press to print Bibles.)

INSPIRED?

I was listening to a radio call-in program and the theme was seven reasons why you can trust the Bible. A man called in who said he used to be a Christian but now he doesn't even believe in God. He railed against the Bible and any belief in it. There are a number of reasons why people reject the Bible. Some are afraid they will meet the author; and they are not ready. They are like the thief who can't find a police officer. To some, any message that threatens their autonomy is automatically rejected, no matter what it is.

Nevertheless, the question must be asked, "Is the Bible worthy of its claimed status?" In this section, we will examine a small portion of the evidence for the divine inspiration of the Bible.

Earlier we learned what kind of men wrote the books of the Bible and how God's people compiled the various inspired works. But what about after they were written? Are the manuscripts that we have today a true representation of what the authors penned years ago? Is there anything in the Bible itself that points to the supernatural? Are there any reliable historical sources outside of the Bible which give it credibility?

Scholars use certain rules to judge the authenticity of a certain document. When we test the Biblical manuscripts using these tests we find they pass with flying colors, far better than any other classical document, better than even some of Shakespeare's writings.

Josh McDowell recounts the following story in his book *A Ready Defense*, that occurred while presenting to a college history class. It started when Josh said confidently that he believed there was more evidence for the reliability of the New Testament than for almost any ten pieces of classical literature put together. Quoting now from his book...

> The professor sat over in the corner snickering, as if to say, "Oh, gee - come on."
> I said, "What are you snickering about?"
> He said, "The audacity to make the statement in a history class that the New Testament is reliable. That's ridiculous."
> Josh replied, "Tell me, sir, as a historian, where are the tests that you apply to any piece of literature of history to determine if it's accurate or reliable?"

The amazing thing was he didn't have any tests to apply. Josh answered, "I have some tests."

Josh uses the same tests established by military historian C. Sanders in his book entitled *Introduction to Research in English Literature History.*

The Biblical documents should be tested by the same criteria used on all historical documents. Mr. Sanders lists and explains the basic tests:

- The bibliographical test; an examination of the transfer of the original documents to what we have today.
- The external evidence test; are there any reliable historical sources that confirm the accuracy and reliability of the document in question?
- The internal evidence test; is there anything in the document itself that would disprove it?[1]

A ***manuscript*** is a handwritten copy of a document in the original language.

The Bibliographical Test:

This test seeks to determine how reliable the copies are on the basis of two criteria:

- how many manuscripts exist
- what is the time span between the original manuscript (remember this is called an ***autograph***) and the earliest existing copy.

There are more than 5300 known Greek manuscripts of the New Testament. Add over 10,000 Latin Vulgate and at least 9300 other early versions and we have more that 24,000 hand written copies of portions of the New Testament in existence.

No other ancient document even begins to approach such numbers. In comparison, the *Iliad* by Homer, common in high school literature classes is second with only 643 manuscripts that still survive.

Sir Frederick G. Kenyon, who was the director and principle librarian of the British Museum, and second to none in issuing statements about manuscripts, says,

> "Besides number, the manuscripts of the New Testament differ from those of the classical authors, and this time and difference is clear gain. In no other case is the interval of time between composition of the book and the date of the earliest existing manuscripts so short as in that of the New Testament. The books of the New Testament were written in the latter part of the first century; the earliest existing manuscripts (trifling scraps excepted) are of the fourth century - say from 250 to 300 years later.
>
> This may sound like a considerable interval, but it is nothing to that which parts most of the great classical authors from their earliest manuscripts. We believe that we have in all essentials an accurate text of the seven existent plays of Sophocles; yet the earliest substantial manuscript upon which it is based was written more than 1400 years after the poets death."[2]

F. F. Bruce in *The New Testament Documents* vividly pictures the comparison between the New Testament and ancient historical writings:

> Perhaps we can appreciate how wealthy the New Testament is in manuscript attestation if we compare the textual material for other ancient historical works. For Caesar's Gallic Wars (composed between 58 and 50 B.C.) there are several existent manuscripts, but only nine or ten are good, and the oldest is some 900 years later than Caesar's day. Of the 142 books of the Roman history of Livy (59 B.C. - A.D. 17), only 35 survive; these are known to us from not more than 20 manuscripts of any consequence, only one of which, and that containing fragments of Books III and VI, is as old as the fourth century. Of the 14 books of the Histories of Tacitus (A.D. 100) only four and a half survive; of the 16 books of his Annals, 10 survive in full and two in part. The text of these existent portions of his two great historical works depends entirely on two manuscripts, one of the ninth century and one of the eleventh.[3]

Use this chart to apply the bibliographical test to the New Testament. If critics accept the other ancient works (which they do) they must then accept the New Testament manuscripts.

Author	When written	Earliest copy	Time span	No. of copies
Caesar	100-44 B.C.	A.D. 900	1000 yrs.	10
Aristotle	384 - 322 B.C.	A.D. 1100	1400 yrs	49
Plato (Tetrologies)	427 -347 B.C.	A.D. 900	1200 yrs	7
Homer (Iliad)	900 B.C.	400 B.C.	500 yrs	643
New Testament	A.D. 40 - 100	A. D. 125	25 yrs	over 24,000

Hundreds of volumes of books are written by scholars from all around the globe attesting to the reliability of the New Testament documents. We can be assured that what those men wrote has been accurately transmitted to us today.

Remember the party game called telephone? Someone starts off by saying a phrase like "Marcy would like a motorcycle" to someone in the circle. The phrase circulates around the room and the last person tells what they think the phrase is. It usually comes out something like, "My mother could find a bearded man."

A common criticism of the Bible is that because it was hand copied by men, what we have now is not accurate to the original and cannot be trusted. Let's look at the evidence for the claim that what we have now *is* reliable and accurate to the original.

Over the last four thousand years, Jewish scribes, and later Christian scribes, were very careful to correctly copy and transmit the original manuscripts of the sacred Scriptures without any significant error. Here are some of the requirements for the copyists:

- Each copy had to be made on a brand new writing surface and had to be prepared a specific way.

- Each copy had to be written in a certain number of columns of thirty letter width, with certain number of lines to each column.

- Each copy had to be made from an authenticated original.

- Not even the tiniest letter could be written from memory. Every *letter* was copied from the original.

- No letter could connect or overlap with another letter. The distance between each letter was measured by a single hair or thread.

- Every letter of every page was counted and compared to the original. The number of times each letter of the alphabet occurred in a book was counted and compared against the original.

- The middle letter of the first five books of the Old Testament and the middle letter of the entire Hebrew Bible were computed and indicated in the text. If one of these calculations was incorrect, they destroyed the copy.

As proof of the incredible accuracy of this method of transmission through the centuries, consider the Masoretic and Yemenite translations of the first five books of the Old Testament, called the Torah. Over a thousand years ago, Yemenite Jews were separated from their brother Jews in the Middle East and Europe. Despite separate transmissions and copying of their manuscripts, a thousand years later, only *nine* Hebrew letters, out of some 304,805 letters in the Yemenite manuscript differ from the accepted Hebrew Masoretic text of the Torah. Not one of these variant letters changes the meaning of a significant word. This astonishing fact proves how exceptionally careful, over a thousand year period, Jewish scribes were in copying their original documents.[4]

Archeological finds like the Dead Sea Scrolls have also done much to confirm the reliability of the Old Testament.[5]

The External Evidence Test

We just took a good look at how the Bible sails through the bibliographical test. Now let's move on to the external evidence test. Remember that this test looks at any reliable historical evidence *outside* of the Bible that validates or invalidates its claims.

How does the Bible stand under this type of scrutiny? One of our main views into the past is through a field of study called archeology. These are the people that spend their days digging and probing the dust of the past looking for insights into ancient cultures, treasure, or the next find to keep them on the grant gravy train. Before Indiana Jones and Jurassic Park, I was digging craters in my back yard looking for Native American artifacts or the newest dinosaur discovery. Every hill in the woods near my house *had* to be an ancient Indian burial ground. I just *knew* it. As I grew and learned more about the field of archeology and how patient, meticulous and detail oriented archeologists had to be, I realized I wasn't wired for such an occupation.

Fortunately for us, many world class archeologists and historians have undertaken the huge task to dig, sift and analyze tons of external evidence regarding the validity of the Biblical record; especially as it relates to its historical accuracy. For if the Bibles claims are not historically accurate, then its Divine inspiration and the men God chose to write the scriptures would be cast into doubt.

The English scholar, William Ramsay, traveled as a young man to Asia Minor over a century ago for the sole purpose of *disproving* the

 Bible's history as described by Luke in his Gospel and the book of Acts. Ramsay and his professors were convinced that the New Testament was full of mistakes. He believed that Luke could not be correct in his history of Christ or in his account of the first decades of the church. Dr. Ramsay began to dig in the ancient ruins of sites throughout Greece and Asia Minor. He searched for ancient names, boundary markers, and other finds that would conclusively prove that Luke had invented his history of Christ and his church. To his amazement and dismay, William Ramsay discovered that the statements of the New Testament Scriptures were ***accurate in the smallest detail.***

Finally, Dr. Ramsay was convinced by the overwhelming evidence proving the Bible's accuracy. As a result, he accepted Jesus Christ as his personal Savior. He became both a Christian and a great biblical scholar!

Dr. Nelson Glueck, arguably the most outstanding Jewish archeologist of this century, wrote in his book *Rivers in the Desert* this fascinating statement: "It may be stated categorically that no archaeological discovery has ever controverted a Biblical reference. Scores of archaeological findings have been made which confirm in clear outline or in exact detail historical statements in the Bible."

Dr. Robert Dick Wilson, formerly professor of Semitic philology at Princeton Theological Seminary, made the following comment: "After forty-five years of scholarly research in biblical textual studies and in language study, I have come now to the conviction that no man knows enough to assail the truthfulness of the Old Testament. When there is sufficient evidence to make an investigation, *the statement of the Bible, in the original text, has stood the test.* "[6] (Emphasis mine)

> "BELIEVERS AROUND THE WORLD ARE ATTUNED MORE THAN EVER TO THE SIGNIFICANCE OF ARCHAEOLOGICAL FINDS OF THE PAST CENTURY, AND ESPECIALLY THE PAST FEW YEARS, IN ESTABLISHING THE REALITY OF THE EVENTS UNDERLYING THEIR BELIEFS."
> *Time* Magazine December 18, 1995

Flavius Josephus was a Jewish historian writing accounts of Jewish history for the Romans. We read in his work called *The Antiquities of the Jews,*

> Now there was about this time Jesus, a wise man, if it be lawful to call him a man; for he was a doer of wonderful works, a teacher of such men as receive the truth with pleasure. He drew over to him both many of the Jews, and many of the Gentiles. He was the Christ. And when Pilate, at the suggestion of the principal men among us, had condemned him to the cross, those that loved him at the first did not forsake him; for he appeared to them alive again the third day; as the divine prophets had foretold these and ten thousand other wonderful things concerning him. And the tribe of Christians, so named from him, are not extinct at this day.[7]

Here is a man who was not a follower of Christ, living during the times of the Early Church, an historian by profession, *giving us an account that exactly matches that of the New Testament;* very solid external evidence.

Let's take a quick look into a handful of the recent discoveries that add weight to the historical accuracy of the Bible as reported by the December 18, 1995 issue of *Time* Magazine.

- In 1990, Harvard researchers working in the ancient city of Ashkelon, north of the Gaza strip, unearthed a small, silver-plated bronze calf figurine reminiscent of the huge golden calf mentioned in the Book of Exodus.

- In 1986, scholars identified an ancient seal that had belonged to Baruch, son of Neriah, a scribe who recorded the prophecies of Jeremiah in 587 B.C.

- A team of archaeologists uncovered a 9th century B.C. inscription at an ancient mound called Tel Dan, in the north of Israel, in 1993. Words carved into a chunk of basalt refer to the "House of David" and "King of Israel." It is the first time the Jewish monarch's name has been found outside the Bible and appears to prove that he was more than a mere legend.

Archaeologists working in the Nile Delta unearthed the remains of a house that is completely different from the Egyptian houses around it. This house follows the pattern of houses that the Israelites later built in Canaan. In fact, the floor layout is know as the "Israelite-type house." And this Israelite house was discovered in Tell el-Dab'a - the location of the biblical city of Ra'amses. That's where, according to the biblical text, the Israelites lived in slavery to Pharaoh.

That's confirmation of the biblical account of the Israelites' time in Egypt.

Here's one more example of the reliability of the Biblical account. The Bible says that on their way out of Egypt, the Israelites camped at the ancient city of Dibon. Skeptics insist that Dibon didn't even exist at the time of the Exodus. But Archaeologists kept looking and discovered inscriptions in Egypt, at the temple of Amon at Karnak, describing an ancient trade route from Egypt into Palestine. One of the cities listed as lying along this route at the time of the Exodus is none other than Dibon.

This shows that the Israelites actually followed a heavily trafficked Egyptian road that did exist at the time of the Exodus. Hershel Shanks, writing in *Biblical Archaeology Review*, concludes that, "We have irrefutable primary historical evidence for the existence of the city of Dibon" in the time of the Exodus.

There's an interesting historical collaboration for one puzzling detail mentioned in the biblical text. There were at least two possible routes that the Israelites could have taken out of Egypt. According to the Book of Exodus, God specifically directed the Israelites *not* to go along the coastal route by the Mediterranean - even though it was the shorter and most direct route back to Canaan.

Scholars have recently unearthed the reason why: The shorter coastal route was studded with Egyptian military garrisons. The Israelites would have walked right into the jaws of a lion.

Christians need to be aware of the factual foundation of our faith. And contrary to the skeptics, the archaeologist's spade is steadily discovering external, historical evidence for the Bible's accuracy.[8]

The Internal Evidence Test

You could only wish that you passed all your tests as well as the Bible passes the first two tests for historical literature. Now let's dive into the last test: the internal evidence test. Remember that this test looks to find any evidence within the document itself that would render it questionable at best, blatantly false at worst.

The structure of the Bible points directly to a supernatural hand. As we learned earlier, men of God were moved by the Holy Spirt to put God's message to mankind into writing.

Take any 40 kids from your school and ask them to write a 10 page paper on all of the following topics: religion, ethics, health, science, morality, heaven, hell, the origin of the universe, the meaning of life, and the destiny of mankind. Then ask them to predict the future in precise detail. What will you get? Literary stew! Nobody could then take these separate papers and combine them together into a unified, sensible, logically consistent book. Yet the Bible has done this and more.

God took about 40 different writers over a period of about 1500 years and had them pen the greatest book ever written. He used men from many walks of life and generations apart - doctors, shepherds, kings, historians, fishermen, tax collectors, and prisoners. They wrote about all the previously mentioned topics and more; *yet the Bible is completely unified, logical in development, and agreed in doctrine.* It has one theme running throughout - God seeking rebellious man. It is the love story of history. How could this happen? It must be a God thing.

Probably the greatest proof of God's fingerprint on the Bible is how this book has accurately predicted much of history. Approximately 2500 prophecies appear in the pages of the Bible, about 2000 have already been fulfilled - to the letter. The remaining 500 or so reach into the future and may unfold before your eyes if you pay attention to the news.

God is not the only one who predicts the future to get people's attention. Satan does too. Through psychics (most are frauds), mediums, and others, come remarkable predictions. They rarely, however, come close to 60% accuracy. These predictions usually fail to include much detail and are usually quite ambiguous.

In his book *The Signature of God*, Grant Jeffries analyzes 17 of over 200 Old Testament prophecies concerning the historical Jesus Christ. We find that by his birth, life and death, Jesus fulfilled them perfectly. Grant also includes well thought out odds of that prophecy being fulfilled by any one man; as we go, the odds become staggering that any one man could fulfill these by chance. For a more detailed analyzation of this topic, see his book. It's a "must have" for your library. We will look at 10 of the 17 prophecies Grant talks about in his book. Please understand that these are just a small amount of the prophecies written in the Bible. Read them for yourself.

Here we go.

The First Prediction:

His birth in Bethlehem from the tribe of Judah

Micah 5:2 "But you Bethlehem Ephrathah, though you are little among the thousands of Judah, yet out of you shall come forth to Me the One to be ruler in Israel, Whose goings forth have been from of old, from everlasting."

New Testament Fulfillment:

Matthew 2:1 "Now after Jesus was born in Bethlehem of Judea in the days of Herod the king, behold, wise men from the East came to Jerusalem."

Probability: 1 chance in 2,400

The Second Prediction:

He would be preceded by a messenger

Isaiah 40:3 "The voice of one crying in the wilderness: 'Prepare the way of the Lord; make straight in the desert a highway for our God.'"

New Testament Fulfillment:

Matthew 3:1, 2 "In those days John the Baptist came preaching in the wilderness of Judea, and saying 'Repent, for the kingdom of heaven is at hand!'"

Probability: 1 chance in 20

The Third Prediction:

He would enter Jerusalem on a colt

Zechariah 9:9 "Rejoice greatly, O daughter of Zion! Shout, O daughter of Jerusalem! Behold, your King is coming to you; He is just and having salvation, lowly and riding on a donkey, a colt, the foal of a donkey."

New Testament Fulfillment:

Luke 19:35-37 "Then they brought him to Jesus. And they threw their own garments on the colt, and they set Jesus on him. And as He went, they spread their clothes on the road. Then, as He was now drawing near the descent of the Mount of Olives, the whole multitude of the disciples began to rejoice and praise God with a loud voice for all the mighty works they had seen."

Probability: 1 chance in 50

The Fourth Prediction:
He would be betrayed by a friend
Psalm 41:9 "Even my own familiar friend in whom I trusted, Who ate my bread, has lifted up his heel against me."
New Testament Fulfillment
Matthew 26:47-48 "And while he was still speaking, behold, Judas, one of the twelve, with a great multitude with swords and clubs, came from the chief priests and elders of the people. Now his betrayer had given them a sign, saying, 'Whomever I kiss, He is the One; seize Him.'"

Probability: 1 chance in 10

The Fifth Prediction:
His hands and feet would be pierced
Psalm 22:16 "For dogs have surrounded me; the assembly of the wicked has enclosed me. They pierced my hands and my feet."
New Testament Fulfillment
Acts 2:23 "This man was handed over to you by God's set purpose and fore-knowledge; and you, with the help of wicked men, put him to death by nailing him to a cross."

Probability: 1 chance in 100

The Sixth Prediction:
He would be wounded by his enemies
Isaiah 53:5 "But he was wounded for our transgressions, he was

bruised for our iniquities: the chastisement of our peace was upon him; and with his stripes we are healed."

The New Testament Fulfillment

Matthew 27:26 "Then he released Barabbas to them; and when he had scourged Jesus, he delivered him to be crucified."

Probability 1 chance in 10

The Seventh Prediction:

His betrayal for 30 pieces of silver

Zechariah 11:12 "Then I said to them, 'If it is agreeable to you, give me my wages; and if not, refrain. 'So they weighted out for my wages thirty pieces of silver.'"

The New Testament Fulfillment

Matthew 26:15 "What are you willing to give me if I delivered Him to you? And they counted out to him thirty pieces of silver.'"

Probability: 1 chance in 50

The Eight Prediction:

He will be spit upon and beaten

Isaiah 50:6 "I gave my back to those who struck Me, and My cheeks to those who plucked out the beard; I did not hide My face from shame and spitting."

The New Testament Fulfillment:

Matthew 26:67 "Then they spat in His face and beat Him; and others struck Him with the palms of their hands."

Probability: 1 chance in 10

The Ninth Prediction:

His betrayal money would be thrown in the Temple and then given away to buy a potters field

Zechariah 11:13 "And the Lord said to me, 'Throw it to the potter' that princely price they set on me. So I took the thirty pieces of silver and threw them into the house of the Lord for the potter."

The New Testament Fulfillment:

Matthew 27:5-7 "Then he threw down the pieces of silver in the temple and departed, and went and hanged himself. But the chief priests took the silver pieces and said, 'It is not lawful to put them into the treasury, because they are the price of blood.' And they took counsel and bought with them the potters field, to bury strangers in."

Probability: 1 chance in 200

The Tenth Prediction:

He would be silent before his accusers

Isaiah 53:7 "He was oppressed and he was afflicted, yet he opened not his mouth; he was led as a lamb to the slaughter, and as a sheep before its shearers is silent, so he opened not his mouth."

New Testament Fulfillment:

Matthew 27:12-14 "And while he was being accused by the chief priests and elders, he answered nothing. Then Pilate said to him, 'Do you not hear how many things they testify against You?' And he answered him not one word, so that the governor marveled greatly."

Probability: 1 chance in 100

If you combine the total probabilities of just these ten predictions you will find that the odds of all ten occurring are one chance in 24,000,000,000,000,000; or 24 thousand, trillion. Jesus fulfilled these and many more.

Just for good measure, let me point out a couple of prophecies that have nothing to do with Christ.

The prophet Isaiah foretold that a conqueror name Cyrus would destroy seemingly impregnable Babylon and subdue Egypt along with most of the rest of the known world. This same man, said Isaiah, would decide to let the Jewish exiles in his territory go free without any payment of ransom (see Isaiah 44:28; 45:1, 45:13). **Isaiah made this prophecy 150 years before Cyrus was born, 180 years before Cyrus performed any of these feats (and he did, eventually, perform them all), and 80 years**

before the Jews were even taken into Babylon.

Joshua prophesied that Jericho would be rebuilt by one man. He also said that the man's firstborn son would die when the reconstruction began and that his youngest son would die when the work reached completion (Joshua 6:26). About **five centuries later** this prophecy found its fulfillment in the life and family of a man named Hiel (I Kings 16:34).

A Titanic Undertaking

We have just touched the tip of the iceburg here in our defense of the Bible. Scope or space does not permit me to write about Ivan Panin's work with Biblical numerics or where the Bible speaks of specific scientific and medical principles long before mankind 'discovered' them. The other 99% of the iceburg remains to be discovered by you.

For your extended study I recommend these books:
- *The Signature of God*, Grant Jeffries
- *A Ready Defense*, Josh McDowell and Bill Wilson
- *Scientific Approach to Christianity*, Robert Faid

Where the rubber meets the road.

The Bible is truly a lighthouse that has withstood the storms of skeptics throughout the ages. There is a long line of people who have set out to destroy the Bible, they're all dead and God's Word to mankind still lives on. Remember, God has put enough in his Word and his *World* to make believing in him a most reasonable undertaking. He has, however, left enough out to keep us from believing in Him by reason alone.

Add these proofs to your faith and let the Bible transform your thinking and *you* into a person that God would write about if he were still writing the Bible today.

1. Sanders, C. *Introduction to Research in English Literary History.* New York: Macmillan Publishing Company, 1952.

2. Frederick Kenyon. *Handbook to the Textual Criticism of the New Testament.* London, MacMillan and Company, 1901.

3. Bruce, F. F. *The New Testament Documents: Are They Reliable?* Downers Grove IL: Intervarsity Press, 1964.

4. Jeffries, Grant. *The Signature of God.* Frontier Research Publications. pg. 14-15, 1996.

5. Josh McDowell. *A Ready Defense.* Thomas Nelson Publishers. pg. 51, 1990.

6. Wilson, Robert. *Speakers Source Book.* p. 391

7. Josephus, Flavius. *The Antiquities of the Jews.* 18, 3; in *The Works of Josephus*, trans. William Whiston, vol. 3 New York: A. C. Armstrong and Son, 1889), 148

8. 1996 Colson, Chuck. *Confirming Biblical History.* pg.8-9. Prison Fellowship

THE SUPREMACY OF CHRIST

There is a God. He has communicated to us through the Bible. According to God's Word, he desires a relationship with us. How do we go about it? Which road do I take? Which plane do I board? It has become increasingly confusing to find your way to a relationship with God.

Not only has God revealed himself through our ability to reason, a moral law, creation and revelation, but he has revealed himself through a divine visitation. God became flesh and dwelt among us. He left heaven to win back the heart of rebellious man. Who was he? What mark did he make on history? What did he show us about himself?

God came down in the person of Jesus Christ. If you want to know what God is like, look at Jesus. The Bible says he was the express image of God and the fullness of deity dwelt within him, (Colossians 1 & 2).

There are those who say God has revealed himself in many different people throughout history. You should be careful to make no mistake about it. Jesus Christ claimed to be the *only way* by which humanity can have a relationship with God. He is said he was the door we must walk through to gain entrance into the kingdom of heaven.

The Bible says there is one God and one mediator between God and man, the man Christ Jesus, (I Timothy 2:5).

Elsewhere it states that there is only one name under heaven given to men by which we can be saved, Jesus Christ, (Acts 4:12).

He is the way the truth and the life, no man comes unto Father but through Him, (John 14:6). Period.

It is becoming increasingly unpopular to say that there is only one way to have a relationship with God. Isn't it a little narrow-minded to say there is only one way? Don't all religions lead to the same God?

Don't forget this: **Truth *is* narrow.** If something is true then anything that contradicts this truth must be false. The world's religions are *not* fundamentally the same. They are fundamentally different. They differ on matters of heaven, hell, creation, the nature of God, and salvation. Because they contradict each other, they cannot all be true.

So logically there must be one way, one truth, that encompasses all reality. Anything that says there are many truths and many ways to God is illogical and self contradictory. If there are many "truths" that contradict each other then they are either all false or all but one is false.

So when Jesus Christ said, "I am the way, the truth and the life, no man comes to the Father but through me," (John 14:6). He made a logical statement. He claimed exclusivity; truth by its very nature is exclusive.

When Jesus claimed to be God and the only way to God, he

> THERE ARE AN INFINITE NUMBER OF ANGLES WHICH A MAN CAN FALL; BUT ONLY ONE AT WHICH HE CAN STAND STRAIGHT.

could have been wrong. So, let us look at the life and influence of Jesus Christ to see if he is the one most qualified to make these statements about himself.

Prophecy: God gave Jesus a miraculous address.

The Old Testament gives us detailed predictions of an event so stunning it would split history in two: God coming to earth, taking the form of a man. Who would be this man? How would we know? His birth, life and death would all match the prophecies written about him hundreds of years before he came on the scene.

There have been approximately 40 major claims by men to be the Jewish Messiah. But only one - Jesus Christ - appealed to fulfilled prophecy to substantiate his claims.[1] And only his life fulfilled perfectly every last one of the over 200 predictions. For more on this, see the section on the Bible's internal evidence, pg. 46.

He lived a perfect life

Search through the records of history and it becomes evident that the founders of various religions or cults fall short in their own lives, not only when measured against the supreme standard of the Law of God, but even when measured by the standards they themselves taught. Read the biographies of these people and one begins to wonder how lives so poorly and immorally lived could be so revered.

In contrast to all of them, the life of Christ stands high above them. Jesus resisted every temptation of lust, greed, and power in its most seductive forms. Pontius Pilate, governor of Judea, said of him, "I find no fault in him," (John 18). One of the convicted criminals hanging next to Jesus on the cross said, "...this man has done nothing wrong." Jesus asked his accusers, "Which of you can prove me of any wrong," (John 8:46).[2]

He performed miracles

Miracles marked the life of Christ. Wherever he traveled, he proved his power over sickness, disease, death, demons and nature by performing miracles. Nicodemus said, "No one could perform these miraculous signs you are doing if God were not with him," (John 3:2). Nicodemus was just finding out that not only was God with him, but *God was him*!

He changes lives

Millions of thieves have become honest. Liars now tell the truth. Cowards are courageous. Those who hated, now love because they met the Savior of the world.

He pointed to a relationship, not a religion.

One bright Saturday afternoon, I opened the door to find a pair of Jehovah Witnesses eager to talk to me. I was wearing a Christian T-shirt and she asked me if I was "religious." I said, "No I'm not; religion is man's feeble attempt to reach God or attain 'godhood.' Christianity is God's attempt to reach man."

The reason for man's existence is not to perform religious duties; it is to have a love relationship with God forever. When people lump Christianity in with *religion* they do it a great disservice. It was the religious people of the day that Christ reviled. Jesus did not speak of ways for man to get good enough to get to God. He spoke of a *good* God making a way for *sinful* man to have a restored relationship with their heavenly father. Buddha was called the way shower; Jesus was the way. This alone sets apart Christ from every other religion on the planet.

The influence of Christ on this planet is unparalleled

Jesus of Nazareth is unparalleled as a **moral influence**. His life and teachings remain unsurpassed in their ability to guide cultures, tribes, and peoples out of moral confusion.

Jesus of Nazareth is unparalleled as an **artistic** influence. He has inspired more of the world's great art and music than any other person. Some of the greatest speeches and hymns in the history of the planet were written about Him or to Him. Bach signed all his works Sola Dei Gloria (Latin for to God alone be the glory). Jesus is the object of more books, music and literature than any other individual. The Library of Congress, considered by many to be the most complete repository of books in the world, has more works about Jesus than any other person.

Jesus is unparalleled in his **humanitarian influence**. More hospitals, orphanages, rest homes, and rescue missions have been dedicated to Him than to all other religious leaders combined. More efforts to help humanity have been founded, financed, and perpetuated by His followers than all others.

Jesus is unmatched in his **scholastic influence**. Though he never founded a college, His teachings and followers have contributed to more literacy and educational institutions of all levels, from kindergarten to graduate school, than all others combined. In America alone, 128 colleges were established in the first 100 years of the nations history; all were founded by a church, denomination, or religious group. Harvard, Princeton, and Yale, which for 200 years served as the headwaters of American education, were created to prepare ministers, missionaries and Christian leaders. For the first hundred years of Harvard's existence, every graduate became a minister of the gospel. The initial charter of Harvard stated unashamedly, "Everyone shall consider the main end of his life and studies to know Jesus Christ which is eternal life. And therefore to lay Christ in the bottom, as the only foundation of all found knowledge and learning."

Before the Gospel ever came to America, it was the followers of Jesus Christ who brought education to the children of ordinary citizens. Prior to the time of Martin Luther in Germany and John Calvin in France and Switzerland, only the rich or royalty or the geniuses of the world were considered fit for education. But these great reformers saw education as the means of teaching the Bible to whole generations who for the first time could read the Scriptures in their native languages

Jesus Christ is unparalleled in his **impact on women**. No one has done so much to raise the status of womanhood and motherhood as has Jesus Christ. He came to a world where women were one step above animals. Many were traded for cattle and few enjoyed personal rights before the law or marriage altar. Where the message of Christ has thrived, women have been ennobled and respected as human beings made in the image of God. Where the message of Christ has yet to fully impact the culture, women are still treated as property

According to the John F. Kennedy School of Government,

- 500,000 women are trafficked each year from Russia and the newly independent states
- Traffickers sell Asian women in North America to brothels for $16,000 each (God help the nation that buys them)
- The number of Nepali girls forced into sexual slavery in Indian brothels now totals nearly 200,000

The followers of Christ led the women's suffrage movements

throughout Europe, England, and America. Secular women in the west may not understand the debt they owe to Jesus Christ and His teachings, but they have the Nazarene and his followers to thank for the exalted status they enjoy today.

Jesus had an unparalleled impact on **freedom and justice** throughout the world. No one has more deeply promoted personal freedom and justice before the law than Jesus's followers, armed with his standard of law. English and American law, once considered the model throughout the world, was made possible primarily through John Locke, William Gladstone, William Wilburforce, William Blackstone (all of England) and James Witherspoon, John Adams, James Madison, and John Marshall of America. All were committed followers of Christ who knew and applied his principles and teachings to the preservation of individual rights and freedom under the law. All of these influential men freely admitted they owed their greatness to him.[3]

This essay called "One Solitary Life" puts the life of Christ into perspective:

He was born in a stable, the child of a peasant woman. He grew up in an obscure village; worked as a carpenter until He was 30; and then became an itinerant preacher for 3 years.

He never went to college.

He never wrote a book.

He never held office.

He never owned a home.

He never had a family.

He never had a lot of money.

He never traveled more than 200 miles from his place of birth.

He never accomplished any of the things that usually mark greatness.

He had no credentials but himself.

Although he spoke with great authority, taught with unusual wisdom, and was widely accepted by the people, the religious leaders of his day opposed him. While he was still a young man, the tide of popular opinion turned against him. He was betrayed by a friend, abandoned by his associates and turned over to his enemies. He was falsely accused, endured the mockery of a trial, and was unjustly condemned to die.

He was crucified between two thieves, and while he was dying his executioners gambled for the only piece of property he had on earth - his clothing. When he was dead, he was buried in a borrowed grave through the pity of a friend. Nineteen centuries have come and gone, and today he is the central figure of the human race, and the cornerstone of world progress.

All the armies that ever marched;

All the navies that ever sailed;

All the parliaments that ever sat;

And all the kings that ever reigned, put together have not affected the life of mankind upon this earth as that one solitary life.

He conquered death and the grave

Go to the graves of all the other religious leaders and they will all be there. Go to the grave of Christ and you will not find a corpse. Christians do not worship a dead man on a stick but a living God.

Both friends and enemies of the Christian faith have recognized the resurrection of Christ to be the foundation stone of the faith. Let us consider some evidence of the resurrection of Jesus Christ.

1. The fact of the Christian church It is worldwide in scope. Its history can be traced back to 32 A.D. These Christians constantly referred to the resurrection as the basis of their faith.

2. The fact of the Christian day. Sunday is the day of worship for Christians. Its history can also be traced back to 32 A. D. Something big must have happened to change the day of worship from the Jewish Sabbath, the seventh day, to Sunday the first day. Christians said the shift came because of their desire to celebrate the resurrection of

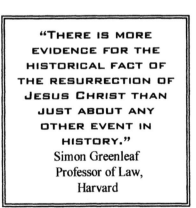

"THERE IS MORE EVIDENCE FOR THE HISTORICAL FACT OF THE RESURRECTION OF JESUS CHRIST THAN JUST ABOUT ANY OTHER EVENT IN HISTORY."
Simon Greenleaf
Professor of Law,
Harvard

Jesus from the dead. The shift is all the more remarkable when we

remember that the first Christians were Jews. If the resurrection does not account for this shift, then what does?

3. Then there is the Christian book, the New Testament. Its pages contain six independent testimonies to the fact of the resurrection.

Two facts must be explained; the empty tomb and the appearances of Christ after his death.

4. Where did the body go? The earliest explanation circulated was that the disciples stole the body. (Mt. 28:11-15). Stealing the body of Christ is something totally out of character for the disciples. Each of the disciples faced tests of torture and martyrdom for their faith and beliefs. Men do not die for what they know is a lie. If they had stolen the body, they knew that their faith was worthless and certainly not worth dying for.

The second hypothesis is that the Jews and Romans moved the body. But why? Having put guards at the tomb, why would they choose to move the body? They wanted to stop the spread of Christianity and the preaching about Jesus. (Acts 4:18). The disciples constantly referred to the resurrection as their motive and proof for the validity of their preaching. There was one simple solution for stopping them: Produce the body. The fact that they didn't tells us they did not have it.

5. What about the appearances of Christ? These occurred from the morning of his resurrection to his ascension 40 days later. Ten distinct appearances are recorded. They show a great variety as to time, place, and people. Two were individuals, Peter and James. There were appearances to the disciples as a group, and one was to 500 people all at one time.

Dr Frank Morrison, a lawyer set out to write a book disproving the claims of Christ's resurrection. He studied the facts and came to a different conclusion. The sheer weight of the evidence compelled him to conclude that Jesus actually did rise from the dead. Morrison wrote his book - but not the one he planned. It is titled, *Who moved the stone?* The first chapter is called, "The book that refused to be written."

Jesus can offer us security in this life and eternal life in the next because his *is* the resurrection and the life. Many religions talk of life after death but only **one** *proves* it can be done.

Jesus Christ has given us plenty of reason to place our trust in him. He is the King of Kings and Lord of Lords. He is God. He gave his life for you; he asks that you would live your life for him. Repent from your sin and believe he is who he said he was and you too can have what you were destined for: A love relationship with the living God. (John 3:16-21, Acts 3:19, Romans 10:9-10.)

He Alone Can Relate to Human Sufferings

When God came to earth, he didn't wear the garments or lifestyle of a king. He didn't dress in royal robes and live in the largest palace. He came to earth in an animals stable. He knew what it meant to work hard growing up as the son of a carpenter. He knew what it meant to be homeless, penniless and friendless. He felt abuse and loneliness; he was a man of sorrows and acquainted with grief. When I experience sorrow and adversity here on earth, I know I have a savior that can sympathize and understand what I am going through. He left heaven to be subjected to the brutality and harshness of fallen men and a fallen world. This sets Christ apart.

For more on this, I recommend the books below on the subject.

1. McDowell, Josh. *More Than a Carpenter*. Living Books. pg 104

2. Zacharias, Ravi. *Deliver us From Evil*. Word Publishing. Appendix A

3. LaHay, Tim. *Jesus, Who is he?* Multnomah Books. 1996 pg 16-19

Also: *Jesus Among the Other Gods* by Ravi Zacharias

HOW TO KNOW GOD

The Good

God has made you for a purpose: to know, love and worship him. You are not on this planet through some cosmic accident. God has made you as part of a divine plan. The plan begins and ends in knowing God.

You can accomplish a lot of things and live a comfortable existence on this planet, but if you have lived your life without a relationship with God you have missed it all. God created you, he loves you, and he desires that you know him. God has placed a hunger in you to know him. There is a hole in your soul that only God can completely fill. (Revelation 3:20, John 17:3, Jeremiah 9:23-24)

The Bad

When God created the universe, he created a moral law to govern it. Through this moral law we know how we should relate to God and to our fellow man. The problem is that we have all broken this moral law. God calls this sin. Sin separates us from God. When we break a law, we deserve justice. Because we have sinned against an eternal God and the image of God in our fellow men, our punishment must be eternal. God created hell for Satan and his demons but it serves a second purpose as justice for all who break God's moral law. Don't think that heaven and hell are metaphorical places here on earth representing good and bad times. They're not.

The Bible speaks plainly about a literal place of eternal fire and agony. Jesus himself talked more about hell than he did heaven. (Matthew

10:28, Mark 9:43-48, Luke 10:15, 12:5, Romans 9:22, I Corinthians 16:22) When someone wrongs us here on earth, we cry out for justice. Our courts are full of people looking for justice. Here, we cry for justice; can we deny God any less? His perfection demands perfect justice.

You may think that because you're not a bad guy or girl that you are good enough to make it to heaven and avoid the judgement of hell. But we too often judge our goodness by comparing ourselves with someone else. We define our own standard and say we are 'good.' But God doesn't use that standard. He uses the moral law as the standard. How do you measure up against that?

Have you ever lied? Have you ever dishonored your parents? Have you ever stolen anything? Have you ever been sexually immoral? Have you ever not served the one true God? Have you ever made God into your image? If you have broken just one of these commandments you are a lawbreaker, guilty before God and deserving of hell. Sounds harsh, but it's true. (Romans 3:23, 6:23, Isaiah 53:6, and 59:2, Revelation 20:11-15)

The Ugly

Even though we have turned away from God - *he still loves us!* He is not willing that any should perish. God has love on one hand and justice on the other. Justice demands our punishment, but his love demands his mercy. God fulfilled both his justice and mercy by coming to earth in the form of man - Jesus Christ. He lived a perfect life and laid it down on our behalf. He took your sin upon himself and took the death penalty on your behalf. He used an ugly, blood stained cross to free us from the justice of God.

Jesus made the way possible for sinful man to reunite with a Holy God. Through him and only him can we have peace with God. God gave two conditions for salvation.

1. Repentance: Turn away from your sin, admit you are a sinner and don't make excuses. Ask God to forgive you, express your sorrow for hurting him and others.

2. Faith: You must believe that Jesus is who he said he was, God

wrapped in flesh. Believe in your heart and confess with your mouth that Jesus is Lord and that God raised him from the dead. (Romans 3:25, John 3:16-36, I Timothy 2:5, I John 5:11-12, John 14:6, Acts 3:19, Romans 10:9-10, II Peter 3:9)

The Beautiful

If you have repented and believed, you are a new creature in Christ. You will begin to have a hunger for the Bible and prayer as never before. You will want to get baptized to proclaim publicly the decision you made. Begin attending a church that believes in the Bible. If you need a Bible or help finding a church in your area, e-mail me and I will do what I can to assist you. See the back of this book for the website. (Ephesians 5:8, II Corinthians 5:17, Romans 6)

What if I choose not to?

Because God wants to rule us through love, he necessarily gives us a choice to serve him or not. You must understand that God gives the power of choice in all areas of life; however, once you make your choices, they exert power over you. If you choose not to follow God, a couple of things will happen.

The Good

You may not choose to follow God but still choose to live by some of his principles written in this book. Because these are universal principles, they will work for anyone - Christian or not. They will not, however, add up to ultimate meaning in life, for without God, even wisdom is meaningless. (Ecclesiastes 1:12-14)

> THOSE WHO PLAN FOR TOMORROW BUT TAKE NO THOUGHT FOR ETERNITY ARE WISE FOR A MOMENT BUT FOOLS FOREVER.

So if you learn these principles and put them into practice, you will probably prosper and live happily for the most part - except, of course, for the nagging fear of eternal punishment.

The Bad

Even if you live by these principles, they cannot fill the hole in your soul and they cannot make you innocent before God - you have already broken God's law.

If you live rejecting God, you will die rejecting him. When a wicked man dies, he loses all hope. Should you never accept the innocence God offers through repentance and belief in Christ, you will die guilty before God. You desired to live unto yourself and in your death God will require you to pay your debt of guilt by yourself. You made a bad trade!

Jesus said, "What would it benefit a man if he gained the whole world and lost his own soul?" (Matthew 16:26)

You bought into the lie that says ultimate fulfillment comes from ultimate autonomy. God did not give laws to harm us, but to allow us to reach our ultimate potential. God does not desire that we worship him because *he* needs it but because *we* need it. When we refuse to worship him, we suffer a double tragedy. We fail to recognize what we have lost and we fail to become all we were meant to be.

To live life to the fullest, you must know the Author of life, then abide in his principles.

When you were born, you alone cried and the world rejoiced. Live your life in such a way so that when you die, the world will mourn and you will rejoice.

I love you,
cw

ATTITUDE

Attitude. We kick this word around a lot. Its official definition is: a mental position, feeling or emotion toward a fact or situation. I also like the second definition which seems to reflect a deeper meaning: a state of readiness to respond in a characteristic way to a stimulus.

Attitude is your outlook on life. It predicts how you will respond to the varied situations life hands you along its journey. The importance of having a right attitude cannot be said any better than how Charles Swindoll put it in his famous essay on attitude:

> "The longer I live, the more I realize the impact of attitude on life. Attitude to me is more important than facts, it is more important than the past, is more important than education, than money, than circumstances, than failures, than successes, than what other people think or say or do. It is more important than appearance, giftedness or skill. It will make or break a company, a church, a home. The remarkable thing is we have a choice every day regarding the attitude we will embrace for that day. We cannot change our past. We cannot change the fact that people will act a certain way. We cannot change the inevitable. The only thing we can do is play on the one string we have, and that is our attitude. I am convinced that life is 10% what happens to me and 90% how I react to it.

In this section, we will explore the impact of attitude. We will explain seven principles everyone must know about attitude including how to recognize and avoid the five 'bad' attitudes.

I love you,

CW

EVERYTHING

It has been said that attitude is everything. At the risk of overstatement, aside from your relationship with God, it is. Growing up, I had never thought much about my attitude. I was mostly concerned about myself and whatever I was interested in at that time. I thought that life would take care of itself. Once I left home (where life tends to take care of itself), I began to slowly learn lessons that would later add up to cumulative wisdom about the all important subject of my *attitude*.

It is impossible to estimate the number of jobs lost, classes failed, scholarships missed, degrees not attained, relationships ruined, careers stunted, marriages destroyed and lives unfulfilled because of the impact of poor attitudes.

There are seven principles we all need to adopt concerning our attitude. Learn these concepts and live by them. They will color every situation, guide your thoughts, conversations and decision making.

They are:

- Your attitude is *your* choice
- To help yourself choose a good attitude, change your perspective

The Fatal Five attitudes are:

- Selfishness
- Ungratefulness
- Fault-finding
- Faithlessness
- Victim-hood

The Fab Five attitudes are (opposite of the Fatal Five):

- Service
- Thankfulness
- Good-finder
- Hopefulness
- Enduring

Your Choice

People have jobs they hate, classes they despise, relationships they tolerate because they are waiting for somebody, somehow, somewhere; a teacher, husband, wife, boss, pastor, Santa Claus, the Tooth Fairy or lottery officials to make them happy. They are looking for that one thing that will finally make their life enjoyable. If they could just get their dream job, their dream physique or their dream spouse, then they would be content.

These people are missing one of life's most important maxims:

Your attitude is a choice.

Nobody can determine your attitude except you. Nobody has the power to control your attitude unless you allow them to.

If you are ungrateful, it is because you choose to be. If you are selfish, it is because you choose to be. If you are irritated, it is because you choose to be. If you are feeling sorry for yourself, it is because you choose to do so. Do you 'hate' math class? It's because you choose to. Do you 'hate' your job? It's because you choose to.

Is there something that always sets you on edge or makes you irritable? Is there someone that really bugs you? Normally, I am a pretty easy going guy but there are a few things in life that will consistently push my buttons.

One of them is when I am in a car and I am late for something and lost at the same time. It's during those times, I feel like taking chunks out of the steering wheel with my teeth. When I am in a situation like that, another thing happens that makes my attitude go from bad to worse: I get behind somebody's granny doing 10 below the speed limit.

I start to talk with her in not so nice tones. I have whole conversations with her and she never hears a word of it. In fact, she is usually oblivious to everything around her. She can barely see over the steering wheel!

Then another thing happens that gets me absolutely seething. The guy behind me is also in a hurry so he tries to pass us both. But he doesn't have enough time, so he ends up cutting me off to squeeze between granny and I. Talk about selfish pigs!

When I finally get to where I am going, my whole mood is affected. Granny and Speed Racer are miles from me, but they are still controlling my attitude. Why? Why should you or I let others control our outlook at that moment?

The fact is that I don't have to get upset. I choose to. These people don't *make* me grouchy. I choose to be grouchy. These people just make it an easy choice.

Anger isn't a bad attitude in and of itself. Anger is amoral. It can be good or bad. Sometimes anger is good like anger at injustice. Most of the time, however, our anger is misplaced and is fed by poor attitudes. The bad attitudes I chose were ungratefulness, selfishness and self-pity. Not to mention, I should always leave earlier and have a map with me.

Sometimes we are surrounded by people or circumstances that

make it real easy to choose a wrong attitude (who are you thinking of???). But with training, we can get better at choosing the good attitudes instead of the bad.

Perspective

The best and easiest way to avoid the Fatal Five is to look at things in their true relationship to reality and relative importance inside the big picture. If you find yourself tempted to choose a poor attitude then change your perspective.

Your attitude is the lens you use to look at life. Most people have a lens that distorts reality and makes unimportant things seem important and crucial things seem trivial. This distorted view is fertile ground for growing bad attitudes.

This lens that we see everything through is primarily a function of our experience and how much we understand of reality. The more experience at living we have and the more we understand how the universe works, the easier it is to choose good attitudes.

The reason young people are so susceptible to poor attitudes is that they don't have much experience at living - they live in small worlds - and their sense of reality is distorted by the media and fed by their peer group (which is also limited by their experience).

How can you change the lens you look through to reflect reality and show things in their relative importance?

- Increase your experience. Try new sports, hobbies and challenges. Lift your vision higher and learn how people other than you live.

- Learn history. Ahhh! No! anything but that! As you sit in history class and ask yourself, "Why do I have to learn this?" realize that knowing history adds context to life. Learn how other people have endured hardships, met challenges and led fulfilling lives. You will find yourself saying, "If _____ did that, I surely can do _____." You fill in the blanks.

- Study the Bible. The Bible gives us the true picture of reality. What it says about life is true. What is says about death is true. What it says about forever is true. What is says about you is true. What it says is important *is important* and what is says is trivial *is trivial*. Knowing and believing what the Bible says about reality is the single most important step in changing your perspective, thus enabling you to choose good attitudes. Much of the time, the culture tells us to see things opposite of how we should really see them.

Culture (Fantasy)	The Bible (Reality)
Human value is related to how much they can produce.	Human value is based on how much God invested in us and how much he was willing to pay to redeem us.
To become great you must look out for yourself first.	To become great you must forget yourself and take the posture of a servant.
Those who die with the most toys wins.	If you gained the world and lost your soul you made a bad trade.
When someone hurts you, avenge your hurt, gossip and slander them.	Forgive them, love them and pray for them.
Ignore your feelings of guilt, forget them, deny them.	Repent and receive forgiveness for your guilt.
Unless you have the best and coolest, your just not with it.	Godliness with contentment is great gain.

Let me give you a couple of examples that illustrate how a perspective change helped me with my outlook on life.

When I turned 16, I received a car handed down through my

family. It was a silver Ford Pinto; we called it my Ferrari. From that point on, I always had a car until my senior year in college. At that time, I lived off campus and worked 10 miles from my house. The car I drove finally died and I had no cash to fix it, so I sold it for junk. That winter I gained some valuable experience walking, using public transportation, riding with friends, and riding my bike. I rode 10 miles each way to work. I learned that I should never be ungrateful for a car no matter what kind it is. Have you ever been jealous or ungrateful because of what you or your family drive? Try walking or taking the bus. This small change in your perspective will help you keep a grateful attitude.

Have you ever watched or played in a sporting event and the referee or umpire made a poor call? When that used to happen to me, I would almost consider it my duty to inform that person what a dolt they had been and my blind dog could have made a better call. My friend was worse than me. He would jump up and down and throw things at the television. This all changed (for the most part) one fall. One of the jobs I had in college was working as a referee for a men's football league. No matter what call you made, one side or the other would harass you. One time, I made a call and this guy got so incensed he put his nose millimeters from mine and screamed about how he would kill me and all my relatives. I found out later that he had just got out of prison and was not joking! Needless to say, I found out how difficult a job it is to referee a game.

I also had experience as a baseball umpire. In my first game working behind the plate, the pitcher pitched the ball in the dirt. I thought the ball was going to hit me, so I flinched. I called it a 'ball.' The crowd on one side of the field erupted all over me. What I didn't see was that the batter swung at the ball and because I flinched and closed my eyes, I didn't see him swing! So I changed the call to a strike and the fans on the *other* side of the field jumped all over me for changing my call. I wished the earth would swallow me up at that time, but no such luck.

Because of this experience and resulting perspective change, I find it easier to applaud the good calls and overlook the bad. Sometimes, however, I still struggle with knowing that my blind dog *could* make some of those calls.

While training for triathalons, I used to swim two or three times a week. When your swimming laps, it's really nice to get your own lane. This day the pool was full and I had to share a lane with another swimmer. When this happens, both swimmers stay to the right and make the best of the situation. But this swimmer aggravated me because he kept bumping into me. I was 'mister serious athlete' trying to concentrate on getting better and this 'rookie, neophyte, guppy man' kept getting in *my* way! A few moments later I had a huge perspective shift that made it real easy to change my attitude about the whole situation. I stopped swimming to take my pulse and I saw that this man was *totally blind!* He tried his best to avoid me and swim at the same time but he couldn't see. I felt like a real toad and tried not to be so selfish after that.

Having trouble keeping a good attitude? Change your perspective......

- Don't like what mom cooked for dinner?
  Go without food for a couple of days.

- Think your life would be better if you just had more clothes?
  Wear the same outfit for a week. (I had to do this because I lost a contest! Believe me, I became thankful for the clothes God has blessed me with.)

- Hate doing the dishes or taking out the garbage?
  Look at them differently. Dishes and our waste are really monuments to God's provision in our lives. You wouldn't have to do the dishes if you didn't eat! Every time you take the garbage out or wash the dishes, thank God for the food, for the running water in your sink and for the garbage man who comes once a week to take it away.

- Hate getting up to go to school each day?
  Thank God for the free education you are getting. I met a boy on a mission trip that wasn't allowed to go to school simply because he stuttered. I became thankful for the education God has

allowed me to receive.

Feeling sorry for yourself? Feeling a little depressed and lonely? Visit a children's unit in a hospital. Visit a cancer ward or a nursing home. Volunteer at the Special Olympics, or help out in a homeless shelter. You will feel that depression begin to lift. (Isaiah 58:10)

One Word

Another trick to help change your perspective is to just change one word in your vocabulary. Change *got* to into - *get* to. Instead of saying, "I *have* to go to work today." Say, "I *get* to go to work today," which is true because there are many people who would love the chance to work and earn money. Don't say, "I have to go to school." Say, "I *get* to go to school!" There are many people who would love the chance at the education you *get* in America.

I could go on and on but you get the idea. Try it for three weeks. Find somebody to hold you accountable and to point out whenever you say the words *"have* to" or *"got* to." You will be surprised at how ingrained this thought process is in your life.

Get Out of Dodge

I encourage every Christian young person to go on a foreign mission trip before they graduate high school because of the tremendous change in perspective it affords. It becomes harder to complain about sharing a room with your sister when you see whole families living in a house the size of your room.

If you haven't served overseas, then get on a team, raise your support and go. It will change your life because it will change your attitude.

OK, time for a pop quiz: To help choose the correct attitude, change your _____ ?

"DAD UNDERSTOOD A FEW THINGS ABOUT MOTIVATION. I REMEMBER A STATEMENT HE MADE WHILE I WAS IN COLLEGE. "I DON'T CARE SO MUCH ABOUT WHETHER YOU MAKE A'S, B'S, OR C'S," HE SAID, MUCH TO MY SURPRISE, "BUT WHETHER YOU *CARE* ABOUT MAKING A'S, B'S, OR C'S."

HE WAS FAR MORE INTERESTED IN MY SPIRIT THAN MY PERFORMANCE, WHICH I BELIEVE DEMONSTRATES A PROFOUND UNDERSTANDING OF HUMAN NATURE. IF A PERSON ADOPTS THE RIGHT SPIRIT, THE PERFORMANCE LEVELS WILL TAKE CARE OF THEMSELVES."

SENATOR JOHN ASHCROFT

SNAKEBITE

The Fatal Five

Do you like snakes? Or do you cringe at the thought of them? No matter how you feel, one would agree that they are fascinating creatures - especially the poisonous ones. The poisons of some of these snakes are powerful neuro-toxins. When bitten by a poisonous snake, the poison initially causes severe stinging. As it travels through the body, it begins to paralyze certain functions of the body like breathing and the heartbeat.

This is the way a poor attitude works. At first it is just something small, an isolated irritant, like a sting. But over time, it spreads throughout all aspects of your life and begins to paralyze your potential.

History tells of an entire generation of Israelites who missed entering the land God promised to them. They failed to live their lives to the fullest; they missed the destiny God planned for them and went to their graves taking only their potential with them. Why? Because an enemy had overcome them? No. Because God had forsaken them? No. Because they didn't have the talent? No. Because they didn't have the desire? No. They didn't attain their destiny because the poison of the Fatal Five attitudes had infected their outlook.

With the exception of two young men, an entire generation died in the desert not reaching the goal they were born for. Why did these two young men (Caleb and Joshua) make it into the promised land while the others didn't? *Attitude*. That's all. They weren't stronger and they didn't have better circumstances to work with. They weren't more talented, more handsome, or more wealthy than the rest of them. *They just didn't allow the poison of the Fatal Five paralyze their potential.* They *chose to* adopt a Fab Five mentality rather than a Fatal Five. This alone made the difference.

The same will work for you. God has placed in you a certain amount of potential and he has given you a destiny to fulfill (Jeremiah 1:5). There are only four things that will keep you from realizing your potential: sin (it steals, kills and destroys), ignorance (not knowing God's best), willful ignorance (knowing God's best but electing not to pursue it), and your attitude. Do you want to live life to the fullest? Take a page out of history and adopt the Fab Five attitudes; don't let the Fatal Five paralyze *your* potential.

So that you will learn to recognize them, let's take the Fatal Five and the Fab Five and contrast the two.

Ungrateful vs. Grateful (I Thessalonians 5:18)

Have you ever known a spoiled brat? Have you ever been one? Nobody likes spoiled brats. What makes us look at a child and call him a spoiled brat? Usually, it's because they act ungrateful. It's that relative of yours that complains because she only got eight presents instead of ten under the Christmas tree. Whenever I see one of these spoiled brats at the grocery store screaming bloody murder because they didn't get something they wanted my right hand gets all tingly; I don't know why.

I think God looks at us and sees much of the same behavior. He blesses us with so much, yet we remain unsatisfied and ungrateful.

We pray for days, weeks, months for something and when God finally blesses us with it we spend 30 seconds thanking him for it. Much of our thinking is: "if only I had...." and it should be: "God thank you for...." Don't live your life as a spoiled brat. Develop a thankful attitude.

When many people say 'grace' before a meal they say, "God bless this food." When Jesus said grace he said, "God *thank you* for this food" (Luke 9:16).

> **"WERE NOT ALL TEN CLEANSED? WHERE ARE THE OTHER NINE? WAS NO ONE FOUND TO RETURN AND GIVE PRAISE TO GOD EXCEPT THIS FOREIGNER?"**
> Jesus Christ

You can develop a thankful attitude by changing your perspective and thinking of things you have that others may not have or things you have that you don't deserve. Sit down and make a list of things for which you are thankful. For the Christian, no matter how bad things get, there is always at least one thing to be thankful for - Salvation. You're going to heaven - forever - because of a gift from God. Thank you Lord! Others include: Health (Exodus 15:26), Food (Matthew 14:19) and Shelter (Luke 9:58).

Every year at Thanksgiving, my family sits down and writes out 20 things we are all grateful for. This helps us keep a thankful attitude all year. One year, a fifteen-year-old girl in my youth group made a list of one-hundred things. She filled pages with things that we normally take for granted (like spoiled brats) and gave thanks for them. When was the last time you gave thanks for your blankets and pillows? That was number 58 on her list. Contact lenses was number 74, the telephone was 75, hot water was 93 and the ability to walk was 95.

God commands us to be grateful. If you would just take the time, you can re-train yourself to become a grateful, pleasant child rather than a whiney, spoiled punk kid.

Selfish vs Servant (Philippians 2:3-11)

Jesus Christ said that to seek greatness you must become a servant. Our inner selves and the prevailing culture both give the opposite advice. But it is true: Greatness is synonymous with servitude. The greatest restaurants have great *service*. The greatest auto dealers have the greatest *service*. The finest stores have the best *service*. Our police officers and elected officials are called public *servants*. The soldier *serves* his country. Calvin Coolidge said, "No man was ever honored for what he received; but rather for what he gave."

This does not prove easy, however, because there resides within each one of us a fountain that secretes pride and selfishness. We are selfish by nature. We want what we want when we want it and how we want it. If something doesn't suit our taste, we don't like it. We grumble and complain.

Jesus calls us to forsake ourselves and live unto him and service to others. In doing so, we will find the essence of life to the fullest and true greatness. (Mt. 16:25 and John 10:10) How do we do accomplish this? Through the cross. The

> "SELF INTEREST IS BUT THE SURVIVAL OF THE ANIMAL IN US. HUMANITY ONLY BEGINS FOR MAN WITH SELF SURRENDER."
> Henri-Frederic Amiel

cross stands as the cornerstone history. The cross is a place of death. Death to your desires, your wishes, your dreams. Until we die to ourselves, God cannot resurrect us to reach the potential and destiny he has for us.

God used a reformed murderer to write most of the New Testament. Paul the Apostle found the secret of greatness and living life to its fullest. He said, "I have been crucified with Christ and I no longer live, but Christ lives in me." The greatness he accomplished came in direct proportion to the amount he surrendered his selfishness unto the Lord and let the Lord live through him. But what about that fountain of selfishness and pride that is in all of us?

On a regular basis, daily, sometimes hourly or even every minute depending on how trying the circumstances - you must die to yourself.

Paul said, "I die daily." You must also. Pray, "Lord I give to you my desires and my wants. I am dead to them and alive to pursuing your best and serving others."

How many happy, selfish people do you know?

Faultfinding vs. Goodfinding. (Proverbs 12:16, 18, 23)

I have the opportunity to talk to groups of people about many different things. One day, I held an assembly in an elementary school and talked about light and color. I had all the kids laughing and having a good time performing experiments while learning about light and color. About halfway through the assembly, I pulled out my funny American Flag. You look at the flag and instead of seeing a blue field of white stars, you see a funny teal color with black stars. Instead of red and white stripes, you see black and bluish-green stripes. After you stare at it for a few seconds and look away, you see an after-image of the flag in its true colors right on your hand. Cool!

I had the entire school of children performing this experiment when it happened - the ultimate public speaker's nightmare. Silence filled the room as the children stared intently at the flag. Ten seconds went by, then twenty, when a little blond haired third grade boy broke the silence with one word...BOOORING! This is BOOORING! Then some other kids started to feed off him. I heard one little girl say, "Yeah, I'd rather be coloring." Then others started to make snoring noises. "Tough crowd," I thought.

Fault-finders, critics, complainers; the world is full of them. Don't become one. It's easy to be a complainer, but you must train yourself to find the good. Become a good-finder! Sometimes we are called to give a life-giving rebuke. Experts say that it takes 20 to 25 positive comments to make up for one negative comment. Aim for that kind of ratio. Reckless words pierce like a sword, but the tongue of the wise brings healing.

Don't fill your house with the poison of negativity. Don't tear people down with your fault finding, build them up! Solomon said, "He who seeks good finds good will." If your parents are negative, you be positive, don't learn their ways. Many a harsh, critical parent (or sibling) has destroyed the self worth of a child by uttering poisonous words like...

"Why can't you do anything right?"

"Why are you so stupid?"

"I wish you were more like your brother."

We place the dangerous poisons out of the reach of our children, all the while we use our careless words to fill them with the deadly toxins of our negativity. Jesus said we will give an account of every careless word we have spoken. God help us. Twenty to one; that's the ratio to shoot for. Become a good-finder; work at it, nobody becomes one automatically. Remember the words of Teddy Roosevelt:

> "Its not the critic who counts; not the man who points out how the strong man stumbled, or where the doer of deeds could have done better. The credit belongs to the man who is actually in the arena, who's face is marred by the dust and sweat and blood: who strives valiantly; who errs and comes short again and again; who knows great enthusiasms, the great devotions and spends himself in a worthy cause; who at best knows in the end the triumph of high achievement; and who at the worst if he fails, at least fails while doing greatly; so that his place shall never be with those cold and timid souls who know neither victory nor defeat."

Faithless vs. Hopeful (Philippians 4:13, Romans 8:31-38)

One of the rules I have when I teach is that the students are not allowed to say, "I can't do this." They must add one more word - yet. That one word adds a great commodity missing in many of the world's citizens - hope.

> "FAITH KEEPS THE PERSON THAT KEEPS THE FAITH."
> Mother Teresa

Times may get tough, circumstances may look insurmountable,

but for the person who knows and is known by God, **there is always hope**. God's book is stuffed with people who, with God's help, defeated armies, withstood fire, prison and poverty to become shining examples of conquering heroes. They understood this reality: God and them are a majority in any circumstance! For the Christian there are no hopeless situations, only people who think hopelessly about them.

Hopelessness sucks the fight out of you. One common war tactic is to make your enemy think that it is futile to fight. "Your force is too weak, too tired, too outnumbered." They may say "Just give up!" Too many of us just surrender. You can do all things through Christ who strengthens you, even algebra!

During World War II, the Germans had the U.S. forces in the city of Bastogne surrounded. Below is the Christmas Eve letter written by General McAuliff, the commander of those forces. Notice his attitude; how many of the fab five can you pick out? Also notice how the enemy tried to infect the troops with an attitude of hopelessness.

> MERRY CHRISTMAS
> HEADQUARTERS 101ST AIRBORNE
> Office of the Division Commander
>   24 December 1944
> What's merry about all this you ask? We're fighting - it's cold - we aren't home. All true but what has the proud Eagle Division accomplished with its worthy comrades of the 10th Armored Division, the 705th Tank Destroyer Battalion and all the rest? Just this: We have stopped cold everything that has been thrown at us from the North, East, South and West. We have identifications from four German Panzer Divisions, two German Infantry Divisions and one German Parachute Division. These units, spearheading the last desperate German lunge, were headed straight west for key points when the Eagle Division was hurriedly ordered to stem the advance. How effectively this was done will be written in history; not alone in our Division's glorious history but in world history. The Germans actually did surround us,

their radios blared our doom. Their Commander demanded our surrender in the following impudent arrogance:

22 December 1944

"To the U.S.A. Commander of the encircled town of Bastogne. The fortune of war is changing. This time the U.S.A. forces in and near Bastogne have been encircled by strong German armored units. The German armored units have crossed the river Ourthe near Ortheuville, have taken Marche and reached St. Hubert by passing through Hompres-Sibret-Tillet. Libramont is in German hands.

There is only one possibility to save the encircled U.S.A. Troops from total annihilation: That is the honorable surrender of the encircled town. In order to think it over a term of two hours will be granted beginning with the presentation of this note. If this proposal should be rejected one German Artillery Corps and six heavy A.A. battalions are ready to annihilate the U.S.A. troops in and near Bastogne. The order for firing will be given immediately after this two hour's term. All the serious civilian losses caused by this Artillery firing would not correspond with the well known American humanity.

The German Commander"

The German Commander received the following reply:

22 December 1944

"To the German Commander

N U T S

The American Commander"

Allied troops are counterattacking in force. We continue to hold Bastogne. By holding Bastogne we assure the success of the Allied Armies. We know that our Division Commander, General Taylor will say: "Well Done!" We are giving our country and our loved ones at home a worthy Christmas present and being privileged to take part in this gallant feat of arms are truly making for ourselves a Merry Christmas.

/s/McAuliffe
McAULIFFE,
Commanding

Reinforcements came and the rest is history.

Knowing there is hope, the question changes from, "Is there hope?" to "Am I willing to put my faith to work to attain it?"

Hopelessness and worry are cousins. Worry is a product of poor preparation and lack of faith. The Bible gives us a simple but effective weapon against worry: pray and prepare.

"Do not worry about anything but pray about everything, with thanksgiving present your requests to God. And the peace of God, which surpasses all understanding will guard your hearts and your minds in Christ Jesus" (Philippians 4:6-7). If you struggle with worry and hopelessness, memorize and meditate on these verses. Make them a part of you. (Matthew 6:25, I Peter 5:5-9)

God also expects us to do what we can about our situation. Stop worrying and start working! If your worried about your basic needs the Bible says you need to *get a job* (certain widows excepted). If your worried about a test - study. If your worried about a relationship - communicate. God will come through for you but he wants to *partner* with you in the working of your miracle. A wise man once said: "Do your best and God will do the rest." Read and memorize I Timothy 5:8, II Thessalonians 3:6-10, 2 Corinthians 12:14, Proverbs 6:6-11, Proverbs 10:4-5.

Victim or Self Pity vs. Enduring

This attitude has become pervasive in our society. The victim's anthem is: I'm a loser and it's *your* fault! If I fail math class, the teacher couldn't teach. If I get a divorce, it's because my parents split up. If I get pregnant before marriage, it's because of my home-life. If I didn't get hired, it's because of the color of my skin. Why do we have such a hard time pinning any blame on ourselves and our choices? When I am perfectly honest with myself I find that I am responsible for most of my problems. If you could kick the person most responsible for your problems you wouldn't be able to sit down for a week! And there is no way to run from your problems because wherever you go, *you'll* be there!

In our society, we find more and more IDI's - I Deserve It's. Their IDIology is self-centered and preoccupied with their wants and needs. In fact, they think they need everything they want and someone should give it to them. If they don't have what they want - it's *your* fault.

When we look to others to blame or we start feeling sorry for ourselves we get a disease. PLOM disease; Poor Little Old Me. PLOM disease is like the snake bite. It paralyzes you. Most IDI's have it. I've had young people come and go through our youth group who just couldn't seem to get life together. Mainly because they wouldn't face the fact that *their* choices had consequences for *them.* It became too convenient to blame Momma, Daddy, the teacher, the church, and the lotto man for all their troubles. When a winner makes a mistake she says, "I was wrong." When a loser makes a mistake she says, "It wasn't my fault."

When your feeling sorry for yourself, your being ungrateful, acting selfishly, finding fault with your situation, your not praying effectively and your not working toward a solution.

Even though most of the time our choices are responsible for our problems, sometimes we are victims of others selfishness or carelessness. That's just the world we live in. You may be the victim of a divorce, disease, downsizing, an accident or abuse.

Don't take the bait to live your life as a victim, choose to live as a *victor* in Christ! God is still on the throne, he is still watching over you, he still loves you! You may be hard pressed on every side but your not crushed; perplexed but not in despair, persecuted but not abandoned; struck down but not destroyed! You must have the courage to release any bitterness or hurt into the hands of your heavenly father. Forgive them! Bitterness is a poison you drink hoping it will hurt someone else.

> SHOW ME A HERO AND I WILL SHOW YOU A TRAGEDY.

Once you have forgiven them, learn to rejoice in the midst of your trouble. Change your perspective. Work at solving your dilemma. Pray, praise, and stop procrastinating!

Success is the best revenge for the victim. If you came from a broken home, stop the trend with you. *You* stay married. If you have been the victim of someone's anger, stop the trend with you. Learn to control *your* anger. If you were abused, stop the trend with you. Set apart your hands and tongue for building up not tearing down. You can't do much about your ancestors but you can do a lot for your descendants! *You* start a godly heritage, a line of victors instead of victims! You can do it; I have!

Show me a hero and I will show you a tragedy. History is full of people who have suffered as victims and came out as conquerors! Names like George Washington, Lincoln, Carver, Booker T. Washington, Wilma Rudolph, Winston Churchill and Napoleon, to name a few. You can do it too! Don't be paralyzed by PLOM! Study these portions of the Bible: Romans 8:28, Acts 16:16-40, I Peter 3:13-18, Matthew 6:14-15, Genesis 37-47, also see the section in this book on Adversity.

Avoid the neuro-toxins of the Fatal Five, let the Fab Five chart your destiny. I'm excited about your future!

cw

AUTHORITY

Just the mention of the word causes some to bristle. In today's world the rebel is glorified and the conformist is vilified. Authority is something to triumph over, depose, and overthrow. Is that really the best way to go about it?

In this chapter, we will explore the reality of authority. We will answer for you questions like: Why does authority exist? How should we respond to it? What about imperfect, unfair authority? When should you ever disobey authority?

The fact is: authority is everywhere. You can't get away from it and much of your future depends on how you respond to it.

I love you,
CW

"BUT DAVID SAID TO ABISHAI, "DON'T DESTROY HIM!
WHO CAN LAY A HAND ON THE LORD'S ANOINTED AND
BE GUILTLESS?" I SAMUEL 26:9

"NO MAN IS ABOVE THE LAW AND NO MAN IS BELOW
IT; NOR DO WE ASK ANY MAN'S PERMISSION WHEN
WE REQUIRE HIM TO OBEY IT. OBEDIENCE TO THE
LAW IS DEMANDED AS A RIGHT; NOT ASKED AS A
FAVOR."
THEODORE ROOSEVELT

WHENCE CAME THIS?

Authority is a weird thing. It is one of those intangible entities that manifests itself in tangible ways. Where did it come from? Why does it exist at all? Why can't we do *what* we want *when* we want and not have to answer to any authority? What gives anyone the right to govern over anyone else?

All authority trickles down from the one who has *all* authority - God. (Rom. 13) There is no higher court, no higher appeal. No army can overthrow God and no revolution can depose Him. No one can justly accuse him or vote Him out of office. All authority and all the power in the universe belongs to and originates with God. It is a good thing he is all loving too. For absolute power corrupts absolutely. But a being who by His nature *always* acts for the highest good is incorruptible.

Just as authority itself originates with God, the *principles* of authority that govern the universe also come from Him. You must learn these principles and align your decisions with them so that - as in the words of Spock - you may "Live long and prosper." The principles of authority are a God-thing. You cannot break these principles. You can either use them as a foundation for your life or you can break yourself against them. It's that simple.

Principle #1: Authority is everywhere

No matter where you go, someone is always in charge. You will never go anywhere where an authority does not exist. If you happen to be someplace where there is no authority, you had better watch your head because anarchy will dominate until someone takes charge. There are no vacuums of authority. When one leaves, another will rush in and take its place. Mankind has fought many battles over who would be the ruling authority in a certain place.

There is authority...

- in heaven
- in the spirit realm of angels and demons
- that governs nations, territories and cities
- in the workplace
- in church
- in school
- in families
- in your own being (flesh or spirit)

Principle # 2: All authority comes from God.

All human authority is borrowed from God.

Romans 13 speaks for itself:

> ..for there is no authority except that which God has established. The authorities that exist have been established by God. Consequently he who rebels against the authority is rebelling against what God has instituted, and those who do so will bring judgement upon themselves.

Principle #3: Authority protects and provides.

So many people dislike the idea of authority. They do so out of ignorance. They don't realize all the *good* things authority gives us. We can place them in two categories: Protection and Provision.

Protection:

Authority is like an umbrella. It's above you, and it protects you from rain. The authorities God has placed in your life protect you from harm.

My wife and I have two small children. Like all good parents, we took the time to childproof our house. Why would we do such a thing? To protect them. Did this limit their freedom? You bet. So many people look at those in charge and think, "I hate having my freedom limited." Maybe they should take the time to be thankful for the protection they offer. What do we need protection from? Other people, ourselves, natural laws (like gravity) and bad physics (force = mass x acceleration; big truck moving quickly, little boy standing in the road = bad physics).

The police do more than limit my freedom. They protect me from criminals and from myself. In fact, some have been so kind as to give me hand written slips of paper to remind me that driving too fast could harm me or somebody else. The United States Government does more to me than tax me; they protect me from enemies foreign and domestic. I do more than discipline my children, I put poisons out of reach (bad chemistry) and little thingy's in the electrical outlets (bad physics). You should have seen the look on my son's face after he put a pair of tweezers in those strange holes in the wall.

Before you despair freedoms lost due to authority, maybe you should be thankful your not getting rained on as much as you could be.

Provision:

When people think of authority, they think it takes things from us; things like freedom, fun, opportunities. Authority does take some things away, but usually only for a season. But it provides us so much more than it takes away. Authority is mainly a giver, not a taker. In fact, it takes only to give us something better.

Authority...

- takes some freedom in order to provide an atmosphere of peace and order instead of chaos. (Your not free to yell 'fire!' in a movie theater when there is no fire.)

- takes some opportunities from me to provide for the common good. A man once offered me a substantial amount of cash - more than I would make in two years of working full time - to airlift cigarettes into Canada for their black market. Authority took that opportunity from me in order to provide for the common good of society. If I had taken the offer, authority would have provided me with a nice place to stay for a few years, complete with cable TV, weight room, and lots of *nice* fellows to *socialize* with.

- gave me food and shelter when I couldn't provide for myself

- provides me with employment

- provides me with accountability

- provides me with knowledge and power to achieve goals

To remove all authority would remove our sources of employment, accountability, the rule of law, order, peace, protection and security. Humanity would degenerate to the lowest common denominator and chaos would reign. *Think differently.* See authority from a different, biblical perspective. Be *thankful* for authority. Authority does many good things for us. If you choose to rebel, you will miss out.

Principle #4: Authority works through a chain of command

God establishes authorities on different levels. In fact, without different levels of authority, authority itself would not exist. Understand this: *When working with authorities, it is best to work through the chain of command, not independent of it.*

When I was a flight instructor at a small college, the chain of command went like this: Staff Instructors, Chief Flight Instructor, Aviation Department Head, Dean of the College of Engineering. Well, it so happened that the staff instructors worked long hours for low pay and sometimes no pay. After awhile, a couple of instructors didn't think our plight was very fair. So they dutifully prepared a proposal that pled our case for more pay. They circulated the petition amongst the staff so they could sign their names, putting their support behind it. It came to me and being caught up in the spirit of Lec Walesa, solidarity and all that, I signed my name.

What was the problem? Well, these boys bypassed two levels of authority and marched the proposal/petition straight to the dean's office. This was a big mistake. The dean listened to the proposal and the boys left her office in seeming triumph. The dean then called our department head and ask him what in the world was going on in his division. Because we had bypassed two levels of authority, he had no idea. He was made to look like a fool.

If you want to stay on good terms with your authorities, don't make them look like a fool. He came back to the department and called a meeting with all the staff instructors. Wow, was he mad! He basically stated that what we did was poor judgement and that if we didn't like working there, go find another job! He made it clear that the proposal was not bad but the big mistake was *bypassing the chain of command.*

After learning that lesson, I had another opportunity to test this principle. While traveling to Costa Rica on a mission trip, we had a girl lose her ticket during a layover. We went to the ticket counter (first in the chain) and explained to him our dilemma. He listened then directed us to another counter (second in the chain). This man listened to our story and confirmed via his computer that she was indeed registered on the next flight, however he said that I would have to pay $600 for another ticket. After they helped me up from the floor, I explained to him that it seemed unreasonable to pay for a ticket we already bought. We went back and forth on the issue and he maintained his ground. So what do you do? Go up the chain of command. Maybe he didn't have the authority to make that decision. I politely asked to speak to his supervisor. He disappeared for a few minutes and came back with permission to write us another boarding pass. I never saw his supervisor, but it's obvious he had the authority to make that decision.

What if the supervisor denied my request? Just keep going up the chain. I would have politely asked to speak to his supervisor and so on. I never raised my voice or made a threat. I just calmly climbed the chain of command. My ultimate trump card in this case (besides the favor of God) was any company's highest authority - the customer. Had I needed to I would have planted in his mind the idea of all these teenagers going home and dedicating hours of their time telling a worldwide audience on the internet how unfairly this particular airline treated them.☺

The chain of command:

- keeps you from embarrassment
- keeps your authority from embarrassment
- keeps the lines of communication open
- develops trust between authorities and those under authority
- keeps those in charge from being overloaded
- keeps those most knowledgeable about a situation closest to it
- allows people to specialize and thus enables them to perform certain tasks at a higher level
- divides up responsibility and rewards those who are willing and able to handle more

There is one situation in which I would bypass the chain of command. I would do it carefully and prayerfully if I felt that my authority was involved in some corrupt, perhaps unlawful activity. Then I would bypass that authority to the next honest authority. But overall, if you use the chain of command, it will be to your benefit. If you consistently bypass the chain of command, it will be to your own detriment. (Luke 14:7-11, Matthew 18, Exodus 18:20-24)

Principle #5: All human authority is imperfect

God's authority is perfect. But once that authority is delegated to a human, no matter how altruistic they may be, that authority becomes tainted. You may have noticed this trait (imperfection) in one of your God given authorities, like maybe your parents, teachers or a boss.

Principle #6: God uses imperfect authority to make us more like Him.

Have you ever been under an authority that treated you unfairly? Maybe your parents blamed you for something you didn't do or an employer snapped at you. Perhaps they made a decision you didn't agree with. Perhaps this decision made things harder on you and in your opinion it was a bad decision. Have you ever had an authority that was not only unfair but just plain ornery? They went out of your way to do you harm?

The Bible gives us an account of just such a situation. We can all learn from what happened. This account is found in I Samuel.

Saul was king of Israel and David was a shepherd who had just been promoted to busboy. While taking food to his brothers who were on the front lines of the war with the Philistines, David encountered Goliath. With the power of God behind him, David conquered the giant Philistine and he became a hero. Saul hired him to be on staff in the palace and also gave him his daughter's hand in marriage. So here was David, under the authority of the king (like everyone else in Israel), under the authority of a boss (who happened to be the king), and under the authority of a Father-in-Law (who happened to be his boss and the king).

All of this was not that unusual until something bad started to happen. Saul became jealous of David and began to plot against him. David's authority acted unfairly and unrighteously. It came to the point that Saul tried to kill David a number of times. Picture yourself coming home from your first job and your parents asking you how your day went and you reply, "It was ok until my boss tried to kill me. It was downhill after that."

At this point David had a choice. It's the same choice we all must make when confronted with imperfect authority - *rebel or trust*.

It would have been so easy for David to rebel. After all, he was the next king in line anyway. He did nothing wrong, and it was obvious to all that Saul was misusing his authority.

> **THROUGH PATIENCE A RULER CAN BE PERSUADED, AND A GENTLE TONGUE CAN BREAK A BONE.**
> Proverbs 25:15

David chose to trust in the God who judges justly (I Samuel 24:15). What did God bless him with for trusting - a life on the run in fear and a home in the desert. Here was David, the future king, running like a scared rabbit.

What was God doing? The same things he does to us. God was breaking him and purging out the "Saul" that was in David.

When God wants to do something fantastic, he looks for a man (or woman) and then he crushes him. In his book *A Tale of Three Kings*, (you must read this book), Gene Edwards puts it this way: "What does this world need: Gifted men, outwardly empowered? Or broken men, inwardly transformed?" God wants you to be a broken vessel, one that he can use. *He will often use imperfect authorities to be his grinding mill.* If you choose to rebel you will miss out on this crushing process. Many people choose to drop out and they never reach their godly potential. And God desires much but ends up with very few men and women who will live broken before him.

God also knew something else about David that is also true for you. In his time, he would be king. And deep in his heart there was a Saul. There was anger, bitterness, jealousy, deceit, and lust. During this process God used imperfect, unfair authority to purify David of the "Sauls" within him so that when he became king, he would be more like the King of Kings. One day, you too will be king. You will be the one in authority. You will be the mom. You will be the dad. You will be the employer, teacher, lawmaker, pastor or Sunday school teacher. The problem is *you* are imperfect. You have character flaws that God wants to smooth over. There are 'Sauls' in you like pride, laziness, deceit, and selfishness. Many times the very same things that really grind you about other people are also in *you*. When you become king, he wants you to be more like the King of Kings. And many times, he will use imperfect authorities to root around in your character to remove flaws and bring into balance your personality.

So the choices are there.

- Rebel against imperfect authorities. Rise up in defiance because *you* know *you* are right! If you choose this you will become like them and repeat their patterns. Patterns of divorce, abuse, addiction, deceit, laziness, wickedness, and selfishness will be deeply entrenched in you.

- Bear up under it. Let it drive you to a deeper trust and intimacy with your Lord. And in the process you will submit to God's grinding mill. He will crush you into someone he can use; someone more like him. (I Peter 2:13-25, I Peter 4:19)

God took a crushed man name David and made him into the greatest king, songwriter and comforter of broken hearts the world has ever known; what will he make of your brokenness?

There is one time when you should respectfully go against what an authority directs you to do. It still puts you in the position of trusting God. When an authority asks you to do something that is against God's law, you must answer to the higher authority. There are many employers out there that will ask you to lie, cheat, steal, or some other dishonoring deed. You must never dishonor God to honor an earthly authority. (Acts 4:19, 5:29, Daniel Chapters 3 and 6)

Principle #7: Rebellion is a thief

Rebellion will make you more like the Devil than anything else. That is why the Bible links rebellion and witchcraft together. (I Samuel

15:23) In John chapter 10, Jesus describes Satan as a thief that comes to steal, kill and destroy. Since rebellion and Satan are so closely linked, it only make sense to see that authority gives, (principle #3) rebellions steals.

If you rebel against your teachers, you will lose wisdom. (Proverbs 13:13) It's a big world out there and God has given you authorities to provide you with godly wisdom to help you better navigate your way through this life. If you rebel against your teachers and cultivate an unteachable spirit, I guarantee your life will hit some rocks. It's hard enough to avoid them when you *are* following the map. Those who are unteachable get the privilege of learning things the hard way, through failure, embarrassment, pain or punishment. How much better to learn from God and those he puts in our lives. It's what you learn *after* you know it all that really matters. Life is too short to make all the mistakes yourself; learn from the mistakes of others. Jesus said, "Take my yoke upon you and *learn* from me..." (Matthew 11:29).

If you rebel against discipline you will lose freedom. (Proverbs 13:18) Everybody loves freedom. It is a great thing. But how do we go about attaining it? Only through discipline. It is the disciplined musician that has the freedom to move people with his skill. It is the disciplined athlete who enjoys the freedom of running a mile in four minutes. It is the disciplined student who possesses the freedom of a scholarship. It is the disciplined businessman who delights in the freedom the fruit of his labor brings.

> "KIDS ARE FOOLING THEMSELVES IF THEY THINK THEY CAN OBEY GOD AND BE DISOBEDIENT TO THEIR PARENTS. THEY'RE FOOLING THEMSELVES IF THEY THINK THEY CAN LOVE GOD AND NOT LOVE THEIR PARENTS."
> The late Rich Mullins

Discipline brings freedom, period. If you want freedom, get disciplined. God places people in along our path to help us gain self-discipline. People who rebel against these authorities grow up without the freedom and benefits of forbearance. They slum through life never seeming to get off the ground while the self-disciplined around them enjoy the freedom to soar into the heights God planned for them.

If you rebel against correction, you will lose yourself. (Proverbs 15:32) Rebelling against correction usually takes the form of lying and manipulation. You are accused of some dastardly deed and rather than confess it and repent of it, you take the bait and lie or manipulate with some excuse. Over the long haul this pattern of deceit and manipulation become entrenched in your character. You begin to act differently around different people. Around your church friends you act like them. Around your work or school friends you act like them. You begin to lose sight of who *you* are. Fyodor Dolstoyevsky in his book "The Brothers Karamazov" put it this way,

> "A man who lies to himself, and believes his own lies, becomes unable to recognize the truth, either in himself or in anyone else...Having no love in him, he yields to his impulses, indulges in the lowest forms of pleasure, and behaves in the end like an animal."

If you rebel against obedience, you lose the protection authority provides you. (See principle #3) (Proverbs 20:20, 19:16) Many of those in graves and hospital beds around the world are there because they disobeyed authority. Authority acts as a buffer between you and pain. If you choose to rebel, be ready for the pain. A young boy I know of is dead now because he rebelled against numerous buffers and wandered down to an off limits swimming area. He took a dare from some other kids to play on some of the apparatus. He fell into water over his head, became trapped under a raft and drowned.

They say the movie that started it all was "Rebel Without a Cause" with James Dean and Natalie Wood. Those two, along with Sal Mineo, Nick Adams, and producer David Weisbort all died young in a set of deaths so strange that it has become known as the 'Rebel Without a Cause' curse. Coincidence? Maybe. One of the ten commandments is "Honor your Father and Mother." It is the only commandment with a promise "..that it may go well with you and that you may enjoy long life on the earth." (Ephesians 6:2-3)

As you travel through life, you will notice unwise, undisciplined, duplicitous people with more than there fair share of pain. You can be reasonably sure they allowed the thief called rebellion to loot and pillage their life and potential.

Creative ways to rebel and be robbed:

- *You don't do what your authority asks unless you feel like it.* You will grow to be ruled by your emotions. You will be unstable, impetuous and selfish. You will miss out on the greatest things this life can provide: love, truth, integrity, salvation, and a moral compass. None of these depend on feeling. Learn to rise above your feelings. Do not do what you want but what you *ought;* this is true freedom. You will learn to persevere instead of becoming a quitter. God calls them "More than conquerors" (Romans 8:37).

- *Do what they ask but grumble and complain about it.* You will steal honor and value from other people if you are a complainer. What you are really saying is that what *they* want is not as important or valuable as what *you* want. You will miss opportunities to add value and honor to people. You will become a taker not a maker. People get tired of those who continually take without producing anything of value.

- *Forget to do tasks assigned.* You will have missed opportunities to learn attentiveness and responsibility.

- *Make him explain every detail why he wants it done before you do it.* This action shows how inconsiderate you have become;

inconsiderate of others time and talents.

- *Point out to others the failures and shortcomings of your authority.* You have learned the skill of the faultfinder. Don't be robbed of the opportunity to pray for your authority and train yourself to be a goodfinder instead!

A tale of two campers

Brenda was a sharp girl who came from a Christian home. Every year she would come to camp to grow closer to God. While at camp, she learned these principles of authority. According to Brenda, (and others), her parents were over-protective and over time the relationship with her mom and dad eroded. Instead of using these principles of authority and trusting God, Brenda rebelled. She couldn't bring herself to believe that God had her best interest in mind. Brenda wanted to do what she wanted to do. She had only one more year before her 18th birthday. She could leave the house with her parents' blessing. But she couldn't wait.

Brenda seemed to love God and desired his best most of the time. She remained a virgin and purposed in heart to stay that way until she married. She dreamed of a good home with a great husband and children. But during this time of tension with her parents along came Jeff. Jeff showed an interest in her but he was not a Christian. Her parents did not really approve of the relationship. Brenda disregarded her parents' guidelines and left home to live with Jeff before she graduated from high school. Soon she lost her virginity, involved herself in drugs and Jeff became violent towards her.

At one time God had a great future for her. Now the desires of a high school graduation, good home, godly husband, and pure wedding night are all but gone. I pray and believe God can restore Brenda. But she will have to live with the pain and regret her decisions brought upon her for the rest of her life. If she had only realized that authority gives and rebellion steals.

Stephanie was another camper at the same camp. She also learned these axioms. When she returned home, her beliefs about authority were put to the test. Stephanie was ready for college. She felt a calling to a school of art. Her father, who was not a Christian (and who happened to be paying for her school) opposed the idea. He didn't feel it was practical and felt she should go to a state school.

Stephanie could have thumbed her nose at her father but instead she chose to operate by Biblical principles. She went to God in prayer and gave the situation over to him. With tears, she relinquished her rights and placed them into the hands of the Lord.

The day came to send the money in for Michigan State University. Her father had the check in hand ready to send when something strange happened. He suddenly had a change of heart. He felt that Stephanie should go to the school of art! He tore up the check and sent her to her school of her choice. God had changed the heart of the king. Had Stephanie rebelled, she would have lost the respect of her father, her Christian testimony, and money for school. Because she trusted in the Lord, he gave her all of these things plus an intimate trust she never would have gained by rebelling.

Where the rubber meets the road

Don't let the prevailing thought of the crowd dictate how you should think, especially about authority. Yes, sometimes the authorities in our lives can be a pain, just as you will be a pain to those under your authority one day. But they keep you from much more pain. They provide you with opportunities to reach your potential and become more like your Creator. Learn to give grace and honor to those around you and you will be given grace and God will see to it you are honored.

Understand that when you make a decision that opposes the crowd it will be tested. You will be tempted toward deceit rather than truth, selfishness rather than love. These are just subtle forms of rebellion. Fill your mind with the Truth of God and prepare yourself for these crossroads, then choose the best. Wisdom is its own reward.

Let God determine how you think about authority. Start with meditating on these portions of God's word. When you are facing difficulty with an authority, these will help you trust in God's motives and power. They will keep you from a distorted picture of reality and help you see the bigger picture.

(Ephesians 5:22-33, 6:1-8, I Timothy 6:1-3, I Samuel Chs. 17-Romans 13:1-7, Hebrews 13:17 through 26, I Peter 2:13-23, 4:19
Acts 4:19, 5:29 I Samuel 24:11-15 I Samuel 26:8-11)

Also, you must read "A Tale of Three Kings," by Gene Edwards. And for more insight, try "Spiritual Authority," by Watchman Nee and "The Bait of Satan" by John Bevere

I love you,
cw

THE PURSUIT OF PLEASURE

One of the keys to finding meaning in life is wonder. There exists in each of us a desire to pursue the 'wows' of life. Since this need for pleasure exists, many questions come to mind. How do we find genuine freedom to enjoy life in its best offerings? How do we choose that which is legitimate pleasure and reject that which is illegitimate?

There are very few issues that we need to think through and address as much as this one. You are forced to swim in a culture filled with an incredible number of pleasurable options. Our culture feeds you a steady diet of all that appeals to the eye and the imagination, with so little to nurture the conscience. Then it manipulates you to believe that because you hunger for something, it is sufficient reason to consume it. And what is worse, new appetites are being created that leave you hungrier than before while you sit under the illusion that those hungers could be met if one could only remove all restraint.

I am sad to think of the damage done to many people long before they have the maturity or inner strength to accept the good and reject the lies.

Sights, sounds, images, tastes, feelings, passions and experiences abound, all offered up in a glittering array. This section explores how God would have you drink of life's pleasures without drowning in them.

cw

"I DENIED MYSELF NOTHING MY EYES DESIRED; I
REFUSED MY HEART NO PLEASURE...AND
EVERYTHING WAS MEANINGLESS."
KING SOLOMON

"I HAVE HAD MILLIONAIRE BUSINESSMEN COME TO MY
OFFICE AND TELL ME THEY HAVE BIG HOUSES, YACHTS,
CONDOMINIUMS IN COLORADO, NICE CHILDREN,
BEAUTIFUL MISTRESSES, AN UNSUSPECTING WIFE,
SECURE CORPORATE POSITIONS - AND SUICIDAL
TENDENCIES. THEY HAVE EVERYTHING THE WORLD HAS
TO OFFER EXCEPT ONE THING - INNER PEACE AND JOY.
THEY COME TO MY OFFICE AS A LAST RESORT, BEGGING
ME TO HELP THEM CONQUER THE URGE TO KILL
THEMSELVES."
DR.'S FRANK MINIRTH AND PAUL MEIER IN THEIR BOOK
"HAPPINESS IS A CHOICE."

SWIMMING IN THE RIVER OF DELIGHT

While flying home from Poland, I read a story more oft repeated than almost any other I know. It's a story of a man destroyed by illegitimate, unrestrained pleasure.

Chris Dawes was a computer software tycoon. He founded a business in his attic and turned it into one worth hundreds of millions of dollars. He quit the company called Micromuse and sold his share for over $48 million dollars. He was not yet forty with all the toys money could buy, including a seven million dollar jet, seven million dollar helicopter, and mansions around the world. Six months later he was dead. His choices about money did not destroy him. His choices about pleasure did.

He joined a very long list of seemingly successful people who appeared to have the right stuff for life. Everything they to touched turned to gold - except the things that mattered most, their relationship with God, their marriages, families, and their sanity.

Alexander the Great conquered the world but he couldn't conquer his alcohol addiction. Elvis Presley had everything the world had to offer, and his half brother found his dead, bloated, drug ravaged body lying prone on the floor with a Bible and a book on the Shroud of Turin open beneath him. Friedrich W. Nietzshe, a German philosopher who popularized the saying "God is Dead," lived life on his own terms until the pursuit of illegitimate sexual pleasure left him insane from syphilis. Everything in life, he thought, could be reduced to the assertion of self will, yet the last 12 years of his life he remained a prisoner of his sister's will.

History does not record the millions of nameless men and women who destroyed everything meaningful through the pursuit of pleasure without the proper wisdom or restraint. Perhaps a part of this great tragedy has played itself out in your own home.

But now it is your turn - your turn to learn how to harness pleasure for good or evil. How you handle the pursuit of pleasure will most definitely affect your future. Pleasure can lift you into the fullness of life or it can make that same life meaningless.

Guidance?

As I entered trigonometry class my freshman year of college, someone told me that the space shuttle exploded. When I returned home, the story unfolded on the evening news. Six astronauts and a school teacher were tragically killed when an o-ring failed and flames from the solid rocket boosters cut into the main fuel tank like a blow torch. During times like these we find it easy to question God as to the how's and why's of tragedy and adversity. But why is it we often times fail to seek God for guidance when it comes to the pursuit of pleasure? The fact is pleasure and prosperity ruin more people than adversity and tragedy.

The pursuit of happiness for its own sake is a frustrating, disillusioning, and often futile effort. Happiness usually hides from those who are spiritually addicted to its sugar, while it chases after those who make wise choices and who are caught up in something more lasting than momentary excitement. Ultimately, meaninglessness does not come from being weary of pain, but from being weary of pleasure. (Luke 8:14)

In our pleasure driven culture, unrestrained gratification robs much of our society of real joy and full lives. The idol for the new millennium is fun. And like any idol it takes more than it gives. Young people compromise God's protective and nurturing guidelines because 'it's fun.' They avoid rewarding challenges because it feels too much like work and everyone knows work is not 'fun.' Mindless pursuits chew away time while eroding away the discernment and thinking abilities of a generation.

The lie is you can have it all, all at once. The truth is you can't have it all and only some of it is worth having anyway. Only knowing and following God's principles of pursuing gratification will enable you to live your life to the fullest. God is not out to limit your fun; he is out to limit the pain illegitimate pleasure will bring you. His principles accomplish this while at the same time freeing you to experience true joy and ultimate living! (Psalms 16:11, 19:7-11)

English writer F.W. Boreham has addressed this theme masterfully. Some of the following thoughts are his with Dr. Ravi Zacharias' as found in Ravi's book *Cries of the Heart*.[1]

Principle of Pleasure #1

Any pleasure that refreshes you without diminishing you, distracting you or sidetracking you from the ultimate goal is a legitimate pleasure. This obviously means that there is a fundamental prerequisite for defining any legitimate pleasure in life, and that is to establish the purpose of life itself. All pleasure is built upon why you and I live in the first place. Without knowing the ultimate purpose of life we tend to treat pleasure as a cafeteria, picking and choosing what suits us with no thought for the bigger picture. Without knowing life's purpose, it becomes impossible to distinguish between fulfillment and disappointment, between fun and destructiveness.

Susannah Wesley had this purpose in mind when she answered her son John's request for a definition of sin. (John and his brother Charles led the great revival in England.) She answered him,

> "Whatever weakens your reasoning, impairs the tenderness of your conscience, obscures your sense of God or takes away your relish for spiritual things; in short, if anything increases the authority and the power of the flesh over the spirit, that to you becomes sin, however good it is in itself."

Life's ultimate purpose is to know God and worship him forever. Any pleasure that diminishes that relationship is illegitimate and will ultimately steal from you. God also has unique personal purposes for us that fit into his 'Grander Scheme.' **Pleasure that distracts us from our personal missions and God given goals along life's journey are also illegitimate.**

Samson is the perfect example of this. From the beginning, God marked his life with purpose. Not only the grand purpose of knowing God but a unique personal purpose that fit into the 'Grand Scheme.' God uniquely gifted Samson to become the deliverer of Israel.

Samson continually failed to keep these purposes in mind. He routinely ignored the big picture and pursued pleasure cafeteria style, with no thought to the bigger consequences. He could not tame his passions and bring them under the control of his greater call. (Judges 13-16)

If a person does not understand that the purpose of life defines lifestyle, then the lifestyle itself is hollow and the life is squandered. Samson should not have frequented the places he did and he ought not to have flirted with the pleasures and people he did. Wisdom is proved right by her actions and Samson's tragically lived life underscores the truth of this principle.

This simple fact has deep implications. The places we go, the friendships we embrace, the hobbies we choose, the language we use, the shows we watch, the books we read, the thoughts we entertain - all must be aligned with the purposes to which we are called by God.

The active ingredient in rat poison - the stuff that kills - is bromethalin, but the poison contains only .01% of it. Ninety-nine point nine percent of it is harmless! Many times life presents us with good, edifying pleasures *mixed* with poor, diminishing, sinful, pleasures. The bait is to partake in the activity, justifying the ingesting of the poison because it's 'fun.' We are willing to ingest the poison because we are addicted to the sugar of pleasure.

When this happens a disturbing progression many times happens. At first, we are aware of the poison, and we may say, "That's not right." But as we permit it in our lives, we build a tolerance to it and we stop noticing the diminishing effect it has on us. Then, we begin to not only

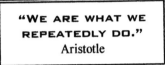

"WE ARE WHAT WE REPEATEDLY DO."
Aristotle

tolerate it, but we start to *hunger for it*. We have slowly trained our appetites to take pleasure in things that grieve God and diminish us.

Life is a series of goals and transitions. The larger goals of the big picture contain smaller objectives that you must keep in mind when questioning specific pleasures. If one of your long term visions is to become a doctor, then sometimes you must choose between study and play. When you can truthfully say that a chosen form of recreation will refresh you without taking away from your smaller goal (as well as the larger purposes of life), then go for it! At this point you can drink in pleasure for all it is worth without facing the consequence of a poor choice. For you, the sky will be bluer and the grass greener, because you will not have the nagging feeling that you should be doing something else. There is a time for everything. This leads us to principle number two.

Principle of Pleasure #2

Sometimes you must choose the best over the good. Life is full of trade-offs. You cannot have everything. Many times life presents you with the choice of two or more good things to do. If you would live your life to the fullest you must choose the best over the good. Get in the habit of asking, "Is this God's best for my life or is it just the good?" The Apostle Paul prayed, "That your love may abound more and more in the knowledge and depth of insight, so that you may be able to **discern what is best** and may be pure and blameless until the day of Christ." (Phil. 1:9)

Sometimes life is like playing on monkey bars. In order to reach the next ring, you must let go of the one you now have. At any moment you must be willing to trade the good for the best, the temporal for the eternal, the pleasure of things for the pleasure of life, everything you are for everything you can be.

Principle of Pleasure #3

Delay your gratification; less now for more later. One of the greatest indicators of maturity and success is the ability to delay gratification. Mature, successful people make a habit of trading less now for more later.

The difficulty of resisting short run temptations for the long-run gains of enjoying a more satisfying life has been borne out in experiments with children. The experiments started with four-year-old children at Stanford University's pre-school.

Researchers took each child into a room and gave to them one marshmallow. They told each child, "You can eat this marshmallow as soon as you want, but if you wait and don't eat it until I return in a little while, then I will give you a second marshmallow." When the researcher left, they observed the children through a one way window. Several of the children ate their marshmallows immediately, others tried to resist temptation but soon devoured their's as well. Others stayed determined to wait, and soon received a second marshmallow.

The result of each child's experiment was recorded, and then researchers followed their academic performance through their later school years. Those children who had saved their first marshmallow until they received the second were later found to be, according to researchers, better adapted and more popular, and they exhibited more confidence and responsibility than those children who could not delay gratification. Also, those who had resisted temptation scored an average of 20 to 25 percent higher on the Scholastic Aptitude Test (SAT), the test most widely used by colleges and universities to help predict academic success.[2]

Our culture is willing to give you a dollar's worth of pleasure *NOW* if you are willing to forfeit the $100 worth of pleasure God has for you *LATER*. God does not want to deny you pleasure; he wants to make sure you have the *character to handle it*.

Culture shows you the dollars worth of pleasure and hides the $100 worth of pain it may bring you. Ask the man working for minimum wage if skipping high school to have 'fun' was worth it. Ask the young mother

> "HOW LITTLE PEOPLE KNOW WHO THINK HOLINESS IS DULL."
> C. S. Lewis

with thousands of dollars in credit card debt if it was worth it. Ask her what it's like to get call after call from creditors demanding payment. Ask her what it's like to be consumed with worry and have to beg people for rent money; then ask her if the new outfit was worth it.   Ask   anyone dying of lung cancer if the pleasure(?) of smoking was worth it. Ask someone with herpes or AIDS if the momentary pleasure was worth it. Ask the pregnant teenager if it was worth it. Then ask the child raised without a father if it was worth it. If you could, I would like you to ask the child being sucked out of the womb with a vacuum hose if it was worth it.

Ask a father who is too obese to play a game of tag with his son if all that food was worth it. Ask him what it will be like to die young, then ask him if it was worth it. Ask him what he thinks a heart attack will feel like, then ask him if it was worth it. Ask the man going blind from diabetes if the food was worth it. Obesity related health problems cost Americans $102 billion in 1999.[3] Gluttony is still a sin.

The commercials show you the fun of the party but they hide the hospital scenes and the funerals of the people killed by drunk drivers. Ask the drunk man who has orphaned two children by slamming into their mother with his truck if the buzz was worth it. Stare into the eyes of a screaming crack baby and ask the mother if it was worth it. Ask the prostitute if the heroin high is worth it.

Ask Esau if the cup of soup was worth it. Ask David at the end of his tragic, pain filled life if Bathsheba was worth it. Illegitimate pleasures are seasonal; they come and go. God wants to give you eternal pleasures! Sometimes living the Christian life is difficult; ask the man in heaven if it was worth it. (Genesis 25-27, Luke 16:19-31, Psalms 16:11)

All pleasure costs you something. Legitimate pleasure makes you pay the price up front. You delay your gratification. Illegitimate pleasure lets you have the gratification now, but you pay a hefty price later. Life presents to you this question: Will you play now and *pay* more later or pay now and *play* more later? It is far better to shun the bait than to struggle in the snare. If you pick the blossoms, you can't eat the fruit. If you would live your life to the fullest, learn to pass on the Washington and keep your eyes on the Franklin.

Principle of Pleasure #4

The story was told by Rich Wilkerson, who had just finished speaking at a junior high school assembly when the principal approached him and told him this story.

He said the previous year they had an eighth grade student in the school whose situation brought much grief to the school community. All of a sudden and for no apparent reason, this thirteen-year-old boy had started coming to school one hour late every day.

"I couldn't get this boy to come to school on time. First, I sent notes to his parents. He would bring the note back the next day signed by his parents - an hour late!" the principal said. No matter what disciplinary method the school administrators tried, the following day the boy would still come an hour late. Finally they suspended him for a few days. His first day back he returned - an hour late.

"I just couldn't take it anymore, so the next day I contacted the Department of Welfare. The welfare agents accompanied me to the boy's home. We walked up to the front door and knocked. No one answered. So I turned the doorknob. It was open so we walked in, and what we found wasn't very pretty. We discovered that two months earlier, while he was at school, the boy's parents had left home." They had left a large supply of groceries in the cupboards and refrigerator, but they themselves were gone. The boy had no idea where they were. He felt abandoned and betrayed, ashamed to tell the story to the school authorities. So every day he would get his eight-year-old sister and six-year-old brother out of bed, bathe and dress them for school, and then walk them to their elementary school two miles away. Try as he might, he could never run fast enough to get to his own school earlier than one hour late.[4]

What you are feeling right now illustrates the fourth principle of pleasure: **Any pleasure that jeopardizes the sacred right of another is an illegitimate pleasure**.

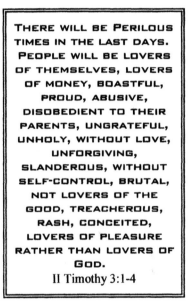

THERE WILL BE PERILOUS TIMES IN THE LAST DAYS. PEOPLE WILL BE LOVERS OF THEMSELVES, LOVERS OF MONEY, BOASTFUL, PROUD, ABUSIVE, DISOBEDIENT TO THEIR PARENTS, UNGRATEFUL, UNHOLY, WITHOUT LOVE, UNFORGIVING, SLANDEROUS, WITHOUT SELF-CONTROL, BRUTAL, NOT LOVERS OF THE GOOD, TREACHEROUS, RASH, CONCEITED, LOVERS OF PLEASURE RATHER THAN LOVERS OF GOD.
II Timothy 3:1-4

The question on the surface: how can anyone be so irresponsible and cruel? The average person would not be so heartless as to abandon their children but how often have we violated this principle without realizing it?

Having sex before marriage takes away the sacred right of you and your future spouse. Pursuing the ultimate deal at the expense of your family violates this principle. Using the television as a babysitter does too. Permissive parents who allow their children to experience pleasures they are not ready to handle rob them of the self discipline and a pure conscience. Allowing children to fail their way through school because it's not fun to lean on them a little steals from them a fair chance at life.

I have seen parents divorce because of their own selfishness, and fathers who refuse to support their children.

I know teenagers who have a chronic cough because of a parent's second hand smoke. At least 6200 children die each year in the United

States because of their parents smoking, killed by such things as lung infections and burns. More young children are killed by parental smoking than by all unintentional injuries combined.[5]

And how many more children need to become butchered at the hands of the abortionist before we realize the child has a divine right to live! The fact is: most abortions are done out of convenience, and we have sold the soul of our nation for the illegitimate pleasures of 'reproductive freedom.'

The seeds of all injustice rest in this principle. When the pursuit of pleasure becomes nothing more than the rape of another's divine right it becomes an illegitimate pleasure, rooted in selfishness instead of love. It's why stealing, slavery, rape, adultery and many other actions are wrong. It is also why doing something that becomes a stumbling block or a hindrance to another is wrong.
(I Corinthians 8:9-13, 10:31-33, 2 Samuel 23:17)

Principle of Pleasure #5

Any pleasure, however good, if not kept in balance, will distort reality or destroy healthy appetites; this then becomes illegitimate.
Solomon put it this way: "If you find honey, eat just enough of it. Too much of it and you will vomit" (Proverbs 25:16). Simply put: too much of a good thing is a bad thing.

I have a friend who used to collect baseball cards. He dedicated an entire room in his house to them. You name the card, he had it. He didn't possess his cards, they *possessed* him. He finally realized they occupied too much of his time, money and thinking so he drastically cut down his collecting. What's wrong with baseball cards you ask? Nothing, but too much of anything distorts reality and destroys healthy appetites.

My weakness is the 'flurry.' You know, those ice cream treats with candy mixed in them? When I eat one I feel God's pleasure! But eating too many makes me a poor steward of my money and body while at the same time destroying my appetite for nourishing things. What about you? What things do you do that if they are done too much, distort reality and destroy your appetite for good things?

Too much food and you become a glutton. Too much sleep and you become a lazy sluggard. Too much television and you become a zombie (more on that in the next chapter). None of these is necessarily bad alone, but too much of them and you risk missing out on the abundant life.

The question becomes one of stewardship. God has given us time, talents, a body, relationships, money and a mind to manage. Any pleasure that takes away from the proper management of these things will keep us from experiencing the best life has to offer.

Principle of Pleasure #6

Just because something is not pleasurable does not make it unrewarding. How many people do you know that at one time in their lives played an instrument? They tell you that they took piano lessons when they were eight or they played in band for five years or something like that. Why did they stop? Usually they lost interest in practicing. Practicing isn't always fun but it is rewarding. Just think how good they'd be by now if they didn't give up. Sometimes we choose the easy and pleasurable over the difficult but rewarding. Over time this becomes a poor trade-off. (I Corinthians 10:23) By and large, we are overly entertained and under challenged. Only discipline brings freedom and *freedom is extremely pleasurable*. I have said this earlier but it bears repeating.

It is the disciplined musician that has the freedom and the pleasure to move people with his skill. It is the disciplined athlete who enjoys the freedom of making the winning shot. It is the disciplined student who possesses the freedom of a scholarship and the pleasure of a goal attained. It is the disciplined businessman who delights in the freedom and pleasure the fruit of his labor brings. It's the disciplined artist that enjoys the freedom to capture imaginations and inspire noble, grand thoughts. It is the disciplined mechanic that enjoys a summer nights cruise in her restored convertible.

Discipline brings freedom and freedom is extremely pleasurable.

Don't work toward fun, work toward freedom and the lasting pleasures will follow.

While you are young, you must search out different activities that you find both rewarding in the end and pleasurable in the process. These will become keys to your future interests and careers. However, you must keep in mind that there are no easy, 100% pleasurable roads to anywhere worth going. All matters of worth and excellence require great effort and sacrifice (trade-offs). There will be times in your life when in order to accomplish anything worthwhile, circumstances will force you to do something you do not want to do. At these times, you must forget about likes and dislikes; they are of no consequence, just do what must be done. This may not always be happiness, but it is greatness.

Sometimes I don't want to exercise. The couch has this gravitational pull on me I find impossible to break. There is a great rule of thumb used by many world class trainers that will help you do things that don't sound that appealing at the moment. This rule of thumb encompasses a great principle that carries over into any area of life where you must do something you don't *feel* like doing. Ever had to do something you didn't *feel* like doing? Good , this will help you.

It's called the **five minute rule**. If you don't feel like exercising and the thought of a long work out keeps you on the couch, just try it for five minutes. If after five minutes, you still don't feel like it, then stop and do something else. You will find that most of the time after five minutes you will feel like exercising. Amazing! Here is the principle: **Feelings follow actions, not precede them**.

If you don't feel like doing something - like homework - just give it five or ten minutes and you will feel like doing it! Don't wait until you *feel* like it; start doing it and the feelings will follow. **Emotions follow the will**. Sometimes you have to grab yourself by the will and say, "C'mon will, we are going to study." Then the will may say, "But, what about the emotions, they don't *feel* like it." And you must respond, "They'll be along eventually, but nevertheless you and I are going to study."

I have watched this principle work in all the areas of my life that require discipline - my personal, marital, professional, athletic and academic life.

Principle of Pleasure #7

Worship. The ultimate expression of pleasure will also be an expression of worship. You will find ultimate pleasure in doing whatever you do to the glory of God. Even drudgery can become alive if performed as worship. (Colossians 3:23) Worship is not just something you do at church.

The Christian does not go to the temple to worship, the Christian brings his temple with him to a building and worships. For the Christian, all of life should become an expression of worship. (Romans 12:1-3) Worship binds the various strands of life into one cohesive strand. The exhilaration of a football game or the quiet pleasure of classic literature can be bound up in worship. Our lives find various methods of expression according to our interests and talents; all of these expressions, if caught up in worship, are legitimate. And pleasure that doesn't somehow nourish spirit will leave you with small nagging doubts as to its legitimacy.

God has given us a tool to help us bring our harried pace within the realm of sanity and to help us realize that all of life should be an expression of worship: The Sabbath. One day of every seven God wants us to dedicate to rest and the worship of Him. God has given us the Sabbath not to fragment our lives between the sacred and the secular but so that we may remember the *weekday* and keep it holy.

Let your work, play, study and relationships become worship unto God and you will find God's secret treasure of ultimate pleasure.

Where the Rubber Meets the Road: Questions of Commitment.

Below are a few questions that encapsulate the seven principles of pleasure and help me enjoy the river of life without drowning in its delights. Print them out and place them on your refrigerator or in your Bible which ever you open most.

1. Is it forbidden in the Bible?

2. Am I willing to let the Bible be my authority?
3. Is it God's best choice for me?
4. Will it weaken my ability to discern truth?
5. Will it diminish my hunger for spiritual things?
6. Would this promote any impure thinking?
7. Would Jesus do it?
8. Will this help or hinder me in any area that I may be struggling with?
9. Will it deny another something they have a right to have?
10. Will it be a stumbling block to another?
11. Would it be more rewarding if I delayed my gratification?
12. Can I legitimately do it as an expression of worship as unto God?

Is Pleasure an Idol in *Your* Life?

Here's how to know if fun or pleasure is an idol in your life:

- Do you regularly compromise Biblical standards because "it's fun?"
- Do you enjoy things that diminish your sense of God and destroy your hunger for spiritual things?
- Do you spend too much time on mindless, passive pursuits and not enough with God?
- Do you often jeopardize sacred rights of others or do you cause others to stumble because of what you enjoy doing?
- Do you choose the good over the best because the good looks more appealing at the time?
- Are you lazy?

If you answered 'yes' to any of those questions I would seriously pray about this. God bless you.

> **PLEASURE IS A SERVANT, NOT A MASTER.**

Scripture Meditations:
Hebrews 11:25, James 4:3, Proverbs 10:23, 36:7-8 and 21:17, I Timothy

5:6, II Timothy 3:1-4

1. *Cries of the Heart*, Ravi Zacharias, copyright 1998, Word Publishers, Nashville TN All rights reserved

2. Goleman Daniel, *Emotional Intelligence*, New York, Bantam, 1995 pg 3

3. CNN news, December 13th 1999

4. *Cries of the Heart*, Ravi Zacharias, copyright 1998, Word Publishers, Nashville TN All rights reserved

5. *Archives of Pediatrics and Adolescent Medicine*; July 1998

"MY BROTHER AND I DIDN'T WATCH TV FOR A WEEK,
AND WHILE HE WOULD PROBABLY HATE ME FOR
SAYING THIS BECAUSE HE LOVES TV, WHEN MY
BROTHER ISN'T WATCHING TV ALL THE TIME, HE'S A
LOT MORE FUN TO BE AROUND. WE ACTUALLY HUNG
OUT TOGETHER AND JUST TALKED, SOMETHING WE
HAD NOT DONE IN A LONG TIME."
BETH LUBOZHISKI, SEVENTH GRADER, MINNEAPOLIS

"WE WERE MEANT TO SEE THROUGH THE EYE WITH
THE CONSCIENCE. MODERN COMMUNICATION IS
GETTING US TO SEE WITH THE EYE DEVOID OF A
CONSCIENCE."
DR. RAVI ZACHARIAS

VAIN IMAGINATIONS

The number one leisure activity in America is watching television. This generation is being bombarded and blitzed with fantasy, fiction, illusion and myth. They are not being bombarded by the purposeful creativity of a sanctified imagination, but a world of fiction that smuggles in deceiving philosophies while stealing the mind of Christ from our young people, killing their sensitivity to God's Spirit and destroying their godly potential.

The goal of this chapter is to make you aware of the influence of the things you allow your mind to feed on, and to raise your level of discernment regarding these issues so you can hold to the good and reject the defective.

The Truth Feels Good?

Melvin Nurse grew up on the streets of Jacksonville, Florida. He had asked his pastor for a chance to speak to the youth group about the dangers of gun use, drugs and gang life. So at a youth rally about 250 parents and children at Livingway Christian Fellowship Church watched as Melvin got his chance.

For an illustration during his sermon, Melvin loaded a .357-caliber pistol with a blank and began to play Russian roulette. He said, "Sin is like playing Russian roulette. Sooner or later, using drugs, carrying a gun and running with gangs will catch up to you. At each point, Melvin pointed the gun at his head and pulled the trigger. The tension mounted as the hammer finally found its mark on the primer of the blank cartridge. The audience - including Melvin's wife and four daughters - watched as the force of the explosion shattered Nurse's skull killing him.

What his pastor told the media illustrates a crucial principle. He said, "We were absolutely stunned. Nobody moved. We thought it might be part of his sermon and he would pop back up. *We knew he was using a blank, so I wasn't uncomfortable with the demonstration.*"

You see, it wasn't what Melvin didn't know that hurt him. It was what Melvin thought was true and wasn't that killed him. You have heard it said, "What you don't know won't hurt you." This is true much of the time but the principle you need to know is: **It's not what you don't know that hurts you; it's what you think is true but isn't that will. Because you *act on* those things you think are true but if they are really false they have no power to sustain you in the real world; thus they are dangerous.**

Think of it this way. If Melvin went to an expert on guns prior to his demonstration and asked, "Do you think firing this blank toward my head will kill me?" And the expert replied, "I don't know, maybe yes, maybe no." Do you think Melvin would have tried it? Absolutely not. So in that case not knowing saved him. But what if the expert said, "There is no way that the blank will kill you." Melvin would have acted upon bad advice. He would have acted on what he thought was true but really wasn't and falsehood has no power to sustain you in the real world.

As a teenager I went ice-fishing a lot. We had a nice little ice shanty with a heater so we wouldn't get cold. Where I live, ice fishing is still popular. There is a problem, however - every winter people fall through the ice and die. Why would they do such a thing? Because they think the ice will sustain their weight so they act on what they think is true. But this is false and falsehoods have no power to sustain you in the real world; in the fantasy world, yes, but in the real world, no.

Hence the problem of a generation. **While the culture bombards them with fantasy, fiction, illusion and myth, they soak in lies and deceptive philosophies like a sponge. They make decisions based on those lies and they get burned because falsehoods have no power to sustain them in the real world.**

All through scripture God links lies with evil and truth with godliness. All sin is founded on falsehood. (Romans 1:20-25, II Thessalonians 2:9-10, Titus 1:1, I Peter 1:22) Truth will sustain you; fantasy will fool you.

Electric Avenue

I stood before an audience discussing this topic and I asked them this question: Through which avenues do the lies come? They responded with these areas: T.V., Movies, Music, Video Games, Role Playing Games, and Advertising.

Do you notice what they all have in common? They are all tools of amusement. Why is it that it's easier to take in a deceptive philosophy when you are amused and entertained? The secret is in the word itself. What does it literally mean? The "a" in amusement is a negative prefix meaning "non." The root word in amusement is "muse" which means "to think." Amusement literally means - non-thinking!

When a medium is entertaining us our minds often times go into neutral. Our discernment level drops so we can "get into" the story or song or game. At that moment, dangerous philosophies can gain free entrance into our psyche.

We need to realize that much of what is in the media is make believe. It's made up! The world that it speaks about doesn't exist! The sets are fake, the characters are fake, the story lines are fake and the endings are fake!

Let's look at the areas a little closer to show you what I mean.

Television: The industry prides itself in the saying 'We just reflect reality.' Do they? The average prime-time T.V. schedule presents the viewer with 350 characters each night, seven of whom will be murdered on screen. If this rate (2% of the population killed per day) applied to reality, then in just 50 days everyone in the United States would be killed!

Have you noticed the things you don't see on television that you see all the time in real life? Things like people who say goodbye on the telephone and people who flub up their words? You never see someone flub up their words on television. Why not? They just re-take that scene. In life, you don't just get to re-take. Then there are things you do see on television that you don't see in real life; things like people who wear make-up in bed. And people who just wake up that look better than most do right out of the salon.

And what's this deal with the laugh track? You know, taped laughter played in spots where the producer wants you to laugh. Why can't they let me determine what is funny and what is not? Why must they insult my intelligence and pay people to laugh into a microphone so that they can tell me when something is humorous or not?

A Center for Media and Public Affairs study found that seven out of eight sexual encounters on TV involved extramarital relationships. Hollywood would have us believe that the best sex is unmarried sex. Yet a 1994 University of Chicago study revealed that sexual satisfaction and frequency is greatest among married religious couples, not among swinging singles. So much for reality. How many sexual encounters on television lead to an unplanned pregnancy? How many lead to an abortion? How many characters acquire a sexually transmitted disease? Of the sexually active population in America today, one out of every five has herpes. Why don't they show you that in fantasy land?

T.V. real? Let's consider the 25 year life of television character Erica Kane of ABC's *All My Children*. Erica originally eloped with Dr. Jeff Martin, divorced him, married Phil Brent, miscarried, had a mental breakdown, seduced Nick, almost slept with half-brother Mark, married

Tom, opened a disco, escaped a murder charge, married and divorced Adam, fell for a monk, almost killed Natalie, married Travis, gave birth to Bianca, committed adultery with Jackson, was kidnaped, divorced Travis, married Dimitri, was found by rape-conceived daughter Kendall (who married Anton, who loves Julia, who's loved by Noah), stabbed Dimitri, and returned to modeling! Sound like anyone you know in real life?

Movies: Everything in the movies (more and more on television also) is laid over music. How much of your real life is played to the Rocky theme? Sound studios labor to create interesting sounds for fight scenes, car chase scenes and love scenes. Those sounds don't happen in real life. Special lighting, special film, camera angles and effects also help to take you to a land of make believe.

Fifty-seven percent of all leading characters smoked in movies a few years ago as compared to only 14% of the real population.

Corporations pay mega-bucks to have their products placed strategically in movies. Whenever you see any product with the label readable you can bet the company paid the studio thousands of dollars to have it there. Why would they do that? They understand the power of the fantasy. So does movie director Bill Meyer who said in his book *Hot Topics Tough Questions,*

> "As a writer and director my primary objective is to manipulate you. I'm only successful if I can get you to cry, to laugh, to ache, and be thrilled exactly when I want you to. All the years I've trained, all the dialogue I write, every camera angle I choose, and all the music I use is designed for one reason and one reason only: to manipulate your emotions. If I succeed and really grab you, you'll tell all your friends, they'll tell their's, and suddenly I have a hit. That's the name the game. And few things feel as good to movie-makers as watching the audience cry when we want them to cry and laugh when we want them to laugh.
>
> Now don't get me wrong; manipulation is not necessarily bad. I like getting caught up in a good story as much as the next guy. All I'm saying is when you step into the theater or turn on the tube, be aware that somebody out

there is trying to manipulate you; then decide if that is the picture or show you want to manipulated by. If it is, fine. If not, pass. Because you will not go away unaffected. Let me repeat that: *You will not go away unaffected.* We've gotten too good at what we do." (Emphasis his)[1]

Music: Music is powerful. God designed it that way. Music has the power to focus your mind, manipulate emotions and inspire your actions. Dr. Richard G. Pellegrino, a neurologist (brain researcher), said, "In twenty five years of working with the brain, I still cannot affect a person's state of mind the way one simple song can."[2] This is not necessarily bad. The Bible has over 800 verses relating to music. God created it to focus your mind on excellent thoughts, to stir your emotions and to inspire noble actions.

Music isn't dangerous, it is the false philosophies that are sown into your thinking that are dangerous. What does your music communicate to you about love, purity, sex, authority, God and a host of other profound themes? Do they agree with the Scriptures? If not, you shouldn't feed your brain on them. From thoughts come actions, from actions, habits, from habits, character and from character, a destiny.

Media insider Bill Meyers relates more about the fantasy world of music entertainment:

> "I just talked to a guitarist who plays with a super-famous rock star known for his crazy, anything goes lifestyle. On stage this superstar will stagger over to the bottle of Jack Daniels and chug down a healthy swig to everyone's cheers and applause. What no one bothers to tell the audience is that it's all a show. A way to grab them and make them believe he's living a wild, reckless, carefree life. A life that they also can enjoy. No one bothers to tell them that they're being manipulated. No one bothers to tell them that it's Lipton tea inside that bottle."[3]

Video Games: These can be loads of fun but they are pure fantasy, a computer generated virtual world.

Role playing games: These require a prolific use of the imagination but many are based on occultic and sorcerous themes.

Advertising: Or Madison Avenue mind control as I call it. Here is an entire industry invented for the sole purpose of making you feel inadequate, ungrateful and discontented. Their primary tool in doing this is fantasy. They create a fake, computer enhanced fantasy land and they place you in it. Your natural response is to feel inadequate. Why? Because you live in the real world. In the real world, old, ugly bald guys don't get a group of young beautiful girls ogling them. So what is the solution? Just purchase and drink brand X beer!

> IN THE 1960's, IF THE TOY SOLDIER GI JOE WERE EXPANDED TO THE SIZE OF A REAL PERSON HIS ARMS WOULD HAVE BEEN THE SIZE OF A NORMAL MAN - 12 INCHES. TODAY THE ARMS OF GI JOE ARE THE SIZE OF A SMALL MAN'S WAIST - 26 INCHES. AND IF BARBIE WERE A REAL WOMAN HER MEASUREMENTS WOULD BE 36 - 18 - 33.

Print advertisers manipulate the pictures of models in their magazines. They use computers to change the shape of the face, to erase wrinkles, brush out blemishes, make lips fuller and eyes bigger. Technicians make models taller, thinner and wider in all the right places. They have a box of tricks to enhance the look of anybody. When you compare yourself to them you have no choice but to feel inadequate and buy something you don't need while paying more for it because someone's name is on it. Don't worry; what you are comparing yourself to isn't real, it's fantasy.

Marketing guru Jay Levinson writes in his book *Guerilla Marketing* that the decision to buy is made by the subconscious mind. He says that marketers can manipulate the subconscious part of the mind through repetition. The more you see an ad for a product the more likely you are to buy it. That's why ads are everywhere!

Why do you think people pay almost two million dollars for a 30 second ad during the super-bowl? If they can sell you a car, a drink, or a pair of jeans in 30 seconds, what are they selling you in a two hour movie?

Don't ever touch?

Am I saying that we should never indulge in the world of fantasy? Absolutely not. Sometimes it's great just to kick back and relax and take in a movie or play a video game. You must, however, keep fantasy from stealing the mind of Christ in you, killing your sensitivity to the spirit and destroying your Godly potential.

Hitler said that if you tell a lie loud enough and long enough people will start to believe it. When you take in and believe defective information, you will make defective and dangerous decisions. There are dangerous behaviors that are nourished by false philosophies fed to you through the culture. If you struggle with any of these I would seriously look at what you are taking into your mind.

Destructive Behavior

Behavior	Underlying Myths
Doubting your faith, bored in church	The God of the Bible isn't real, God and serving God is boring
Feelings of inadequacy, inferiority, eating disorders	You are not good enough, you have little value unless...Your too fat, too tall, too skinny....
Lust, masturbation Boy-craziness, impure romantic fantasies	If it feels good, it won't hurt you. There is nothing wrong with sex outside of marriage, it's natural. Everything else is OK as long as we don't go "all the way." You need a boy to make you feel fulfilled. It's OK as long as he *loves* you (gag)

Poor attitude toward authorities	Rebellion is cool, submission is for whimps. Rebellions pays, not costs. Only gee*ks* obey their parents! *They* don't know anything, you do!
Drugs, nicotine and alcohol	You will be cool! It is fun! Your problems will go away. You can be someone you are not, someone better!
Peer pressure	Nobody will accept you if you don't.... You will be *weird* if you serve God. *Nobody* will like you if you don't..... You are doomed to spend every Friday night *for the rest of your life* with your parents if you don't get with the group, man!
Greed, materialism, shopaholics	You will be a better person only if you had....If you buy ____ you will finally be happy. All the girls will finally want you if you buy____ You will not be cool wearing that label, only poor, stupid, geeky people wear that. You have little personal worth unless you buy......

Laziness

Slacker. Why do they label an entire generation this way? Could it be that laziness is one of the most pervasive sins in this era of young people?

Mike Kane is the football coach at Olean High in New York. Sports Illustrated reported his growing frustration over getting kids to try out for his team. He said, "The hard work of passing, blocking and tackling aren't as popular anymore. Why? Kids can play Nintendo football now, they don't see the point."

We are slowly becoming a nation of consumers instead of producers, takers, not makers, copiers, not creators. We eat the fruit of someone else's creativity, study and hard work. We are not producing fruit of our own. We are overly entertained and underly challenged. Because hard work is foreign to many of us, character is foreign to many of us.

Whatever you feed grows. The more you watch TV, the more you want to watch TV. The more you play video games, the more you want to play video games. The more movies you watch, the more you want to watch movies. The more you pray, the more you want to pray. The more you study, the more you want to study. You get the idea.

Do not allow laziness to become a part of you. Your potential is too valuable. (Proverbs 24:30-34, 12:24, 13:4, 14:23)

Poor Stewardship of Your Most Precious Resources: Time, Thinking Ability, Health

According to a recent study, 21% of the average teenager's **time** is spent in front of a screen (tv, movie, video game, computer). Over the course of an average lifetime, that amounts to over 14 YEARS![4] What could you do with 14 years? Become a doctor, lawyer, astronaut, master artist, travel the world? The cry of our nation is 'I'm busy.' Yeah right.

Life is just a vapor; you're here and soon your gone. One shot and that's it. There is no recycling plan. The fantasy world calls us and lures us to immerse ourselves into its realm. As we do, the hours click by never to be regained. There are grander things to experience then the newest game; search them out. (Proverbs 25:2)

Much of our communication today has eroded the **thinking ability** of our society. Any teacher will tell you that the learning process is hindered by short attention spans.

Television has played a major role in reducing our ability to concentrate for extended periods of time. One study focused on the number of shifts of attention (one plot to another, flash forward, flash back, news break, or commercial) on television. It found as many as **78** shifts per hour excluding shifts in commercials. When including commercials, the number of shifts rose to over **800** times per hour: 14 times per minute. One manager for a marketing agency that targets younger consumers was commenting on the attention spans of their target market and said, "It's an entire generation with ADD."[5]

Television moves too fast to promote thinking and creativity. When you read, your imagination remains sovereign over it. Your brain is forced to create the setting, the looks and voices of the characters, the smells and tastes of everything in the story. Music and the visual have the capacity to bypass reason and go straight to the imagination. When you are given a picture, that image remains sovereign over your imagination. We've become entertained by consuming rather than producing and our imaginations have atrophied as a result.

The mediums through which fantasy come to us all require sedentary, passive postures. As a result, our **health** is suffering. Since 1985, researchers have initiated over 12 studies linking excessive television watching to increasing rates of obesity.[6] Something is wrong when a sixteen-year-old, red blooded, able bodied American male cannot do one push up! Every year at camp I run into many of them!

God gives us all one body through which we live our lives. He expects us to become good stewards of our health. And too much fantasy land will not help build your biceps. Find pleasure in at least one thing that requires some movement: walking, hiking, biking, ballet, golf, something! When you're old and still active, you'll not regret it.

Lack of True Vision

Every week in my youth group we have the visitors fill out a small questionnaire. The last question is, "What are your long terms goals and dreams?" Over the past three years, 40% of the teenagers left it blank or responded with something like, "I don't know, go to college or something."

Where is their vision? Our outlets for fantasy have buried it. God planted seeds of greatness in all of us, seeds meant to be nurtured during our school years. But when we spend so much time bathing in someone else's vision via TV or the theater screen it's hard to see our own.

Turn off the television. Get to know God, get to know yourself and start trying different things to find out what you like and what you're good at. Through that process the seeds God planted in you can get the sunlight they need to grow!

Where the Rubber Meets the Road

Train yourself to notice how you are influenced by what you feed to your mind; and raise your level of discernment regarding these issues so you can hold to the good and reject the defective. Do not allow things that may seem true but aren't to become the foundation of your life decisions. Fantasy has no power to sustain you in the real world.

1. Bill Meyers, *Hot Topics Tough Questions*, Victor Books, 1987 pg 65

2. *Billboard Magazine*, January 23, 1999

3. Bill Meyers, *Hot Topics Tough Questions*, Victor Books, 1987, 66

4. This figure is taken from three different sources: A.C. Nielson Co. and the American Medical Association and T.V. Free America

5. Good Morning America, 3-15-99

6. T.V. Free America Statistics, August, 1998

WHATSOEVER THINGS ARE TRUE

As stated in earlier chapters, the nourishment of the mind on God's truth is paramount to making decisions that will empower you to live the most satisfying life possible. This chapter briefly discusses ways to get your mind on the same wave length as God's.

Something About Brains

In the brain there is an organ that God has given us to help us renew our minds. The Reticular Activating System (RAS) sits where the spinal cord meets the brain. The RAS is a filter that keeps you from going insane by filtering out the thousands of messages your senses send your brain each second. Your RAS system filters out those things you tell it are not important and allows everything else through to your brain. You have the power to tune this system. *Whatever you spend your time thinking about, whatever emotionally impacts you and whatever you see as dangerous, the RAS system deems important.*

You have all watched and experienced how this works. Have you ever been to someone's house that lives by an airport? While you eat, a jet begins its final approach and you think it is landing in the living room. You look around at your friend's family and they act like nothing happened. You ask them, "How can you stand it?" They say, "Stand what? Oh, the airplanes? It used to bother us but we hardly notice it any more." Why don't they notice it? Because they have tuned their RAS to ignore it. It's not important to them.

Have you ever stood in a group of people talking and having a good time while the music in the room plays softly in the background? All of a sudden a person shouts above the rest of the crowd, "Everyone be quiet, this is my favorite song!" While most people didn't even notice the music playing, someone picked out their favorite song out of the many sounds mixing in the room. How did they do it? Through their actions they have tuned their RAS to allow that particular band through, straight to the brain.

My wife is one of the soundest sleepers I know. As a teenager she acquired a number of baby-sitting jobs. While baby-sitting one night, she fell asleep on the couch next to a sliding glass patio door. The parents arrived home only to notice they had locked themselves out of the house. Not to worry, surely the baby-sitter (my wife Kim) would let them in. They rang the door-bell and pounded on the door to no avail. Kim lay sound asleep on the couch. The parents moved to the patio where they saw her sleeping. Only feet from her hearing, they pounded on the door screaming and yelling. Kim never woke up. They had to break a window to get in!

After our first child was born something changed. She still slept soundly, but whenever the baby moved, cried, burped or rolled over she woke up even though he slept in a room on the other side of the house! Why would that wake her up? Because she had told her RAS to tune into any sound the baby made; it was important to her. Why can a mother pick out her baby's cry in a nursery full of crying babies? The RAS, they have tuned it to be so.

What is the point? The RAS not only takes input from your physical senses, but it also hears from your spirit. Both your flesh and your spirit send information to your soul where your decisions are made.

If you are going to live your life to the fullest you must tune out the world and tune in the heart of God. You must train your RAS system to allow in the truth of God while filtering out the lies of our culture. You must hear more loudly the call of God than the call of gold, the call of purity rather than the call of popularity.

When the Bible speaks of its heroes, it tells us like it is. It doesn't attempt to hide us from information that speaks negatively about them. We know of Noah's drunkenness, Abraham's lying, David's adultery, and Peter's denial. Of all the main characters in the Bible, one comes through without any negative marks on his reputation. His name is Daniel. Daniel lived his life surrounded by immorality, greed, envy, beauty and spiritual options. Throughout all this he lived pure. What was his secret? How did he pull it off?

We find the answer in Daniel chapter six. Three times a day Daniel got alone with God for a spiritual tune up. Daniel took the time and made the effort to tune his heart, mind and will to the heart, mind and will of God. If you desire to become a Daniel in your day, you must do the same.

The type of things you feed your mind are extremely important to the discerning ability of your conscience. Why do you think God said to think about whatever is true, noble, right, pure, lovely, excellent, admirable and praiseworthy? (Philippians 4:8) He wishes to guide you moment by moment into the abundant life. By thinking about such things, you tune into the heart of God because God is true, noble, right, pure, lovely, excellent, admirable and praiseworthy. The Bible says that only when your mind is renewed can you discern God's will. (Romans 12:1-2). When you can sense the voice and heart of God above the din and disarray of the crowd, you are on your way to the vestibule of heaven.

Loving God with All Your Mind

Nothing develops your discernment, enhances your creativity, gives you a foundation for God given direction and makes you an excellent steward of your mental resources like the nourishment of your mind on God's truth.

The two best ways to nourish your mind on God's truth are to memorize and meditate on God's Word.

Tips on Memorizing and Meditation:

- Repetition; put it through your head. Learn how you memorize. Use spare moments and 3x5 cards.

- Get to a quiet place. Keep a notebook and write down thoughts that come to you. Spend some time using God-centered music to focus your thoughts.

- Meditate on a scripture that speaks to an area you are struggling with. There are about 30,000 promises in scripture. All of them are great food for meditation.

- Give to God and receive from God. Give to God your anxiety over a situation. Receive from God his peace. (Phil. 4:6-7) Give to God your anger or bitterness against someone. Receive from God his love for them. (Mt. 5:43-48) Give to God a problem. Receive from God wisdom in handling it. (James 1:5)

- Just do it

The third best way to nourish your mind with God's truth is to purposely study God's truth in other areas like the sciences, arts and philosophy. Most people don't realize how much you can learn about the creator by 'reading' his creation. Pay attention in school! Train your brain!

George Washington Carver was the son of a slave. God gifted him in the areas of chemistry and agriculture. He almost single-handedly saved the south from poverty and starvation after the Civil War. He invented hundreds of products from the peanut, soybean and sweat potato. In 1921, the Congress of the United States asked him to speak before the Ways and Means committee concerning potential uses of the peanut and other new crops to revitalize the economy of the south.

Initially, Congress only gave him 10 minutes to speak but George so enthralled the committee that they gave him unlimited time. His presentation lasted one hour and forty five minutes. At the end, the chairman of the committee asked, "Dr. Carver, how did you learn all of these things?" Carver answered, "From an old book." "What old book?" "The Bible," Carver replied.

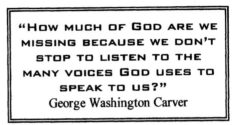

"HOW MUCH OF GOD ARE WE MISSING BECAUSE WE DON'T STOP TO LISTEN TO THE MANY VOICES GOD USES TO SPEAK TO US?"
George Washington Carver

Then the Senator asked, "Does the Bible tell about peanuts?" "No sir," came the answer, "but it tells about the God who made the peanut. I asked Him to show me what to do with the peanut and He did."

Carver named his laboratory 'God's Little Workshop' and he never took any scientific books into it. He just sat down and asked God to show him how to perform the experiments.

When asked the secret of his success he said, "Every morning I get up at 4 am and ask God what am I supposed to do today. Then I go out and do it."

If you plan to drink out of life everything it has for you then you must learn to discern truth from lies and make your decisions based on the truth. In order to know truth you must spend time with it, learning it, handling it, tasting it. May God bless you with discernment.

146

RELATIONSHIPS
& SEX

People. The world is full of people, six billion or so. And God has created us to live in relationship with some of them. Relationships present to us a key to the ultimate meaning in life. And if we plan on pursuing the best that life has to offer, we would do well to learn about relating to others.

Relationships move in and out of different phases: acquaintances, friendships, deep friendships, romantic relationships, family relationships and so on. Thrown into the mix of our relationships is the very important act of sex.

God did not create us to be alone. He created us to live in the midst of others, all under God. But if you mishandle relationships and sex, you will miss out on much of the sizzle and poetic drama life has to offer and you will experience some of the deepest regret and sorrow mankind can endure.

In these next chapters, we will explore God's best in handling friendships, romantic relationships and sex. Let these principles guide into the abundant life and steer you away from lasting grief.

I love you,
CW

"LOVE SEEKETH NOT ITSELF TO PLEASE,
NOR FOR ITSELF HATH ANY CARE,
BUT FOR ANOTHER GIVES ITS EASE,
AND BUILDS A HEAVEN IN HELL'S DESPAIR.

LOVE SEEKETH ONLY SELF TO PLEASE,
TO BIND ANOTHER TO ITS DELIGHT,
JOYS IN ANOTHER'S LOSS OF EASE,
AND BUILDS A HELL IN HEAVEN'S DESPITE."
WILLIAM BLAKE IN THE "THE CLOD AND THE
PEBBLE"

"ABOVE ALL ELSE, GUARD YOUR HEART FOR OUT OF
IT SPRING THE ISSUES OF LIFE."
KING SOLOMON

ROMANCE

What's it all about? Why this thing called romance? And why does it cause so much pleasure *and* pain? To pursue the best in the area of romance, you must understand its original purpose.

God's plan for romance is first, to mirror on earth a shadow of our relationship with God. Our mortal romances should point us to our sacred romance. Secondly, true romance inspires us to become more loving - like Christ. It affords us great opportunity to lose our life while finding it at the same time. Thirdly, when done correctly, it provides us with deep intimacy, trustworthy life-long companionship, and legitimate pleasure. Fourthly, it provides a continuation of the first institution God created: marriage and the family. Purposeful romance prepares us for providing the best atmosphere for raising children - a godly home.

Sounds good, doesn't it? With the purposes of romance now established, the question becomes: "If romance is supposed to do all of those nice things for us why does it cause us so much heartbreak?"

Let me share an actual letter written by a fourteen-year-old girl about her father, published in *American Girl* magazine. She wrote;

"When I was ten, my parents got a divorce. Naturally, my father told me about it, 'cause he was my favorite.

"Honey, I know it's been kind of bad for you these last few days and I don't want to make it any worse, but there's something I have to tell you. Honey, your mother and I got a divorce."

"But Daddy..."

"Now I know you don't want this, but it has to be done. Your mother and I just don't get along like we used to. I'm already packed, and my plane is leaving in half-an-hour."

"But, Daddy, why do you have to leave?"

"Well, honey, your mother and I just can't live together anymore."

"Well, I know that, but I mean, why do you have to leave town?"

"Oh, well, I've got someone waiting for me in New Jersey."

"But, Daddy, will I ever see you again?"

"Oh, sure, you will, honey. We'll work something out."

"OK, Daddy. Good-bye. Don't forget to write me."

"I won't. Bye. Now, go to your room."

"Daddy, I don't want you to go."

"I know, honey, but I have to."

"OK. Well, I guess that's the way life goes sometimes."

After my father walked out that door, I never heard from him again.

This becomes more painful when you realize this scene plays itself out every day in our culture. A generation ago, a child could reasonably expect to grow up with his or her father. Tonight, 40% of children will go to sleep in homes in which their fathers do not live.[1]

Fatherlessness is America's most urgent social problem. Kids from fatherless homes account for 63% of those who kill themselves, 85% of young people in prison, 71% of high school dropouts and 90% of homeless and runaway children. Divorce is the most painful outworking of misused romance, but it is not the only one.

People mope through marriages intended to be a slice of heaven, but ended up more like hell. Thousands of young marrieds and singles carry the scars and regret that the misuse of romance brings. Broken hearts litter the landscape as former boyfriends and girlfriends rip apart their emotional attachments for each other. Why? **Because people have failed to learn, understand and apply the purposes and principles of true romance.**

Instead of learning these principles, people have abandoned intelligent guidelines and did whatever felt right at the time. Today in our culture, we have a system of romance that does not mirror our sacred romance, teaches us little of true love and prepares us better for divorce than for intimate, committed marriage.

Missed Approach

Marriage is foremost a spiritual relationship. Its foundation rests in both parties knowing, loving and obeying God more than anything. Our cultural system of romance places little importance on cultivating a spiritual bond. Many Christian young people find themselves distracted and useless for the Kingdom of Heaven when they start dating. Because their focus is no longer on the Lord, they find it harder to keep up their devotional life, their worship becomes dead, and they are distracted by intense emotions and sometimes feelings of guilt brought about by premature physical involvement.

If these couples marry, they may struggle because they never practiced a spiritual relationship while they dated. Then they realize that there is *much more* needed to keep a marriage together than emotions and the physical.

Many young men regret that they have never learned how to be priest of their home; and they married a woman who never learned how to inspire spiritual leadership. Many young women regret marrying a man not equipped to lead spiritually. Because marriage is foremost a spiritual relationship does not mean that non-Christians cannot have a fulfilling marriage, some do. They cannot, however, experience the full love and intimacy brought through a covenant under God; they can only attain a shadow of it.

Our system of romance often mistakes physical and emotional passion for love. Just because bodies have touched doesn't mean souls have joined. And just because people involve themselves physically, doesn't mean they are right for each other.

Many couples evaluate the seriousness of their relationship by the level of their physical involvement. Couples who have feelings for each other can easily express those feelings through holding hands, kissing and everything that follows. Therefore, it becomes easy for people to believe that going out with someone means physical involvement. Intense feelings come with physical involvement. This presents two problems.

First, it sets a pattern of thought in our minds that says, "Feelings of passion equal love." The concept that love is synonymous with warm fuzzy feelings is deadly within a marriage. **Love is a choice for the supreme good of another person, not a feeling.** This philosophy has become the basis for some of the most cowardly and sissified statements ever spoken within a marriage, such as: "I just don't feel the same about you as I once did" and "I'm just not in love anymore."

Why do people place so much weight on their romantic feelings? They have little to do with true love. Most likely, during their pre-marriage relationships they focused too much on physical touch and emotional warm fuzzies.

Second, the intense emotional feelings brought on by physical relationships often push the relationship further than it is ready to go, while at the same time obscuring qualities in the partner that may make them relatively incompatible. These qualities will come to light later, after the passion cools a little. During this time many couples realize they have little of lasting substance in common. What they had in common is now gone. Now what? Many times they wait until someone else can light those fires again. Then they have affairs of the mind, body or both. Women lose themselves in romance novels and men dabble in pornography. Why? They are just following a pattern of so called 'love' they established during their younger years.

Marriage has certain ownership rights. Many say that all is permissible as long as you are not sexually involved before marriage. This goes against the marital pattern. For in marriage, one does not just claim ownership rights to the spouse's body, but also exclusive rights to their romantic emotions.

You would break your spouses heart if you gave them your body but in your heart you treasured and loved another. Why? Because marriage has emotional ownership rights.

In our culture's system of romance, we are expected to give away our emotional love unreservedly long before we know if we will marry that special someone. We don't realize that intimacy comes at a price: commitment. **Our culture encourages intimacy without commitment.** Our culture has cheapened intimacy to the point where we expect little or no commitment to attain it.

Our girls give themselves to attain a vapor of intimacy and boys give a vapor of intimacy to attain a girl. They break up and both are cheated. This system really hurts those who go from one romance to another.

Most junior and senior high dating is short term, serving our desires for the moment. Most people want somebody so they can enjoy the emotional and physical benefits of intimacy without the responsibility of a life-long commitment.

An intimate relationship is a beautiful experience that God wants us to enjoy. But he has made the cost of intimacy true commitment. Our system of romance falls far short of this goal. It sets forth patterns of emotional promiscuity that will have to be broken. Proverbs cautions us to guard our heart above all else (4:23). We would do well to do this.

Married couples keep themselves from sources of temptation. We avoid places, people and entertainment that would tempt us to cheat our mate. We remove ourselves from situations that might tempt us to enter into an emotional, mental (fantasy), or physical relationship with someone other than our spouse.

Yet our culture expects you to jump right into the lap of temptation by telling you, "It's OK to cultivate strong emotional ties and spend time alone together...but don't get carried away physically." That's like asking me to spend the night alone in a music store, but please don't play the drums! It's dangerous to head down the same course as those who have fallen and hope that in the critical moment you'll be able to stay in control.

God is not impressed with your ability to withstand temptation. He is more impressed with your obedience when you *run* from it. (I Corinthians 6:18, 2 Timothy 2:22, Philippians 3:3, Genesis 39)

The best marriages are the best friendships. Have you ever known someone who worried about dating a long-time friend? If you have, you probably heard that person say something like, "He asked me out, but I'm just afraid that if we start actually *dating* it will change our friendship." People who make statements like this recognize that the culture's system of romance includes "romantic expectations." In a true friendship you don't feel pressured by knowing you "like" the other person or that he or she "likes" you. You feel free to be yourself and do things together without spending three hours in front of the mirror, making sure you look perfect.

Friendship can be described as two people walking side by side toward a common goal. Their mutual interest brings them together. Young people often skip the commonality stage by asking each other "out" where their "coupleness" will be the focus.

Joshua Harris points out in his fabulous book *I Kissed Dating Goodbye,*

> "In dating, romantic attraction is often the

relationship's cornerstone. The premise of dating is, 'I'm attracted to you; therefore, let's get to know each other.' The premise of friendship, on the other hand, is 'We're interested in the same things; let's enjoy these common interests together.' If, after developing a friendship, romantic attraction forms, that's an added bonus."[2]

Most improper romantic relationships isolate couples from their friends and family. Have you ever had a friend that started dating someone and then they forgot about you? And when you did get together all they talked about was their special someone? But after they broke up you gained a friend again? Sound familiar?

During life, before and after marriage, it becomes increasingly important to have one or two very close friends. Keeping romantic relationships in the proper context allows your social life to blossom. You remain free to associate with many people without worrying that someone may become threatened by your "other friends."

Whatever you label your system of romance, it remains important that you align your system with the ultimate purposes of romance. What follows are some guidelines for pursuing romance wisely.

Keys to Wise Loving
Principle of Wise Love #1

Commit to trust God to bring into your life the one He has for you. The righteous shall live by faith (Romans 1:17). Hey! Listen! Do you believe that God has your best interest in mind? Do you think he is trustworthy enough to base the second greatest decision of your life on his principles? Have you trusted him with your salvation? If you have trusted Christ to deliver you from the flames of hell, then it should be easy to trust him to deliver you from the pitfalls of the dating game. I don't care if you're a Christian or not. God is not mocked; you will reap what you sow. If you sow fleshly seeds of romance you will reap an overwhelming whirlwind (Galatians 6:7-9).

Everything in life, your big decisions and your small ones, boil down to one question: Do you trust God? I can't even count the number of times I've had to trust God and his principles over *my* feelings during times in my marriage. It happens almost daily! I only got into trouble when I didn't believe God. How do you learn to trust God during critical times in marriage? You trust him during critical times before marriage. Simple.

So how does trusting God work itself out in this case? People who trust God with their love life,

- Trust God's timing. They know that until they are reasonably ready for marriage there is no good reason to cultivate a romantic relationship. They understand that romantic relationships should have a purpose (to end in marriage). They understand that the right thing at the wrong time is the wrong thing. (See also principle #2)

- They trust God's standards for a mate. They will not cultivate a romantic relationship with someone that has no potential to become their spouse. (See chapter on "Becoming" to learn to recognize a true man or woman of God.)

- They commit to becoming a "one-woman-man" or a "one-man woman" even before they are married. Before they even meet their future spouse, they commit to saving themselves emotionally, as well as physically for that one person. They will not get emotionally attached to anyone unless they are quite sure that he/she at least meets the standards of someone that they could marry.

> **"FOR I KNOW THE PLANS I HAVE FOR YOU, PLANS TO PROSPER YOU AND NOT TO HARM YOU PLANS TO GIVE YOU A HOPE AND A FUTURE."**
> Jeremiah 29:11-13

Do you trust God? Can you trust him to put your life's calendar together and allow him to schedule your life's relationships? Can you trust him even when others pressure you to pursue romance not fitting with his principles? When God knows your ready for the commitment of a lifetime, he will reveal the person for a lifetime.

What do you do in the mean time? I'm glad you asked.

Principle of Wise Love #2

Commit to "becoming the one" instead of "looking for the one." If your trusting God, you are not cultivating romantic relationships until you are reasonably ready for marriage emotionally, financially and spiritually. (I say "reasonably ready" because no matter how much you prepare, it is still hard making two people into one.)

Many people become trapped by the "hunt" or "rescue" mentality. They constantly hunt for that special someone that will fulfill all their dreams, that one who will rescue them from their pitiful life. They are fond of asking their parents, "When can I date?" They focus their life on *looking* for the one when they should concentrate most of their energy on *becoming* the one.

God has a school. In fact, he has a number of schools. He wants to enroll you into his school of manhood or his school of womanhood. He wants to make you into an awesome man or woman of God. God has given you a season of time to graduate from this school. (Luke 2:40,52)

The culture would rather you flunked out. It pushes you to skip class and spend this season of time chasing after fantasies and meaningless, fruitless pursuits (Proverbs 12:11). It hopes you will involve yourself with premature romance so that it will siphon crucial energies and efforts away from God's school.

Unfortunately, many do drop out because of the time, effort and self denial it takes. Those who make it through reap a bountiful harvest of righteous treasures that fill their life to overflowing.

How can you assure yourself of an awesome woman of God or man of God for your spouse? Just concentrate on *becoming* awesome and you are assured an incredible mate.

Men are designed to *lead* in a relationship and women are designed to *inspire*. If a guy becomes an awesome man of God, God will not send him a mediocre Mrs. Why? She is not capable of inspiring him. God is obligated to sending that awesome man of God an awesome woman of God because that's what it takes to inspire him. Now, if he skipped manhood classes and he is only an average Joe, a mediocre Mrs. will do. Mediocre people have mediocre marriages. Awesome people of God have awesome marriages!

If a girl becomes an awesome woman of God, God becomes obligated to send her an awesome man of God. Why? Because an average Joe does not have the capability of leading her into the marital promised land, only an awesome man of God does!

Your best guarantee of an incredible spouse and marriage is to take this season (generally from age 12 to age 20, a tithe of your life) and dedicate it to becoming the best person in God you can be. We will talk more on what that entails later.

If you missed this schooling opportunity when you were young, don't fret. You just have to go to night school. When the world sleeps you must stay up and get tutored, one on one with the Holy Spirit. Study the Bible, pray, read books on marriage, becoming a man or woman of God, money management and so on.

I have had many young people come to me saying they have found the one God has for them. So what's their problem? They are still in high school or their first years in college. They are really not ready for marriage. What should they do?

They should take much of the time and energy used to cultivate their relationship and re-direct it into becoming the husband or wife God would have them become. They should limit the time they are together, the time they spend on the phone, writing letters, day-dreaming and use those resources more wisely. Won't the relationship cool down? Yes, it will. But if they truly are the one that God has for them, this won't be a problem. They can trust God to light the flame at the proper time.

If I were the male in one of these relationships I would approach the subject like this: "(Insert girls name here), I feel that you are potentially the one for me. However, I am not the man of God I need to be yet. Please allow me to use much of the time and energy I spend on our relationship to make myself into the man I need to be so that at the proper time, I will be everything you deserve." If she is a woman of God, she will honor your request. If she doesn't, the relationship is for her pleasure and not God's.

There are a few more principles to loving wisely I will share in a later chapter. Right now, we must turn to our local stations for a late breaking chapter on what it takes to *become* a man and woman of God. Stay tuned.

1. David Blankenhorn. *Fatherless America*, Harper Collins, 1995 introduction.

2. Joshua Harris, *I Kissed Dating Goodbye*, Multnomah Press, pg 35, 1997

> "MEN ARE GOD'S METHODS. WHILE MEN LOOK FOR BETTER METHODS, GOD LOOKS FOR BETTER MEN."
> E.M. BOUNDS

> "CHARM IS DECEPTIVE, AND BEAUTY IS FLEETING; BUT A WOMAN THAT FEARS THE LORD IS TO BE PRAISED."
> KING SOLOMON

THE ART OF BECOMING

Have you ever heard people say things like, "You're not a man yet" or "You're not a woman your still a girl?" Growing up, I always wondered what it took to become a man. How do you achieve that mythical status of a "woman" or a "man?" Is it merely a function of age? Is it related to puberty or sexual conquests? Much confusion surrounds this issue. In this chapter, we will outline biblically what it means to become an awesome man or woman of God.

This chapter, as all the sections of this book, could become a book of its own. There, are however, some good books already written on this topic that you should read: For guys- *The Four Pillars of a Man's Heart* by Stu Weber, *Courage* and *Maximized Manhood* by Ed Cole. Girls should read: *Becoming a Woman of Influence* by Pam Farrel. For both, *Youth Aflame* and the *Daniel Files* by Winkey Pratney.

Becoming God's Man (For the guys)

Congratulations! You're male. In the beginning, God created them male and female. He created you male. Being male is an intensely special thing. Only males get a chance at becoming men, real men, men who love their God and their families, men who are led by their God and lead their families and His church. He created you male; now he wants to make a man out of you. You pass the first test - you're male. That means deep within you lies the potential, strength, heart and guts to become the leader he has destined for you to be.

You don't become a man overnight. You are born male but God makes you a man. There is a lengthy process God uses to bring out the strength, heart, tenderness and courage he placed in you. This process never really stops unless you choose to stop it (and many do). But at this time, while you are still young, God chooses to put you through school - the school of manhood. Unfortunately, most drop out because of the time, effort and self-denial it requires. Because of this dropout rate, our nation suffers from a deficit of godly leadership.

Becoming a man is about living under authority, establishing priorities, becoming balanced and self controlled, accepting responsibility and providing leadership and guidance.

Your not a man...

..until Jesus Christ is Lord and your priorities are in line with what he says really matters. Jesus asked a great question, "What would it benefit a man if he gained the whole world and lost his own soul?" (Matthew 16:26) He would make a very foolish trade-off. Jesus Christ defined what it meant to be a man. It is not living as the captain of your own destiny, master of your universe, creator of your own reality! It involves surrendering your life into the hands of God and letting him give back to you whatever *he* desires. If you seek to chart your own course, your life will slip through your ever tightening grip. Matthew 10:39

So how is your relationship with God? Have you surrendered to his authority? How often do you talk with him? Have you established a regular time talking with him and studying his Word? If not, you must carve out time in your life to make God and his kingdom the very first priority - period. (Matthew 6:33, Philippians 4:6)

How well do you know the Bible? Have you read it through even once? Do you want to be a man? You must become a man of the Book - period. (Psalms 1, Joshua 1:7-8)

Is church a blow-off for you? Do you think of excuses to miss church or to go to church? Do you sit there and pass notes along with the other average Joe's? You need church and the church needs you. A man of God is a man of the body of Christ. (Hebrews 10:23-25, I Corinthians 12:12-26)

How is your worship? Are you a man of worship, unafraid to lift his hands and sing unto the Lord in front of people? Can you publicly give thanks to God for food? If not, concentrate on becoming a man of worship. Before you can fully love a woman, you must first learn what it means to love Jesus. (Psalm 150)

Have you allowed Christ to tame your tongue? Are you still entertained by off color jokes and slang? If so, allow God to purify your heart and your words will become fountains of blessings. God's men do not allow any unwholesome talk to come out of their mouths. (Ephesians 4:29)

What about your music? Does it honor God? Does it feed your spirit and draw you closer to God? If you do not surrender your music and other forms of entertainment to the Lord you will stunt your growth as a man. (Philippans 4:8, see also chapter on fantasy)

Have you given God control of your money? Do you spend it on his priorities or yours? What you spend your money on tells the world who your god really is. Is it *the* God? Do you tithe? Do you give to world missions? Or is your money exclusively spent on your own desires and pursuits? **God's man spends God's money on God's plan.** (Matthew 6:19,21, Malachi 3:8-12, Luke 12:15)

Are you in harmony with the authorities that God has placed in your life? Or are you a rebel without a clue? Do you honor your parents? How you treat your mother is a good indication of how you will treat your wife. God's man loves authority and is given authority. (Romans 13:1-7, Ephesians 6:2 also see section on authority)

What does it take to become a man? The first step is surrender. In this you will find the freedom and power to become much more than you could ever think or imagine. (Ephesians 3:20)

...until you have allowed God to balance your personality and control your passions. God has created us all unique with unique personalities and dispositions. If we try to seek gratification outside of God and his plan our personalities work against us to keep us enslaved to some very unproductive and destructive things. God wants to bring into balance your passions and personality. He wants you to live free of enslavement.

For example, some guys are real hard driving, 'get it done' types. There comes with this a danger to let anger and perfectionism get the best of you. Some guys are real laid-back kind of "whatever" types. The danger here is laziness and apathy. Any personality trait out of balance harbors danger.

Once the testosterone in your body mixes with the images of our culture, many boys become enslaved by lust. God has put in you passion, a drive for life; he wants to harness it for his and your good. Many boys let lust and masturbation rob them of the self control and the healthy sex life they are supposed to have. (see section on defeating lust in the chapter on Sex)

In order for you to allow God to balance your personalities and control your passions, you must renew your mind. Every battle for self-control begins in your mind. You must embark on an extensive and specific scripture memorization program. Here are some for starters:

Lust: 2 Timothy 2:22, Proverbs 6:25,27-29, I John 2:15-17

Laziness: Proverbs 10:4,5, 6:6-11, 19:15, Hebrews 6:12,

Anger: Proverbs 29:11, 14:29, 15:1, Ephesians 4:31

Lying: Proverbs 12:17, 19:22, Leviticus 19:35-36, Revelation 21:8

Peer pressure: Romans 12:1-2, I Peter 3:15-16, Luke 12:4-5

Friends: II Corinthians 6:14-15, Proverbs 17:17, 13:20, 18:24

Speech: Colossians 3:18, Ephesians 4:29

Don't settle for enslavement! Live free! God's man knows the truth and the truth sets him free. (John 8:32-36, Romans 6:18) Don't let personality imbalances and poor habit patterns keep you from reaching your godly potential.

...until you are prepared to accept responsibility for yourself and for others entrusted to you and you can produce more than you consume. I tell the boys in my youth group that they are not ready for marriage until they are ready to take the blame for everything. Why? Because that's the price of leadership. **Leaders accept responsibility for and learn to serve those entrusted to them.** But before a boy can become a man, he must take responsibility for himself. If he proves himself faithful in little things, he will find that people will give him greater responsibilities   (which are greater areas of freedom and liberty in disguise).

What about you? Can you do your own laundry yet? Can you cook your own meals, fix your own car, manage your own money? Can you keep your room clean and make good grades without anybody harping on you? Can you get to school and work on time without your momma having to wake you up? If you can't take responsibility for yourself, how can God trust you with others (a wife, kids,

> WHEN WE ARE FOOLISH WE WANT TO CONQUER THE WORLD. WHEN WE ARE WISE WE WANT TO CONQUER OURSELVES.

employees)? How about your role in your home? Do you fulfill your obligations to your family? If not, take the time to learn to serve your mom, dad, brothers and sisters. The family life is a training ground for life after your family. Don't skip or excuse yourself from it.

Can you provide enough income for you plus someone else? Or are you just barely getting by now? (I Timothy 5:8) God desires to make you into a fruit-bearer! Learn the secrets of producing more than you consume and watch God use you to bless not only your family but nations! (John 15:1-17, Luke 16:10-12, Matthew 13 see also the section on production)

...until you are able to provide Godly leadership, vision and guidance for yourself and for those entrusted to you. God created men with leadership in mind. II Corinthians 11:3 If you are male, there is some leadership potential in you. You may never become president or a CEO but you most likely will lead a family - which is hard enough. You need to know how. You don't just become a leader. You must take the time and effort to learn the skills.

Leaders show the way. Leaders know the secret of greatness - servant-hood. Leaders set standards by their own lives that are a cut above those they expect to lead. Leaders take risks. They risk failing, being criticized and second guessed. They risk loneliness and the unknown. But they would rather take the risk than be numbered with those poor, timid souls that know neither victory nor defeat. At best, they know the triumph of high achievement; at worst, when they fail, they fail doing greatly.

Leaders inspire people to move in a certain direction. They say, "This is the way, let's go!" Now if you don't know where *you* are going, how can you show others? You must learn to discern the will of God. Learn God's answers to tough questions. Learn how to find God's *best way,* then others will soon come to you. When this happens, you're on the right trail to manhood. This process takes much time, study and prayer. But better to learn this now then to wait until your responsible for others and a crisis comes.

Leaders communicate. How well can you talk to your parents? Do you run to your room after supper or do you hang around and talk with your family? Do you give more than one word answers to your parent's questions? The fundamental skill in marriage is communication - not just small talk but deep, thoughtful communication. How well do you communicate now? You're training yourself for how you will communicate to your wife.

Leaders persevere. As you grow you must understand that perseverance is a habit - and so is quitting. If you start something, finish it. If you join a sports team or a club, finish the season. Become reliable; finish what you start. Quitters never taste the sweetest fruit God has reserved for the 'never give up'ers.' (Galatians 6:9)

Don't skip the school of manhood. Becoming a man takes a lot of initiative and work. This is why you must remain focused on your primary task while you are young - preparing for your future. Don't let non-purposeful romance or a thousand other distractions divert precious energy and time away from becoming the man God has destined you to become.

Don't force your wife to secretly wish you would just grow up. The life you are living now, the responsibilities you have, the God you know and the self control you must develop will pay huge dividends when life gets a little more complicated.

Becoming a Woman of God (For the gals - my wife edited this section, as I have a hard time knowing what it's like to be a woman!)

Congratulations! Your female! Being female is an intensely special thing. Only females get to be daughters, sisters, wives, mothers, and grandmothers. Only females get to be women of God. You are part of an elect sorority, a sorority that has a terrific history of changing the world for the better.

But just because you are female, however, doesn't mean you automatically become a real woman. Becoming a woman of God takes time, self-sacrifice and devotion. If you allow him, God will give you all the tools and resources to become ALL he intends you to become - an awesome woman of God that shakes the rafters of heaven with her prayers and robs the cradles of hell with her service!

To become an Awesome Woman of God you must...

...find and deposit your worth, value and security in Jesus Christ. The girls of our nation face a crisis of epic proportions. To describe them in one word: vulnerable. They have a gaping void in their lives that leaves them open to the burglary of their most precious gifts. In their trying to fill the void they obsess about their bodies, boys, friends, authority figures, their hair, their make-up, their wardrobe and their complexion. They grasp for security in insecure things. They haven't learned the secret of peace in the midst of the storms of life: To place their lives totally on the Rock - Jesus Christ. (Matthew 7:24-27)

Take the time right now to answer this question - Who are you? Go ahead, in one paragraph or less define yourself. Who are you? After you answer the first question, answer this one: What makes you valuable? Why are you worth anything? Until you have the right answers to these questions you will remain extremely vulnerable to the thievery of your most precious gifts.

Why are you valuable? Contrary to what you may think, your looks don't make you valuable, your body doesn't make you valuable, neither do your talents, your friends, your house or your possessions. You have value for two reasons: First, God has invested a part of his glory and dignity in YOU! (Psalm 139:13-14, Psalms 8) Whether you are a Christian or not, if you are human, you have incredible value. It doesn't matter how athletic, pretty, smart or popular you are - *you are priceless*. God has invested his glory and honor in you.

Secondly, God has purchased the opportunity for you to know him again. Sin in our lives has put us in bondage and separated us from our most important relationship - God. Rather than force us to pay the penalty for our sin and impart his well deserved wrath on us, Jesus Christ paid the price for us. He took the wrath and justice of God on our behalf. He paid the ransom to free us from sin and the penalty of it (hell). How much did our ransom cost? It cost God the life of his only Son. You are worth whatever God paid for you. What did it cost him? It cost him Jesus; you are worth Jesus to God. How much is Jesus worth? He is of infinite value and then so must you be. Regardless of your complexion, body-fat content, grades or job, you are priceless.

You have just read why you are valuable, but who are you? Could you come up with an answer? As a Christian, you no longer have to fumble with your identity. Your identity is hidden in Christ. Until you find your identity and worth in God and him alone, you have yet to become a real woman.

In Christ:

- You are God's child. (John 1:12)
- You are a new creation. (II Corinthians 5:17)
- You are holy and acceptable to God. (Romans 5:1)
- You are a temple where the Holy Spirit lives.
  (I Corinthians 3:16 and 6:19)
- You cannot be separated from the love of God. (Romans 8:35)
- You can do all things through Christ who gives you strength. (Philippians 4:13)
- You are complete in Him. (Colossians 2:10)

Do you have an insecure heart? Here are some **symptoms of someone that hasn't found their security in Christ.**

- Sexual promiscuity, fantasy (romance novels), unhealthy emotional attachments, lust, infatuation, boy-craziness

- Immodest dress, dressing in a manner to draw attention to ourselves in a bold or seductive manner. Defining who you are by what you wear.

- Allowing what you look like or other external circumstances to determine your outlook (attitude) on life. Self pity

- A woman who cannot control her tongue, gossip: loud, brazen, nag. She must define herself by what she says. She's not comfortable with silence or keeping the confidence of others. Loves to control with her words.

- Overindulgence, poor diet, alcohol, tobacco, anti-depressants, money, materialism

Symptoms of a secure heart:

- Able to delay gratification to secure God's best for them. Stays pure sexually, rejects unhealthy emotional attachments. Isn't always hunting for the one, but working on becoming the one. Isn't boy crazy.

- Dresses in a manner that pleases God. Concerned that her dress will not cause someone else to stumble. She does not define herself with 'the latest fashion.' (I Timothy 2:9-10)

- Displays a quiet and meek spirit. (Meekness isn't weakness; it's power under control.) She does not need to defend herself needlessly; she does not need to talk all the time and control every conversation.

- She is a good steward of the body God gave her, protecting it from overindulgence and neglect. She recognizes the need for exercise and careful grooming without becoming obsessed with the world's standard of beauty. If she can't take care of herself, how will she take care of others?

... learn to harness the power of your femininity to inspire good in others. God has vested in you a power, a power to inspire. This power of inspiration is one of the mysteries of femininity. I have seen many a boy suddenly get his act together because a certain female has caught his eye.

You can inspire for good or for ill. Your power can build or destroy. The wise woman builds her house, but with her own hand the foolish woman tears her's down. (Proverbs 14:1) You can cause Samson to shave his head, or you can save a nation by persuading a king. (Judges 16, Esther)

Sadly, many women have not learned how to inspire. Instead, they nag. Nagging produces bad fruit. It causes people to shrink up, not blossom out. Would you like people to know you as that lady that nags her husband to death?

Some women just have wonderful lives. They have wonderful marriages, children, or maybe careers; things always seem to go their way. One of their secrets is that they have learned to inspire greatness out of those around them and together, they conquer life's challenges. Here's how you could do the same:

- Stay positive. Avoid the fatal five attitudes like cheap cologne. They will just make you stink in the eyes of others. Learn to choose the fab-five attitudes and people will love to hang around you. (See section on Attitude)

- Make a habit of using (and meaning) inspiring words to everyone you know. Try these on: "I'm proud of you." "Wow, I can really see you have a lot of potential in that area." "I believe in you; you can do it." "I really admire how you..."

- Learn to speak other people's 'love language.' A number of years ago, Dr. Gary Chapman wrote a ground-breaking book on love called *The Five Love Languages*. Dr. Chapman pointed out that human beings communicate and receive love in five main ways: acts of service, words of affirmation, physical touch, giving of gifts and spending quality time. And each human being - including you and your family and friends - has a *primary* way they receive love: one of those five. (You will also have a secondary love language that is not as strong as your primary but it still plays a factor.) Your job is to learn the love languages of those around you and then speak it to them on a regular basis. If words of affirmation really light up your father, then make a habit of telling him what a great guy he is. If quality time means the most to your mother then spend time with her on a regular basis and watch her bloom. Go get the book.

- Learn to serve. The secret of greatness and *inspiring* greatness is servitude. If you want others to see further, let them stand on your shoulders. Do you feel comfortable serving others? Get over the idea that it demeans you; it actually lifts you and others at the same time. Serving keeps ego and selfishness in check. Both will kill a marriage.

• Keep the lines of communication open. When something doesn't go your way, don't clam up. Immature, selfish people give the silent treatment. When he asks you what's wrong don't say 'nothing' if there is something. Communicate, communicate, communicate.

• Smile and be a good listener.

• Learn to trust God in prayer. Rather than nagging when somebody will not respond in the way you wish, learn to pray. *You* will not change anybody, only God can. Learn to release people from your control and into the control of the Holy Spirit.

Dr. E. V. Hill has one of the greatest national speaking ministries in America. He relates how his late wife Jane used the power of her femininity to inspire him during a crucial time in their lives together.

They faced financial difficulty as E. V. had foolishly invested in a failed gas station. Not long after the fiasco with the gas station, E. V. came home one night and found the house dark. When he opened the door he found that Jane had prepared a candlelight dinner.

E. V. thought the dinner was a great idea and he went into the bathroom to wash his hands. He tried unsuccessfully to turn on the light. He went into the bedroom and tried to no avail to turn the lights on in there. He then asked Jane why the electricity was off. She began to cry.

"You work so hard, and were trying," said Jane, "but it's pretty rough. I didn't have quite enough money to pay the light bill. I didn't want you to know about it so I thought we would eat by candlelight."

Dr. Hill later described his wife's words with much emotion. "She could have said, 'I've never been in this situation before. I was reared in the home of Dr. Caruthers, and we never had our lights cut off.' She could have broken my spirit; she could have ruined me, she could have demoralized me. But instead she said, 'Somehow or another we'll get these lights on. But let's eat tonight by candlelight.'"[1]

Now that's a woman of God inspiring greatness! We need more women like that. Will you be one?

...learn to pursue God's vision for you. Find your dream. What are you doing with your life? Where are you going? Recognize that the choices laid out in front of you are preparing you for the fulfilment of his plan down the road. Too many girls think that this is just free time. "The choices I make right now don't really matter right now." "I can date any old guy, slough off at school, spend my money." Girls with no vision, no dreams or direction make easy targets. Don't let the choices you make today give you baggage that you will struggle with later.

Do you have a dream? Here are some symptoms of a woman without a vision:

- Low standards, anything or anyone will do, physically and emotionally attach myself to whomever

- Spends money like water. Waste God's resources on more and more clothes, music, hair. Has no vision for future expenditures (college, house, car). Has no problem going into debt - especially with credit cards.

- Compares herself with others. Is fond of saying or thinking, "I don't measure up to ..." She criticizes others and becomes easily consumed with self pity and ungratefulness.

- Has poor self-esteem because she places her value on other things than Christ and she doesn't accomplish much. In fact, she doesn't even attempt much.

- Impatient. She's unable to delay her gratification, will not wait for God's best so she settles for the good.

Characteristics of a woman *with a vision*:

- Adopts God's standards for every area of her life. Nothing will prevent her from God's best in terms of a husband. She does not let guys that are not fitting for marriage distract her from her goals.

- She is a good steward of God's money. She doesn't spend money on frivolous things that don't last. Looks toward future financial goals, plans to and avoids debt.

- Realizes that God has given her unique gifts and talents. She spends her energy and time building and investing in her gifts. Finds her passion and follows it.

- Has a healthy self esteem because she places her value and worth in Christ and she *accomplishes* things worthy of esteem. They don't mope around thinking what about what a failure they are because they are too busy attempting and succeeding at many ventures. Get off the couch! Do something! And give it your best; then work at making your best *better*!

- She patiently waits for God's timing, learns to delay her gratification. And she learns to trust God through difficult decisions.

During this season of life, take the time to concentrate on your primary responsibility - prepare for your future. Instead of hunting for the one, concentrate on becoming the one. We need more men and women of God and less average Joe's and mediocre Misses. I'm excited about your future!

Now back to the last two keys of 'Wise Love.'

1. Joshua Harris relating a story told by James Dobson in his book *I Kissed Dating Goodbye*, Multnomah 1997, pg 198

ROMANCE II

The Bible does not offer us a 'one size fits all' pattern for romance. Cultures, people and circumstances are too different to dictate the same format for all people. God has, however, given us principles by which to operate - principles that protect us from the heartache and provide us with the good fruit romance can bring. Here we pick back up these principles with..

Principle of Wise Love #3

Commit to refraining from illegitimate physical contact. Wisdom recognizes that marriage is primarily a spiritual relationship. To properly live this principle through the dating relationship, each person should attempt to draw the other closer to God, all the while considering the possibilities of marriage.

Many young people look at the physical play of kissing, petting and sex as just another form of entertainment. Many more say, "What's

> ILLEGITIMATE PHYSICAL CONTACT IS DOING ANYTHING THAT WILL IGNITE A DESIRE THAT YOU CANNOT RIGHTEOUSLY FULFILL.

wrong with it just as long as you don't have intercourse?"

God calls us to purity. The word 'pure' means to be free from all taint of that which is lewd. It suggests refraining from all acts and thoughts that incite desire not in accordance with one's virginity or marriage vows. It stresses restraint and avoidance of all sexual actions and excitements that would defile one's purity before God.

The kissing and touching that often goes on in today's relationships often leads to confusion and compromise. Such behavior is often based on selfishness and it awakens desires that you can righteously satisfy only in marriage.

Physical intimacy works in stages. People often ask, "Where is the line?" or "How far is too far?" They desire to get as close to the cliff without going over. They don't realize the power of sexual attraction or the 'law of diminishing returns.' God designed physical intimacy to start slow, pick up speed and end in the act of intercourse. When you get the train moving, it's incredibly hard to stop as many regretful young people have found.

The law of diminishing returns states that doing the same thing over and over will give you a diminished thrill each time you do it. At first, holding hands gives you a terrific thrill. But soon it just doesn't give you the same feeling as it did, so you must go a bit farther to give you the same thrill. You start kissing, but soon you need to go further and your hands desire to wander and so on...and so on. Illegitimate physical involvement is like a stick of dynamite. If you light the fuse, it will burn. The next time you light it, you must light it where you left off. Soon you will get to the explosion.

The Bible talks of three types of loves: *Philia* - brotherly, friendship, sharing not selfish love, *Agape* - spiritual, giving not getting, unconditional, Godlike love, and *Eros* -physical love. True marriage is the fusing of all three basic loves, thus the couple become "one" in spirit, soul, and body. God plans the fusing of these loves in stages. The couple must awaken and cultivate friendship and spiritual love before they are allowed to awaken the physical love.

Making out with some one you have not pledged your life to awakens physical love waaaaaaaay too early. That's why it brings confusion and compromise.

If you cannot be satisfied with spiritual, friendly communion and conversation, with just that desire to be together and keep your live's holy and pure, you are NOT in love. Lust can wait five minutes; love can wait five years.

Principle of Wise Love #4

Commitment to living under the protection of your God - given authorities. Today's system of romance tends to isolate us from our friends and our families. The parents of young people just seem to be along for the ride. They no longer actively participate in the romantic lives of their children. They will go with them and advise them, even co-sign for them to by a car. But when it comes to the second most important decision of their lives, many are nowhere to be found. They do their children a great disservice. Parents have a right and an obligation to guide their children through this process.

If you will not commit to living under and including your God given authorities in your romantic life, you are treading in a mine-field without a map. Find authority figures you

> **"LISTEN MY SON TO A FATHERS INSTRUCTION; PAY ATTENTION AND GAIN UNDERSTANDING."**
> Proverbs 4:1

respect and honor. Submit yourself to them and invite them to speak into your life. Allow them to question you if they see you headed toward a questionable area.

Have you ever had a friend who had a boyfriend or a girlfriend you knew was not good for them? You could see what a jerk he was, but she couldn't? Infatuation blinds people. It makes them unable to think straight. It could happen to you. That is why you need authorities in your life to guide you through this process. They will help you think a bit more clearly and logically. They can see the big picture easier because they are not right in the middle of the situation.

If a boy desires to win your heart, talk it over with your parents or another trusted authority first. If this boy meets God's standards for you and you are not in danger of violating any of God's principles, then arrange for him to meet and spend time with your family as soon as you can. He must show honor to your family before they can trust him with your honor.

If you desire to pursue the heart of a girl, have the courage to talk to her parents about it. She is not yours. She is theirs. Let them know what your intentions are. Are you just friends? Do you intend to marry her? What makes you the best man for her? What have you done to prepare for your future?

Marriage transfers authority from the father to the groom. The groom places himself in a new relationship of submission to the Lord. For this reason, it becomes vital for both the man and the woman to understand the principles of authority.

I know for some of you this issue brings some legitimate fear. It may seem like a fate worse than death to have someone your interested in actually spend time with your *weird* family. Or maybe your fear is rooted in the possibility that your little sibling will tell your new friend all of your secrets. Allow me to let you in on a little secret: Everybody's family is weird and all brothers and sisters have dirt on each other. So gather up some courage and spend time together with each other's family.

If you don't have a family unit that cares, then pray for God to give you an authority you can trust - perhaps a youth pastor, pastor or maybe your friend's family could 'unofficially adopt' you.

A word to parents (please have your parents read this)

Hello, Mom and Dad. You should be extremely proud of your son or daughter. They desire to pursue the best things in life.

- Get involved. God has entrusted you with children. He desires that you love them and teach them. God has put together a method of teaching children his principles. He says, "Teach them to your children, talking about them when you sit at home and when you walk along the road, when you lie down and when you get up" (Deuteronomy 11:19). Get involved with your child's life - especially their romantic life. The second greatest decision of their life is who they will marry. Make a concerted effort to get to know any person desiring to win the heart of your child.

- Let love and honor guide you. If a boy desires to win the heart of your daughter, get to know him. Seek to build him, not destroy him. Before they get too involved, find out what he likes to do and go do something he likes. Talk to him, help him to verbalize his intentions with your daughter. Does he plan to remain friends? Does he see potential for marriage? What does he need to do before he is married? What are his plans for life? How can you help him? Seek to honor him and bring honor out of him.

- Pray. Pray protection over your child's purity. Pray that if they are doing anything wrong it will come to light and they will face constructive consequences. Pray for their future spouse and marriage.

Recognizing the real deal

While you concentrate on becoming the man or woman of God you need to become, you should learn what qualities to look for in a future spouse. As you trust God's standards for a mate, maintain awareness of the qualities of the people around you.

Qualities to look for in a man:

1. Commitment to Christ? Is Jesus Lord of his life and are his priorities in line with what Christ says really matters?

- How is his devotional life? Does he spend regular time with the Lord? Does he place a high priority on time with God? Has he ever canceled anything with friends to spend time with God?

- Does he worship God freely? Is he unafraid to lift his hands, dance or bow his knee before God? More importantly, does his entire life reflect worship unto the Lord? (Romans 12:1-3)

- Does church attendance represent a high priority in his life? Does he use his gifts to bear fruit in God's kingdom?

- Does he give thanks for food in public?

- How is his language? Is it clean and pure or spattered with vulgarities and off color slang?

- What about his music and entertainment choices? Do they resemble what a man of God would allow his mind to feed on? Is he entertained by things that grieve God? Does he even know what would grieve God?

- How does he spend his money? Wherever his money goes, that's where his heart is. You can tell a lot about a person by how they spend their money.

2. Self controlled?

Has he allowed God to balance his personality and control his passions? Does he struggle with anger, lust, laziness, or commitment? Can he live without any physical relations? Lust can wait five minutes; love can wait five years. Is he satisfied with just being with you? Does he treat you with respect and display proper etiquette?

3. In harmony with authority?

Is he willing to honor your authorities? Is he willing to spend time with your family? How he treats his mother is a good indication of how he will treat his wife. How does he treat his teachers and pastors? What attitude does he display toward the law?

4. Is he responsible?

Does he take responsibility for himself? Does he take care of the things entrusted to him? Has he developed the life skills to take care of a house and a car? Is he a good steward of his time and possessions? Can he provide for a household?

5. Is he a man of vision?

Does he have a vision for his life? Does it coincide with yours? Does he have direction and motivation? Does he show signs of becoming a Godly leader?

6. What else would you like in a man? _____

What to look for in a woman:

1. Commitment to Christ

- Does she inspire you to walk closer to God? Or does she allow compromise in yours and her life?

- Has she developed a regular devotional life? Is it a priority?

- Does she freely express herself in worship?

- Is church attendance a high priority? Does she use her gifts to build up the body of Christ?

2. Is her security in Christ?

- Does she dress in an immodest manner? Does she like to draw attention to certain parts of her anatomy by the way she dresses?

- Is her language pure? Does she edify others with her words?

- Does she show concern for others? Is she an IDI? (See chapter on Attitude)   Is she free of self pity and PLOM disease? (See section on Attitude)

- Is she materialistic? Does she hear more loudly the call of gold or the call of God?

- Does her music and entertainment agree with God's standards? Does she know God's standards in this area?

2. Submissive spirit or rebellious and controlling?

Is she in harmony with her authorities? How she treats her father is a good indication of how she will treat you. Do her words and actions inspire great things in people or does she tear down her brothers and sisters?

3. Does she take care of herself and others?

How does she keep her room? Is she a good steward of her body but not obsessed with the world's standard of beauty? Is she a care-giver or a taker? Does she look to do for others or look for others to do for her?

4. Life skills?

What skills could she bring into the relationship? Cooking? Money management? Fixing cars? Cardiovascular surgery? Working on life skills may seem un-romantic but they pay great dividends in the real world.

5. Does she have a vision?

Can she see past the end of her nose? Does her life's calling coincide with yours? Does she accomplish things? Does she invest time and energy into her gifts and talents? Is she a good steward of her money? Does she delay her gratification for better things? (Genesis 24:12-21)

6. What else would you like in a woman? _____

These lists may seem unrealistic to you. But to God they are totally in the realm of normalcy. We have accepted mediocrity for so long that when excellence comes our way it seems freakish.

We all can grow. We all should continually strive to become better men and women of God. But most of your growth physically, spiritually and emotionally occur while you are young - before you face the extra pressure and responsibilities of a home and family. If you find yourself coming up short in any of these areas, then work on them!

If you have a friend that needs to work on an area or two, then pray for them and inspire them! As iron sharpens iron so one man sharpens another. (Proverbs 27:17) Don't let anything sidetrack you from your primary goal - to prepare for your future.

Now What?

So your attracted to someone, now what? As mentioned earlier, the Bible gives us some leeway here. There is no hard core blueprint for acquiring the perfect mate. As long as you keep God your focus and you remain in his principles, you should do fine. What follows here is a skeletal pattern to which God and your specific circumstances will flesh out.

Relationships usually progress to one state or another. We have acquaintances, friends, close friends, romantic relationships, engagements and marriages. Every time you are attracted to someone, remember you have obligations to them just as a human being. God expects you to treat them as you would want to be treated. He asks that you would honor and love them as a brother or sister in God.

After reminding yourself of these obligations, you should make becoming close friends your top priority. Get to know them better as people without the distortion that romance brings. Set out to get an accurate, unbiased idea of each other's true nature. Instead of dropping out of your regular activities, try to include each other in some of your normal activities. Find activities that pull you into each other's world of family, work, school, recreation, service and ministry.

I learned much about my wife during our service in ministry together. She volunteered to coach our church's Bible quiz team and help out with youth group. I happened to be the new youth pastor in her church. Before we were anything, we were friends. And as friends we got to know each other without the rose colored glasses of romance (that came later). I watched her during normal activity and she watched me.

During this time you must be very careful not to allow your emotions to take over. Do not allow the romantic train to leave the station. Once it gets going, you need to derail it to stop it. And that is never pretty. Avoid doing things that communicate romantic love. Be careful in the giving of gifts, spending too much exclusive time together, touching, and expressing romantic words.

Take care not to feed infatuations by day-dreaming about them, writing their name on everything you own or talking exclusively to your friends about them. When you feed an infatuation, you place them in a position they were never intended to fulfill - that of an idol.

It will take patience and much self control to keep romantic feelings from blooming prematurely, but it's worth it. Learn to cultivate friendship and spiritual love.

Green Lights?

As you develop your friendship, you should **watch and pray.**

During this time, you must eventually ask yourself the tough question: "Based on the character and personality of this person, would I consider marrying them?" If you cannot say that this person has the qualities you wish for in a spouse, than you must be careful not to allow the relationship to become romantic. Just remain friends. Neither of you has lost anything. You have gained a friend. If, however, you have invested your romantic emotions in them too soon, a broken heart or compromise of values waits just around the corner.

If, however, you can honestly see yourself complimenting, serving and loving this person for the rest of your life, then look for these green lights before you proceed with a romantic investment.

- Have you trusted God's timing and his standards for a mate? Re-read chapter on becoming and what to look for in a spouse.

- Are you ready for marriage spiritually, professionally, financially, and emotionally?

- Do you have the support of your families and friends? If you think your ready for marriage but nobody else does, go back to prayer and be honest with God and yourself. This is not to say that parents or other advisors can never be wrong, but rarely should we proceed without considering their opinions.

- Do you have a prayerful peace about it? Do you have any feelings of confusion or anxiety about it? Do you have a sense of haste? If so, don't move. Hold steady and seek the mind of God. If you have an honest, objective peace about your situation, then consider it another green light.

Let the Train out of the Station

When you get all the lights green, you now face a time when you must clearly define the purpose and direction in your relationship. Are you to remain friends or pursue each other's hearts? Communication is critical here. Do not allow room for each other to wonder what the other is thinking. At the right time, one of you (preferably the man, as he should be practicing spiritual leadership) should broach the subject by saying something like this: " (Insert name here), as we have grown closer during this time I feel I need to be up-front with you about my motives. I'm not a person who dates girls just to date them. I try to pursue romance with the goal of marriage in mind. I just want to let you know that with your parents permission, I would like the opportunity to win your heart."

You may think, "Wow, that is serious!" Yes, it is. We should not play with a person's heart and future.

Talking about such things encourages a habit of courage and communication in the relationship. Courage and communication stand as cornerstones of all good marriages. If more married couples had the courage to admit when they are wrong, or the courage to say, "I love you," or "I'm sorry," we wouldn't have as many bad marriages.

If we learn how to communicate our needs, desires and love effectively without raising our voices, the whole world would reap the benefits. Don't wait to learn them. Take the time now.

At this stage in the relationship you are free to cultivate romantic feelings. Pursue the heart of your prospective bride or husband. Learn to lead them or inspire them in a deeper way. You may feel free to spend more time together, give gifts and express your feelings in romantic ways. Discuss many subjects. Talk about feelings, concerns, visions, hopes and dreams. Attempt to learn more of the differences between men and women, goals and roles, how each other communicates. Learn each other's pet peeves. Take walks together, try different activities and serve together on different projects. Share what you are learning about God; memorize portions of scripture.

During this activity, guard yourselves against the temptations of physical intimacy. Your not married yet; don't treat each others bodies as if you were. Focus on the spiritual side of the relationship. Where physical progression begins, depth progression ends. As soon as your focus turns to the physical side of the relationship, the friendship and spiritual side atrophies. Part of this commitment means avoiding places of temptation. If you delay sexual involvement, you will store up passion for the days when you will be able to righteously unleash them in all their glory with no regrets.

Get the Ring

The period of testing and winning the hearts need only last as long as it takes for you both to feel comfortable about getting married. With all the new information gained through this stage, have you found anything in him/her that would cause you to have doubt about trusting your entire life with this person? If you get a green light here, then it's time to pop the question. And fellas, please make it memorable. Don't cheese out and make it lame.

My wife has a story to tell all her children, friends and grandchildren about how her husband proposed. Believe me, this story rivals that of any one I have ever heard of.

After your engagement, you will face increased times of

temptation to involve yourselves physically. Don't blow it here. Don't let the enemy say, "Well, your going to get married anyway." Your NOT married yet!

Two points about the ring:

- Don't buy the lie put out by the marketing geniuses at DeBeers (the company that operates a monopoly on most of the diamond mines around the world) that a ring should cost you three months salary. You can get her a fantastic ring (and you should) for thousands less than that.

- Don't buy a ring at a mall jewelry store. They mark up their merchandise about 500%. Buy your ring from a discount jeweler this will save you serious cash. And don't buy the 'investment quality' sales scheme. All gems are poor investments. Get one that looks nice to your naked eye. Your better off getting a bigger, 'average' quality diamond than a spec of dust 'investment quality' diamond. Trust me, size does matter here, not 'investment quality.' With that said, don't get a diamond so dirty that it won't sparkle in the sun; these are poor quality.

Two words about wedding planning for guys:

- "Yes dear" - and - "whatever you want dear."

God bless you! I can't wait to hear how God will bless you according to his Word in this area!

"A FRIEND LOVES AT ALL TIMES, AND A BROTHER IS
BORN FOR ADVERSITY."
KING SOLOMON, PROVERBS 17:17

"BE DEVOTED TO ONE ANOTHER IN BROTHERLY
LOVE. HONOR ONE ANOTHER ABOVE YOURSELVES."
THE APOSTLE PAUL, ROMANS 12:10

"JONATHAN BECAME ONE IN SPIRIT WITH DAVID,
AND HE LOVED HIM AS HIMSELF."
I SAMUEL 18:1

MI COMPADRE

Companionship. We have a longing in ourselves for companionship. We consider it a form of torture to isolate someone from others for extended periods of time.

Human relationships have inspired the greatest poetry and literature and we have witnessed the human bond become the grandest of themes in our favorite films. People who isolate themselves from others for extended periods of time we call kooks, hermits and weirdos. God himself said, "It is not good that man should be alone" (Genesis 2:18).

Relationships help bring meaning into our lives. God created us to live in vertical relationship with him and horizontal relationship with others. He has given us three underlying principles that will, if followed, insure that you enjoy the best fruits of human relationships. These principles apply to those people in our family, our friends and those we work with.

Principle # 1: Love

What have we written and talked about more than love? Even as love plays such a prominent role in our culture, most people have a solid misunderstanding of it. The world shows us two bodies embracing on the silver screen and tells us, "That is love." God takes to the foot of a tree, points to an innocent man dying in place of the guilty and says, "This is love."

We often mistake love for romantic feelings. We may possess romantic feelings for someone we love, but those feelings are not love. **Love is a choice that wills the highest good for someone** *regardless of how we feel.* If we love someone, then we consistently make choices that are motivated by desiring the highest good for that person.

The apostle John, often called the apostle of love, said that the greatest way to show someone you love them is to lay down your life for them. This doesn't mean that we all have to die in someone's place to show them how much we love them. What we do need to do, however, is to consistently set aside our own selfish desires in favor of the good of others. Most of the problems we have in relationships we can trace to this root issue - lack of love. Where selfishness rules, conflict and division flourish; hearts grow hard and people grow bitter. If everyone would act in the best interest of others, humans would have no word for war, divorce, racism, conflict and hatred.

> "THIS IS HOW WE KNOW WHAT LOVE IS: JESUS CHRIST LAID DOWN HIS LIFE FOR US. AND WE OUGHT TO LAY DOWN OUR LIVES FOR OUR BROTHERS."
> I John 3:16

No one can know of the immeasurable pain due to fractured families and friendships lost because of stubborn selfishness rooted in pride. God hates pride and selfishness. Maybe someone has hurt you by their pride and selfishness. Maybe *you* have hurt others because of your pride and selfishness.

If we defer our desires for the needs and wants of others then who will take care of our needs - God will. He knows our needs and desires and he has promised to take care of them. (Philippians 4:19, Psalms 37:4, Matthew 6:25-33)

We all reap what we sow. If you want love, give it. If you desire friends, show yourself friendly. The more you give, the more others will give to you. Think about it. Aren't the most giving and selfless people that you know the most contented and blessed? They rarely lack for anything. They continually give yet they receive even more! (Proverbs: 11:24-25)

People often mistake love for tolerance. I often hear people say, "We just need to be tolerant of everyone's beliefs; stop hating and start loving." They usually say this to get certain people to stop expressing their beliefs. Tolerance used to mean - respect all people and their right to their own opinion. Now it means - respect all people and hold their beliefs as equally valid. *The belief that all beliefs are true is false and very dangerous.* Tolerance is not love. The world calls us to tolerate (treat all opinions as equally valid), but God calls us to love.

Tolerance says, "You must approve of what I do." Love responds, "I must do something harder; I will love you, even when your behavior offends me."

Tolerance says, "You must allow me to have my way." Love responds, "I must do something harder; I will tell you the truth, because I am convinced the 'truth will set you free.'"

Tolerance says, "You must agree with me." Love responds, "I must do something harder; I will plead with you to follow the right way, because I believe you are worth the risk."

Tolerance says, "All beliefs are true." Love responds, "Truth by definition is exclusive, and love rejoices in truth."

Sometimes love must be tough. Sometimes love allows people to experience the consequences of their behavior. Love doesn't enable people to keep harming themselves through poor behavior by constantly bailing them out of situations they created themselves.

Love forgives. When someone wrongs us, God calls us to forgive. Love doesn't hold grudges, but releases revenge and retribution to the Lord. As God forgives us, so we forgive others.

Who does God call us to love? Everyone. Our friends, our family, our in-laws, our out-laws, our enemies, those who hate us and those who love us; God calls us to love them all!

If you learn love, it will enrich your life - especially your relationships.

Principle #2 Honor

Honor, Courage and Commitment - these three cardinal virtues have made the United States Marine Corps some of the most feared fighting forces around the world. The first in this creed is the second principle for having good relationships - Honor.

You don't hear much of this word out in the civilian ranks anymore. Honor means to value or esteem to give respect. If you desire good human relationships, *learn to honor others*. Learn to recognize the value of the people around you.

We are to honor parents (Exodus 20:12, Matthew 15:14), church elders and national leaders (Numbers 27:20, I Peter 2:17), older people (Leviticus 19:32) and everyone else (Romans 12:10). We are to honor the gift of God in someone's life, because it honors the God who gives it (Malachi 1:6, John 12:26, Matthew 13:54-57).

The root of division among people is an *independent spirit* - an attitude of self-sufficiency. It's thinking and acting as if you are the whole thing; imagining that because you can do one thing better, you can do all things better. It is to project an attitude - especially to those who have no status or prominence: "I don't need you."

But the Bible likens human relationships - especially the church - to a body. "The eye cannot say to the hand, 'I don't need you!' And the head cannot say to the feet, 'I don't need you!' On the contrary, those parts of the body that seem to be weaker are indispensable" (I Corinthians 12:21).

So what makes the difference in human relationships; how can we avoid the strife and division that seems so prevalent among us? *Honor makes the difference.* "On the contrary, those parts of the body that seem to be weaker are indispensable, and the parts that are unpresentable are treated with special modesty, while our presentable parts need no special treatment. But God has combined the members of the body and has **given greater honor the parts that lacked it**, so that there should be no division in the body, but that its parts should have equal concern for each other. (I Corinthians 12:22-25).

Do not fail to give special honor and encouragement to those who need it.

Principle #3: Purity

None of us can live without contact with other people. Nobody lives to themselves and nobody dies to themselves (Romans 14:7). This can be good or bad. Living around other people brings with it a certain pressure to conform. We call that peer pressure. When that pressure pushes us to compromise God's standards, we violate the third principle of human relationships - purity.

Dr Bob Laurent surveyed more that 400 Christian teenagers about negative peer pressure. Here's what he found:

Statement	Teen response
My non-Christian friends opinions are important to me.	Strongly Agree
I am more likely to act like a Christian when I am with my Christian friends and to act like a non-Christian when I am with my non-Christian friends.	Agree
I get upset when my non-Christian friends leave me out of their activities.	Agree
It bothers me when my non-Christian friends think I'm too religious.	Agree
I try to keep up with the latest fads.	Strongly Agree

Steve, a sixteen-year-old junior says, "My friends want to do things that are un-Christian and it's hard not to go along. I guess it means my friends aren't good for me. But knowing it doesn't make it easier. No one likes to be the oddball."

Janet, a fourteen-year-old says, "I know it's stupid but I end up doing things I'd never do by myself. I get caught up in the excitement and just don't think."

God knows that friendships are important. He also knows that the most important friendship is the one you have with him. News-flash: **You can't always please God and your friends.**

The values and standards of people rub off on us almost imperceptibly like mold spores and flu viruses. **This is why God calls us to keep our closest friends also *his* closest friends.** "Do not be misled, bad company corrupts good character" (I Corinthians 15:33). "He who walks with the wise grows wise, but a companion of fools comes to ruin" (Proverbs 13:20, I John 2:15-17).

We have three different levels of friendships. Acquaintances are people that you have met once or twice; you know *of* them. You may have hundreds of acquaintances. Friends share some common interests or work. You may have 10 to 20 friends. Close friends, soul-mates, share your deepest core values, dreams, ideals and priorities. You may only have one to four very close friends. God calls us to make our closest friends also friends of Christ. If they are not, you are violating the principle of purity in relationships. What fellowship does light have with darkness, what do righteousness and unrighteousness have in common? (I Corinthians 6:14-18)

During the research for this book, I have listened to hundreds of people tell me their life stories. People from every walk of life and economic stratification shared with me what has worked and what hasn't. **Most of the ones that had deep regrets or miserable lives had this statement somewhere in their story: "I began to hang with the wrong crowd."** They violated the principle of purity in relationships.

When you first become a Christian, your likes, dislikes, values, priorities and standards change. When this happens, your friends will see a different you. They will want you to go places you can't take Jesus. They will say things, do things, drink things, smoke things, watch and listen to things you cannot do without compromise. They will either accept the Jesus in you or reject him.

They may say things like, "Your just not the same person you used to be. You used to be more fun."

They're half right! You are a different person, but you still have fun, just in different ways.

What do you do with these friends? The better question is, "What will they do with you?" Will they desire to go to the places you like to go to now? Will they like to do the things Christians like to do? Do not reject them outright. Just love God, love them, and see what happens. What will they do with you when you lovingly refuse to compromise? You may find them becoming less and less close as they share less and less in common with you. **Continue to love and pray for them but avoid the temptation to compromise your purity just to have friends!**

> "IF THE WORLD HATES YOU REMEMBER THAT IT HATED ME FIRST. IF YOU BELONGED TO THE WORLD, IT WOULD LOVE YOU AS ITS OWN. AS IT IS, YOU DO NOT BELONG TO THE WORLD, BUT I HAVE CHOSEN YOU OUT OF THE WORLD. THAT IS WHY THE WORLD HATES YOU."
>
> Jesus Christ; John 15:18-19

Solitude

Even though God didn't intend us to live the Christian life entirely alone, times will come when circumstances will force you to choose between pure and alone or compromised and accompanied. Every great soul must spend time in the crucible of solitude. Noah, Daniel, Joseph, Jesus, every great person throughout history Christian and non-Christian alike all spent time at odds with the crowd.

God will give you great friends, but you must always maintain a willingness to walk alone if need be. You can overcome the problem of loneliness through prayer. You can use times of feeling alone to pour out your heart to Jesus. He is always there! He will never leave you or forsake you! (Hebrews 13:5, Romans Ch. 8)

David learned friendship with God. He said, "When my mother and father forsake me, the Lord will take me up" (Psalm 27:10).

Some of the greatest spiritual times of your life will come when you are all alone with God. No great man or woman of God ever lived without learning to hear God in the silence.

> "AS OFTEN TIMES AS I WAS AMONG MEN I CAME BACK LESS A MAN, THAT IS TO SAY, LESS HOLY...LEAVE VAIN THINGS TO THE VAIN, SHUT THY DOOR ON THEE AND CALL TO JESUS THY LOVE; DWELL WITH HIM IN THY CELL FOR THOU SHALT NOT FIND ELSEWHERE SO GREAT A PEACE."
> Thomas a Kempis

A. G. Sertillanges said: "All great works are prepared in the desert, including the redemption of the world. The precursors, the followers, the Master himself all obeyed or have to obey one and the same law. Prophets, apostles, preachers, martyrs, pioneers of knowledge, inspired artists in every great art, ordinary men and the Man-God all pay tribute to loneliness, to the life of silence, to the night."[1]

How to?

Maybe you have had trouble in your friendships and other relationships before. You may be shy or feel that people will not like you. It is true that some people in this world will never like you. If you live for Jesus, people who runaway from God's love will not want to know you too well. Your life will convict them of their own sin. You will meet hurt, bitter people who do not trust anyone.

Christians don't expect to be popular with everyone. But Jesus had many friends. He was a supremely friendly and understanding person.

You could come to him and always be sure of a welcome.

The world has a funny idea of Christians. They think in terms of being too weird, not tolerant of other faiths, not able to enjoy a little 'fun' in life. The world always creates a miserable picture of Christianity. But that's not why the Pharisees criticized Jesus. They said "He was a friend of tax collectors and sinners" (Luke 7:34). Sinners liked him too much. Jesus had a knack of mixing with people and building them up even when he put down their wrong.

Here are some everyday ways that you can use the same principles Jesus used - Love, Honor, and Purity - to further your relationships.

- **Get pure before God.** Place your security and worth in him, not in what others think about you. Place the highest priority in the opinion of God rather than the opinions of men. Be willing and ready to stand alone with Jesus if need be.

- **Learn to forget about you.** Remember that honor *values* others. Learn to lower yourself to lift others up. Build them up with your words and by serving them. Instead of thinking of what you can get from a friendship, think of what you can give. Stop talking about yourself; instead, ask sincere questions and listen intently to the answers. Stop trying to explain to people how *cool* you are by telling them all the *cool* stuff you do and all the *cool* people you know. Don't be *cool*, be selfless; then you will really be cool.

- **Train yourselves to say uplifting, positive, encouraging words.** The mouth of the righteous should be a fountain of life. Give sincere compliments like, "I really liked how you...," "I thought you did a great job on..." Think of ways to make them feel important. Make a list of good things you can say about them, even if it's only a few. Then ask God to bless them, to help them.

- **Learn names and remember them.** Then say a friendly, "Hi _____, even if they don't say it. To help you remember their name, say it a few times. Use it in conversations with them. They will almost always like you if you remember their name; it means you found them important enough to remember. You honor people by remembering their names and things about them.

- **Look for the lonely and neglected.** Don't just try to hang out with the cool crowd. Don't be proud but be willing to associate with the humble. **Humility comes before honor!** (Proverbs 15:33, 18:12)

- **Admit your mistakes cheerfully, and learn to laugh at yourself once in a while**. When you compete, be a good winner and a loser. Don't moan or brag.

- **When talking with people you disagree with, agree with them as often as you can**. Try not to make them feel stupid; don't belittle them. All people are of infinite value, even if all idea's aren't.

- **Don't call older people by their first names**, honor them by referring to them as Mr or Mrs, Sir and Ma'am.

- **A friend loves at all times and a brother is born for adversity**. (Proverbs 17:17) When a friend is going through a hard time, do what you can to make it easier - don't bail on them during their times of trouble; your time is coming.

- **Wounds of a friend can be trusted.** (Proverbs 27:6) Sometimes we must confront friends about things that they are doing wrong. We do this out of love. If you let them continue in their sin without saying anything, your heart becomes motivated by their opinion of you rather then your love for them. Before you rebuke someone, spend some time in prayer about the situation. You may find that God will change their heart even before you say anything. Make sure you have pure and not selfish motives. When confronting, use gentleness and respect. (Galatians 5:23,

Philippians 4:5, I Peter 3:15)

- **Love your enemies and pray for those who persecute you.**
  What do you do when people persecute you? Love them. Let the
  words of Christ guide your thinking. "You have heard that it was
  said, 'Love your neighbor and hate your enemy.' But I tell you:
  Love your enemies and pray for those who persecute you, that you
  may be sons of your Father in heaven. He causes his sun to rise
  on the evil and the good, and sends the rain on the righteous and
  the unrighteous. If you love those who love you, what reward will
  you get? Are not even the tax collectors doing that? And if you
  greet only your brothers, what are you doing more than others?
  Do not even pagans do that? Be perfect, therefore, as your
  heavenly Father is perfect" (Matthew 5:43-48).

- **Forgive, forgive, forgive.** You will not go through life without
  experiencing hurt and injustice. Through misunderstanding, mis-
  communication and rank selfishness, we will all be hurt. You
  must release your right to harbor anger and revenge against those
  people to God. Do not take your own revenge, allow room for the
  wrath of God. Do not repay evil for evil, instead look for ways to
  do them good. Do not overcome evil with more evil, overcome
  evil with good. (Romans 12:17-21) Forgive others as the Lord
  forgives you. (Colossians 3:12-13) Bitterness is a poison you
  drink in hopes that it will hurt others. But it only hurts *you* and
  the state of *your* friendships. If you do not forgive others, God
  will not forgive you. You are making yourself better than God.
  If he finds it in his heart to forgive you of all the hurt you have
  caused him, shouldn't you find it in your heart to forgive all the
  hurt others have caused you? (Matthew 18:21-35, 6:14-15, Luke
  17:3-4)

  Don't hold grudges, they just get your hands dirty.
  Take some time to pray. Ask God who you need to forgive, then
  do it. It doesn't mean you have to forget what they did to you or
  that you even have to trust them again. It just means that you no
  longer hold it against them. You give up your right to revenge to
  the Lord.

- **Cut the gossip.** Gossip betrays a confidence and separates close friends. (Proverbs 11:13, 16:28) People gossip because they want to improve their position in the crowd by tearing others down and because they lack real lives. Instead of getting a life, they just talk about people who have lives. When someone entrusts some personal information to you, **keep it to yourself!** Be a fireman. Everywhere you go you carry two buckets, one filled with gasoline and one filled with water. When someone says something **positive** about another, add your gasoline to that fire and make it even more positive. When someone says something **negative** about another, pour water on that fire. Add positive words so that it will not grow.

- **Pray for godly friends who share your vision and values.** Ask God, he desires that you have great friends. After you pray for friends, show yourself friendly.

1. Quoted in Winkey Pratney's, *The Daniel Files,* under the heading "Making the most of what you are." For a copy of this book surf to: www.moh.org. You must read this book.

"WHAT YOU SAID REALLY HIT ME. IF I COULD HAVE JUST ONE WISH IN LIFE, IT WOULD BE FOR ME TO BE TWELVE YEARS OLD AGAIN AND HEAR THIS SAME LECTURE. I HAVE MADE SOME WRONG DECISIONS IN DATING AND NOW I'M FEELING PAIN FROM MY CHOICES."
UNIVERSITY OF WISCONSIN COLLEGE STUDENT SPEAKING TO LECTURER JOSH MCDOWELL

"WHEN I MET MY BOYFRIEND AT THE BEGINNING OF MY SOPHOMORE YEAR, WE BEGAN HAVING SEX AS SOON AS WE STARTED KISSING. I DIDN'T REALLY WANT TO AT ALL - I DON'T EVEN THINK HE DID - BUT WE COULDN'T THINK OF ANY REASON WHY WE SHOULDN'T DO IT."
LETTER TO SEVENTEEN MAGAZINE

"MAY YOUR FOUNTAIN BE BLESSED, AND MAY YOU REJOICE IN THE WIFE OF YOUR YOUTH...MAY HER BREASTS SATISFY YOU ALWAYS, MAY YOU ALWAYS BE CAPTIVATED BY HER LOVE."
KING SOLOMON, PROVERBS 5:18-19

SEX

There seems to be few things on this earth to match the power of sex. Sex has sparked revolutions, moved people to murder, sold billions of dollars of merchandise, aroused great pleasure, caused confusion and pain and killed millions of people.

We seem to know more about sex and less about love than ever before. Sex has become a master to us instead of the servant God intended it to be. Sex dominates our thinking and colors our motives. Our culture worships sex over life itself. We would rather risk our lives and the lives of our children for sexual freedom without constraints.

We would rather suck an unborn baby down a sink than to have anyone restrict our 'reproductive freedom.' We would risk it all, trusting a thin sheet of latex to save our lives.

We say sex is a private act, then we parade it around like a trophy. We more readily talk about our sex lives than our bank account. We bristle at any attempt to re-establish sexual boundaries because, "It's nobody's business what I do behind closed doors." Our young people are told to wait "until your ready," then we blitz them with thousands of sexual images and messages designed to feed their sexual urges and appetites. We then provide a moral framework that suggests that appetite is sufficient reason to consume anything.

We give them no reasonable boundaries. Some say, "Don't have sex....because it's wrong." Others say, "If it feels good, do it." Still others say, "We'd rather you didn't, but if you can't control yourself wear this latex cover."

So what do we do? Why does sex cause so much pleasure and pain? What, if any, are the boundaries? Why have any boundaries? How can we enjoy the benefits of sex and avoid the pitfalls? We will answer these questions here.

I haven't found anything better at defining and defending the best sexual ethic for human-kind than Josh McDowell and Dr. Joe McIhenny. I will borrow from their work and expertise found in *Why Wait?* and *Right From Wrong* by McDowell and *Sex, what you don't know can kill you*, by Dr. Joe McIlhenny.

Take it From the Master

To hear many talk, you would think that the sole purpose for God's existence is to quench sexual pleasure. The opposite is true. God created sex, not Hollywood. It follows then, that because God is good, he has our best interest in mind and therefore God's sexual ethic has our best interest in mind. He designed sexual guidelines for our good. They protect us from harm and heartache and provide for us all that sex was designed to deliver. To cast off these guidelines is to ignore the stop signs along life's highway. Sooner or later you will run into the truck of cosmic morality coming the other way.

God's ethic, as outlined in the Bible, protects us from guilt, unplanned pregnancies, abortions, sexual insecurities, emotional distress and guilt. They provide for us spiritual reward, a healthy body, peace of mind, the best atmosphere for raising children, trust and true intimacy.

As with everything else, when defining use, we must first discover the purpose. God created sex for four main reasons:

- **Procreation** (Genesis 9:1) Through the sex act, God gave us a chance to participate in creating something that will last forever: a human being. Each child will exist longer than the sun and the stars. Anyone who has witnessed the birth of a child cannot rationally deny the existence of a miracle-working, good God.

- **Family bonding** (Genesis 2:24) Speaking of sex, God said, "the two shall become one." Love isn't just a romantic feeling. Love is a commitment of the will to the true good of the other person. Otherwise, how could a bride and groom pledge to love each other? You can't pledge to have a feeling. In every other biological function, such as eating, digesting and growing, the man and woman are separate organisms. During sex, they join to become a unit. Triggered by physical touch and the penis entering the birth canal, the body releases hormones like oxytosin that cause us to 'bond' to one another.

- **Pleasure** (Proverbs 5:19, Song of Solomon) Yes, sex is pleasurable! God is not against pleasure. He created it to be pleasurable. Sex is like fire though; within it's boundaries, we derive great pleasure from a bonfires, fireplaces, heat and cooking energy. Outside of it's boundaries, it causes us great harm and pain.

- **To help unfold the mystery of God's love** (Song of Solomon,

Ephesians 5:25-33) The apostle Paul said speaking of the union of husbands and wives, "This mystery is a profound one, and I am saying that it refers to Christ and the Church." Ancient rabbi's said that the book Song of Solomon not only portrayed the love between a husband and a wife, but symbolized the love between God and his people. The revelation of John speaks of the "Marriage of the Lamb," a future union between Christ and his church. What does all this mean? We won't know completely this side of heaven.

God's Safeguards

God's book is full sexual guidelines. He knew how powerful and influential a force it would be. Here are few selections:

- Flee sexual immorality. All other sins a man commits are outside his body, but he who sins sexually sins against his own body (I Corinthians 6:18).
- Marriage should be honored by all, and the marriage be kept pure, for God will judge the adulterer and all the sexually immoral (Hebrews 13:4).
- Anyone who looks at a woman lustfully has committed adultery with her in his heart (Matthew 5:27).

Just what exactly does God mean when he says "sexual immorality?" The Bible uses various words to describe the scope of immoral behavior.

- Sexual immorality (Greek: pornea)
- Debauchery (aselgeia)
- Taking advantage of someone (pleonekteo)
- Lust; having immoral desire (epithumia)

These four terms cover the range of these sexual acts. God considers all these behaviors deviant.

- Any intimate touching outside of marriage
- Taking lustful pleasure in seeing another's nakedness
- Depriving another of the moral purity God desires; seduction

- Lust
- Adultery
- Homosexuality
- Incest
- Bestiality

Masturbation

Yes, I said it. The opinions of men vary on this topic and we circulate lots of old wives tales regarding it. Is it OK to do? Is it healthy or not? What does the Bible say about this?

The Bible does not speak specifically about masturbation, just like it doesn't speak specifically about smoking crack. It does, however, give us some principles of sexuality and love that apply toward masturbation.

- Jesus said that anyone who lusted in his mind after someone has committed adultery in their heart. The brain is our number one sexual organ. Masturbation is a sin of the mind. (Matthew 5:28)

- Masturbation robs you of self control. God desires that you develop the fruit of the Spirit in your life: love, joy, peace, patience, kindness, goodness, faithfulness, gentleness, and *self control*. Every time you masturbate, you miss an opportunity to develop more self control. The more you masturbate the more you want to and the less sexual control you have. Thousands of people are enslaved by self sexual gratification.

- Masturbation is inherently selfish. It views sex as "What can it give me?" Loving sex says the opposite, "What can I give you?" Thousands of married couples do not experience the fullness of a great love life because masturbation has helped to teach their partner that the primary goal of sex is *their gratification* instead of their partner's.

- Masturbation teaches us to see others as objects of gratification. It feeds sexual fantasy and makes it hard for you to see people in a light other than a sexual one. Many men struggle with wandering sexual thoughts and perverse fantasies because of their habit of masturbation.

I can't think of any good long term fruit that comes from this habit. Some say there is nothing wrong with it, and that it is a legitimate form of sexual release. But God has given us legitimate forms of sexual release as part of our biology.

Take it from a person who has counseled hundreds of boys who were enslaved by this habit. Quit before you start. Just like any tyrant, sexual sin will continue to exert more and more influence on your life. Pursue the best, and God will reward you with a handsome love life. See section on **defeating lust** later in this section.

Does it Work?

Do God's standards really provide for us the best love life possible? Absolutely. God does not just decree his standards out of an illogical, arbitrary mind. He bases all of his standards directly out of *his character*. His principles of sexuality reflect God's character traits of love, purity and faithfulness. Therefore, any sexual act that is not based on *true* love, purity and faithfulness - as God defines them, not man - does not reflect the person, nature, character of God - therefore is wrong.

Moral behavior is not only right, but it provides for our deepest longings and protects us from our deepest fears.

God's standards protect us from Sexually Transmitted Diseases and provide us with a healthy body and peace of mind.

Every day in America, 4,219 teenagers contract a sexually transmitted disease. In parts of Africa, they face a crisis of Biblical proportions because AIDS has orphaned almost an *entire generation.*

Although AIDS gets all the press, every year four million people contract chlamydia. Well over four million will contract other diseases like pelvic inflammatory disease, gonorrhea, herpes and human papilloma virus. **Yet not one of those instances has occurred between two**

mutually faithful partners who entered the relationship as virgins.

According to the Thomas Eng and William Butler Institute of Medicine in Washington D.C., the annual cost of treating STD's runs into the billions of dollars each year.

- Syphilis....................$106 Million
- Hepatitis B...............$156 Million
- Genital Herpes..........$178 Million
- Gonorrhea.................$1 Billion
- Chlamydia.................$2 Billion
- Human Papillomavirus....$3.8 Billion.

That's some fee for what people think of as *free* sex.

Obviously, there is more to STD's than the economic price they inflict on us. They exact a much more heavy toll on the human side of things - both physically and emotionally.

Chlamydia is the most common bacterial STD in the United States, and teenagers have the highest rate of infection of any group. About four million people in the U.S. develop a chlamydia infection each year. Between 8 and 25% of sexually active college students have chlamydia. *70% of people who carry it have no symptoms thus they can unknowingly infect their partners.* Men who carry it may experience puss from the penis and burning sensations during urination.

Chlamydia infections can be devastating for a woman. It scars fallopian tubes which causes infertility in many cases. It is the most rapidly increasing cause of female infertility. Chlamydia is also often the culprit in causing tubal pregnancies - the leading cause of death among pregnant teenagers.

A baby has about 66% chance of becoming infected during the birth process if the mother has chlamydia. Babies can develop eye infections, pneumonia, or inner ear infections. These chronic inner ear infections can prevent a baby from developing good language skills and listening abilities, which could cause later learning problems.

Dr. Joe McIlhaney recounts this story:

"A young, unmarried, sexually active patient of mine went to college in another city. She called one day to say that she was pregnant and having abdominal pain, and her doctors thought she needed surgery for a probable tubal pregnancy. I told her she needed the surgery. I did not have the heart to tell her that since this was her first pregnancy and it was ectoptic, there was a good chance she might be sterile. That was several years ago. She eventually did marry. She and her husband have been trying for two years now to become pregnant. Unfortunately, she is probably sterile. All this heartache because she thought it was okay to have sex with a couple of guys while she was in college."[1]

Human Papillomavirus wins the prize as America's most common STD. Approximately 33 - 45% of sexually active single people are infected with HPV often without symptoms for many months. HPV infections produce warts in warm, moist areas of your body. It is commonly a genital growth that grows better in women than men, often growing in the vagina or cervix.

Up to 70% of female victims will later develop pre-cancerous changes of the cervix. Some will then develop cervical cancer. Almost all abnormal Pap smears indicating pre-cancerous or cancerous cells are a result of infection from HPV. During pregnancy, venereal warts tend to grow quite rapidly and become quite large. Dr. McIlhaney relates,

"A pregnant teenager was referred to me because of huge venereal warts, bigger than my two fists. The surgical procedure to remove the warts took over two hours. Unfortunately the warts grew back and became so large that they obstructed her vagina and made a cesarean section necessary."[2]

The answer to avoiding HPV is not condoms. Condoms give almost no protection against HPV. It is skin to skin disease that has no reliable prevention - except one - abstinence until marriage.

Herpes is an extremely contagious and common STD. Approximately one third of unmarried, sexually active people have contracted herpes by the age of 30. According to the Centers for Disease Control, one in five Americans over age 12 has the herpes virus and doesn't know it.

In men, the blisters and sores caused by the genital herpes virus may appear on the penis, scrotum or anus. In women, the blisters and sores caused by the virus may appear on the vulva, inside the vagina, on the cervix, or in the anal region. As of the time of this writing, there is no known cure for herpes.

If a woman delivers a child vaginally during her first outbreak of herpes, her baby has a 40 - 50% chance of becoming infected. If the baby becomes infected, it has a 60% chance of dying. Those who survive have a 50% chance of having severe brain damage.

Dr. McIlhaney tells of some college students encounter with herpes:

> "A coed came in one day. She could hardly walk, had a fever and chills, and had such terrible sores on her vulvar area that she would not allow herself to urinate because it burned so badly. A few days before her symptoms began, she had intercourse with a rock star who played on campus. I put her in the hospital, put a catheter into her bladder, and started her on medication for herpes infection.
>
> The next day, I admitted a second young woman with the same symptoms. She had also had intercourse with the same rock star on the same weekend."[3]

AIDS is now the leading cause of death in Americans ages 25-44. Approximately 7,000 HIV infected mothers are delivering babies each year. Between 1,000 and 2,000 of the babies will have HIV. Practically all of the mothers will die of AIDS. AIDS kills. Here is the story of a real person - Sherry Root - who thought it couldn't happen to her as reported in the Austin American Statesman, Tuesday, December 8, 1992:

"She grew up in a middle-class family in northwest Austin. She didn't drink, she didn't smoke, she didn't do drugs. While in college, she began dating a guy she met at school who was from a small town outside Austin. She was nineteen at the time, and they dated for two years. It was her first sexual relationship, and Root says they discussed birth-control methods and decided she should take the pill.

It was not until four years later, engaged to be married, and on a vacation with her fiancé, that Root began to suspect that something was wrong. She was fatigued, running a fever, and would wake up nights soaked in sweat. She also had lost quite a bit of weight and began having problems catching her breath.

She went to see a doctor. He told her it was viral pneumonia and gave her medicine. But three weeks later she was no better. In fact, she was much worse. She could not get out of bed, couldn't even roll over without help. Her father had to carry her into the doctor's office because she was too weak to walk. She took an HIV test that day.

'I knew it was going to be negative. I was confident it would be negative because things like that didn't happen to people like me. I was a good girl. I didn't date people with sexually transmitted diseases.'

Then on July 30, 1991, a day that would be etched in her memory, Root learned that she had AIDS. She discovered later that her first boyfriend, who had experimented with intravenous drugs as a teenager, had known for more than three years that he had AIDS and had not told her. He died in March of 1992.

Sherry asked, (speaking at a school assembly) "What is it that I can say that can convince you that you are at risk? I come here not because I have to, but because I care. I come here because I hope you are never in the position I am in today. I come here today to leave little pieces of myself with you so that maybe some little thing I have said will stick in your mind and make you think before you act the next time.

'I'll never be able to get married, never be able to have children, never able to grow old and get gray hair - all because of a choice I made when I was nineteen.'

Since that time, Sherry Root died of a disease she never in her wildest imagination dreamed she would contract."

Condom Nation?

To many, the solution to the problem of STD's is a thin latex cover called a condom. Condoms are the savior of the sexual revolution. Not only can they prevent pregnancy, but also STD's!

Are they really the savior people make them out to be? Not really. Here are the facts. According to the Minnesota Institute for Public Health, "There are twenty sexually transmitted diseases which are not prevented by contraception."[4] Condoms do little to prevent HPV, Herpes, Chlamydia, Pubic lice and Syphilis.

A 1995 study done by Johns Hopkins School of Medicine in Brazil showed that of 162 women who had sex with HIV positive men, 31 contracted the AIDS virus in spite of using a condom every time.

Dr. Susan Weller from the University of Texas School of Medicine showed that condoms had an average of 31% failure rate in preventing the transmission of HIV from an infected partner to an uninfected partner.

Manufacturers sell condoms that have three or four holes per thousand condoms. Also, 1.7% of condoms break during intercourse, 6.2% of condoms slip off during intercourse and 6.7% of condoms slip off during withdrawal.[5] Condoms have pores up to 50 microns in size. The HIV organism is .1 of a micron in size. Leakage of HIV sized particles was found in as many as 29 out of 89 condoms.[6]

How many Americans play Russian Roulette? Most people consider a one out of six chance of instant death an unacceptable level of risk. As we have seen, using a condom as HIV prevention also gives odds similar to Russian Roulette. Is that an acceptable level of risk?

Suppose nine of your friends invited you to go skydiving. If the pilot told you one of the parachutes would fail, would you jump? You probably wouldn't even get into the plane.

Suppose you joined the football team. At the opening meeting, the coach informed all the players and parents that according to their track record, about 3 out of the 22 players would sustain fatal injuries this season. Would your parents let you play?

Even the "professionals" who are so eager to talk about "safe sex" aren't willing to take that kind of risk. Dr. Theresa Crenshaw, past president of the American Association of Sex Education Counselors and Therapists, and a member of the national AIDS Commission discovered first hand,

> "On June 19, 1987, I gave a lecture on AIDS to 800 sexologists at the World Congress of Sexologie in Heidelberg. Most of them recommended condoms to their clients and students. I asked them if they had available the partner of their dreams, and knew that person carried the virus, would they have sex, depending on a condom for protection? No one raised their hand. After a long delay, one timid hand surfaced from the back of the room. I told them that it was irresponsible to give advice to others that they would not follow themselves. The point is, putting a mere balloon between a healthy body and a deadly disease is not safe.[7]"

But wait - some experts will say that you can use a condom to decrease your chance of becoming infected. Years ago this was called *safe sex*. Now that they have seen the results of condom failure, they use the term *safer sex*.

What if they taught drivers education the same way they taught sex? "Welcome to Drivers Education 101. I would like to go over some ways for 'safe driving.' While a majority of drivers prefer driving on the right side of the road, some of you may choose to drive on the left side. This is a moral choice, and only you can decide what is right - not your parents or your friends. If you decide to drive on the left side, please use protection. Drive only in automobiles that contain air-bags. Air-bags save lives!"

"The same goes for red lights and stop signs. Some will tell you that you should terminate your acceleration at these designated areas. This is another moral choice. I cannot tell you what is right or wrong. You will have to decide whether this particular life choice is for you. But remember, if you choose to go through red lights and stop signs, make sure you wear your seatbelt!"

As you can see, this is nonsense. The only truly safe sex is that which God designed: sex between one man and one woman in the bonds of marriage for life.

God's ways protects us from unhealthy situations and provide us with peace of mind. When two married virgins make love, they do not have to worry about anything. Their minds are settled on enjoyment before, during and after. They have no shots to worry about, no treatments, no life shortening diseases, no regrets just pure, righteous pleasure - just how God drew it up.

God's guidelines for sex protect us from unplanned pregnancies and provide us with the best atmosphere for raising children. In his book, *Why Wait*, we find this letter to Josh McDowell,

"The reason I'm writing this is I'm alone and confused. My boyfriend kept pursuing me for sex. I had sex with him thinking that I owed it to him. Later, when I learned I was pregnant he blew up, said to get an abortion, and that it was all my fault. So to save my parents heartache, and to keep Matt, I did. Now Matt has left me. How can God love me after all I've done?"

Every day in America, 2,795 teenage girls get pregnant and 1,106 have abortions. Those girls who carry their babies to full term often face overwhelming difficulties; many drop out of school, many experience physical problems, many feel left out of "normal" teen activities because of their responsibility to a child. Those who abort their children are not delivered from such consequences; abortion produces traumatic results too. Dr. Anne Catherine Speckard of the University of Minnesota reports the following long term (five to ten years later) consequences of abortion:

- 81% reported preoccupation with the aborted child
- 73% reported flashbacks of the abortion experience
- 54% recalled nightmares related to the abortion
- 23% reported hallucinations related to the abortion

Seventy two percent reported that they had no religious belief at the time of their abortions and 96% percent said that, in retrospect, they regarded abortion as the taking of life or as murder[8].

From an economic standpoint, so called free sex exacts a staggering toll. Seventy five percent of teen-age moms are on welfare within five years of giving birth. Sixty three percent of families headed by an unwed mother are below the poverty line. According to the Alan Guttmacher Institute, we spend about $34 billion dollars on teenage pregnancy every year since 1992.

God's standards for sexual behavior were meant to provide the best atmosphere for raising children. After all, if you play with the instruments, your going to make music. Having children within the confines of a strong marriage is a blessing of infinite proportions. God's plan for every newborn is to be nurtured and loved by a man and a woman who love each other exclusively and are committed to each other for a life time.

This does not suggest that single parents do not perform bravely and admirably to raise their children. (I was raised primarily by a single Mom.) But the evidence overwhelmingly shows that the biological unit of one mother and one father has proven itself to be the most successful in ensuring the physical survival and promoting the social development of the child. God's standard of purity, love and faithfulness had the best interest of every newborn in mind. Obedience to God in this area helps to give you your best chance of creating an atmosphere of love and security for a child that can leave a lifelong, positive imprint on a child spiritually, emotionally, psychologically and even physically.[9]

1. Joe McIlhaney, *Sex, What you don't know can kill you.* Baker Books, 1997, pg 26

2. IBID pg 35

3. IBID pg 42

4. "Young Love: How to Talk to Your Kids About You-Know-What," Minnesota Institute of Public Health, Anoka, MN n.d. 5

5. Joe McIlhaney, Medical Institute for Sexual Health, *Sex, What you don't know can kill you*. Baker Books 1997, pg 89

6. IBID, pg 90

7. Theresa Crenshaw, From remarks made at the National Conference on HIV, Washington D.C. November 15-18, 1987

8. *Right From Wrong*, Josh McDowell and Bob Hostetler, 1994 Word Publishing, Nashville, TN, All rights reserved pg 158-159

9. IBID pg 159

MORE SEX

Depending on viewing habits, the media will expose most people to over 2000 sexual acts per year. Of those, more than 80% will depict sex outside the boundary of marriage. They will show us what sex is supposed to be: beautiful, enchanting, fantastic, and supremely satisfying. Or is it? How many of those illegitimate sexual episodes depict the real life consequences of unmarried sex? How many get the disease, how many get pregnant on television or the movies? How many broken hearts do they show? How many sexually satisfied married people do they show?

The media wishes to push an agenda that promotes what they call sexual freedom but what really leads people to sexual bondage. The reality is: **The most sexually satisfied people in this nation are married, religious people.** According to two studies, one by the University of Chicago in 1994 and another by American Demographics done in 1989, the percentage of people who are very satisfied with their sex life was highest amongst married religious traditionalists - 72.3%.

Those that the media portray as the swinging single rated **lowest** with only 41% being very sexually satisfied.

According to an article in *Focus on the Family* magazine by Marianne Hering in September of 1994, **"The most religious women were most satisfied with the frequency of intercourse and felt free to discuss sex openly with their husbands, and most surprisingly, were more orgasmic than were the non-religious."** So much for the stereotype of the religious prude!

Compare this to lead singer of rock band Limp Bizkit, Fred Durst's comment in *Billboard Magazine*, January, '99, "I play the pimp thing on purpose. Like, when I'm on MTV, these chicks are fanning and massaging me. It's not like I attracted 'em off the street. We ---- hired them. I want everybody to be thinking I'm having the time of my life, **but I'm single and I'm miserable**."

Want great sex? Do it God's way.

God's standards protect us from sexual insecurity and provide us with an atmosphere of trust within marriage. The power of sexual interaction is something that you will carry the rest of your life. God created the sexual process to bring a flood of emotions and sensations that dramatically imprint on the brain. Sex will bring the most vivid and oft recalled memories of your life. As a result, sexual immorality can produce haunting effects. Stacy and Paul Rinehart in their book, *Choices*, describe one man's discovery of this fact:

> "One young husband admitted that his relationship with his new wife wasn't what he had hoped it would be. "It's really my fault," he admitted. "Before we were married I had several physical relationships with girlfriends. Now, whenever I kiss my wife or engage in love play, my memory

reminds me that this girl could kiss better than my wife, that girl was better at something else and so forth. I can't concentrate on loving my wife with all that I am - there have been too many women in my life to be wholly committed to one."

Because sexual immorality is not exclusive, it creates insecurity and jealousy, and hinders sexual freedom and expression.

Sexual purity and faithfulness before marriage contributes to an atmosphere of trust within marriage. That trust provides a peace of mind for both partners. They don't ever have to battle with memories of previous sexual partners. They don't ever have to wonder if their partner is thinking of someone else while they are loving them. They don't have to worry about their partners faithfulness while they are apart. Why? Because before they married, they proved themselves trustworthy by saving themselves for each other exclusively.

Pre-marital sexual activity can be a source of distrust in a marriage. "If he couldn't control himself before marriage, what makes me think he will control himself in marriage?" A study of 100,000 women concluded, "Pre-marital sex...does not necessarily lead to extra-marital sex - it simply increases the odds."[1]

God's standards for sexual behavior protect us from emotional distress. The emotional costs of sexual immorality are immense. Take a lesson from those who have gone before you:

> "...Having premarital sex was the most horrifying experience of my life. It wasn't at all the emotionally satisfying experience the world deceived me into believing. I felt as if my insides were being exposed and my heart left unattended...I know God has forgiven me of this haunting sin, but I also know I can never have my virginity back. I dread the day that I have to tell the man I truly love and wish to marry that he is not the only one, though I wish he were...I have stained my life - a stain that will never come out."[2]

"I lost my virginity at age 16. That was the worst night of my life. I was so drunk, I puked for an hour then I passed out. The next thing I knew when I woke up there's this guy on top of me and my clothes were all off. I couldn't do anything because my body was so weak and I was so sick. Who knows, I probably said yes."

A girl from Michigan

"After you've done it, you're really attached to that guy. It's as if he's your life; you feel really vulnerable. (When the relationship ended, I felt,) really awful. I can't describe it. About a week after we had sex we broke up because I found out he was dating other girls. It really hurt."[3]

"I love him. He said he loved me too. But after we did it, he called me all sorts of names and left me. The reason I'm writing, I don't understand it. We went together for months and I thought we had something special...I really need help. I have this feeling that no one cares about me, and no matter what I do I am not able to make any man happy."[4]

"I never realized that I felt cheated until my wedding night when we got to our hotel room. As I was getting ready for the most romantic evening of my life, I looked in the mirror and realized I had already done this. What a let down. What was there to be excited about? This was nothing new. It was as if all the life has been drained out of me.

As months went on, we got frustrated and uptight. Sex used to be so much fun before we got married. What happened? Sex had been just a game before. Now, when it should have been the ultimate expression of love between a husband and a wife, it had no meaning.

We struggled with this for almost a year. It was about to destroy us when we finally went to some close friends and received counseling, prayer and forgiveness from the Lord. Now things are as they should be."[5]

Contrast those letters with this one from a girl and guy who did it God's way:

> "Last July, God gave me the most wonderful man in the world to be my husband. I had asked for Prince Charming, and the Lord gave me much more than that. He gave me someone I can talk to God with, someone I am glad I waited for.
>
> On our wedding night, I experienced sex for the first time, and it was with my husband. I wouldn't have wanted to share my first time with anyone else. I had no riches or jewels to offer my husband, but he asked for none. All he wanted was me, and that is just what I had to give him -all of me, untouched, his alone. That meant a great deal, and we both knew it."[6]

God's standards of sexuality provide for a level of intimacy that can only be found inside of marriage. Couples can feel free to share their innermost feelings and desires without any regrets or ghosts from the past. They can feel free to explore each other emotionally and physically without the fear of any skeletons falling out of their closets.

God's standards for sex protect us from guilt and provide for us spiritual reward. Because God defines right and wrong, when we break God's laws we will suffer guilt. Many people experience guilt and a sense of loss after pre-marital or extra-marital sex. Many report feeling dirty or grimy inside and out. Married people can express their love sexually without guilt! They can go through their day with a clear conscience before God!

I remember my wife and I going back to our new apartment to leave for our honeymoon. At that moment it felt so weird but so freeing to know that we could do anything we wanted and not feel guilty! In fact, we had God's blessing!

God's standards will always provide you the best opportunity to live life to the fullest. Sex is a part of that. Don't let the culture dictate to you their standards. Don't live low, live large!

What if you've already blown it?

Go to God. You will face temptation to run from him, resist this and run to Him. God is a God of mercy. No matter what you have done, go to God and ask him to forgive you. Don't allow the enemy to draw you deeper into sin. You may hear something tell you, "Well, you've done it now, you might as well not stop." Don't buy it; stop and run to God. If you confess your sins he is faithful and just to forgive you of your sins. (I John 1:9) Repent and renounce the use of your body or mind in a sinful manner.

Once you are forgiven, don't let guilt and condemnation ruin your perspective. If God has forgiven you, you are no longer condemned for that action. (Romans 8:1) The prophet Micah put it this way: "Do not rejoice over me, my enemy! Though I have fallen, I will rise. Though I sit in darkness, the Lord will be my light."

Get forgiveness from the person or persons you committed the sin with. Tell them you are sorry for using them in that manner and for not setting a proper standard or failing to act as a Christian. Once you are engaged to be married (or maybe even before depending on how you feel), **ask your future spouse to forgive you also.** This will release a great burden off you. If you need to forgive anyone, you must do so.

Start over. Make a new commitment - from this day forward - to remain sexually pure. Get yourself a ring to signify your new commitment. Make sound Biblical decisions that will not cause you to go deeper into sin. If you are pregnant, do not get an abortion. You will face even more regret and torment for that decision. Look in your phone book for a crisis pregnancy center, one that promotes life.

Forgive yourself. You will face memories and flashbacks of these times. Do your best not to rehash them over and over. As they come, change the channel in your mind by thinking of something else. Say to yourself, "Yes, I blew it, but God has forgiven me and so I must forgive myself." Every time a memory comes back, pray for the person you were with. Pray aloud that they would come to know God better, that they would also remain sexually pure.

Renew your mind. Do not allow your mind to wander. You stay in control of your thoughts. Fill it with the Word of God.

Understand that God will restore you. You can and will have a great love life. The world is full of people who have blown it and rededicated their lives back to living within the purity of God. Although I do not believe their sex lives are as free from baggage as two virgins marrying each other, God can still bestow a great love life upon you. Remember, there will come a time when God will make all things new!

Tell others your story. The culture wishes to glorify pre-marital and extra-marital sex. You now know the truth from experience - that it's not all it's cracked up to be. You fell through the ice; take the time to tell others that it's not worth skating on that lake until the proper time. Don't be afraid to let others learn from your mistakes. You will find it a great release for your frustration and disappointment.

Defeating Lust

Our cultural obsession with illicit sex has built a vast wasteland full of people in the clutches of lust. People struggle with fantasies, pornography, masturbation, immoral sex, rape and even murder.

If you habitually fall into sexual sin of one form or another and you wish to regain your freedom, here's what you must do:

Be brutally honest. Don't justify it or rationalize away your guilt. Call it what it is - sin. Then go to God, get forgiven and restored. (I John 1:9) Don't tell yourself the lie, "I can't help it." God can free you. If you are a Christian, God makes you this promise: "No temptation will come to you that you are not able to overcome if you take the way of escape that I will provide for you" (I Corinthians 10:13 Memorize this). God gives you the ability and authority to resist temptation. "Submit to God and resist the devil and he will flee from you" (James 4:7).

We win and lose our battles with lust in the mind. **You must continually renew your mind.** (Romans 12: 1-3) Train yourself to think only pure, true, and praiseworthy things. When a temptation comes to your mind, change the channel. Submit to God and resist the devil - out loud - for he cannot read your mind. Say something like, "Lord, I submit my thoughts and actions to you, and devil, I resist you and command you to leave in Jesus name." Every time you are tempted to lust after a person, ask God to draw that person to himself and to keep them pure. Ask God every day to cleanse your mind.

You must memorize parts of the Bible that will help you in your situations. There is no shortcut for this! Here are some to look at: Proverbs chs 5, 6, 7, Job 31:1, Matthew 5:28, I Thessalonians 4:5.

Along with spring cleaning your mind, **spring clean your environment.** Identify things around you that pull at you to lust and get rid of them. Check out posters, pictures, your music, what you watch on T.V., the movies you see and so on. Get quiet before God and ask him to reveal to you sources of temptation.

Make a Job 31:1 covenant with your eyes. Train yourself to look people in the eyes. If something comes your way that will tempt you to lust - look away!

Stay busy. If the battle over lust begins in the mind, it ends in idleness. Find productive things to do. Get a hobby or a sport or a job or a life! Don't sit around too much; use that energy to make a better you! Make an 'I'm bored' list. Sit down and write "15 things to do when I'm bored." Don't include watching T.V. or a movie or listening to music. Those are primarily passive, consuming things. Put down only active, producing things. Instead of watching a movie, go make one with some friends. Practice an instrument, take a run, walk the dog, write a letter or whatever your into. Tape the list next to your bed. When you find yourself bored or vegging in front of the T.V., get up and pick something on the list to do. I have had kids in my youth ministry do this and it helps them greatly.

> "SOME TEMPTATIONS ATTACK THE INDUSTRIOUS, BUT ALL TEMPTATIONS ATTACK THE IDLE."
> Charles H. Spurgeon

Never give up. When you fall, get up. People don't drown by falling in water, they drown by staying there! Get up, get clean. Use the FIDO motto. Forget It and Drive On! (Philipians 3:13) I believe in you and so does God!

Read these books. They go more into this realm of total freedom from the bondage of sin. *Bondage Breaker* (Youth or Adult addition) by Neil Anderson, *Counter Attack* by Jay Carty.

God bless you in your pursuit of the best in this area of your life. I can't wait to hear how God is blessing your life with his wisdom in the area of relationships and sex!

1. Robert J. Levin, The Redbook Report on Premarital and Extra-marital Sex: The End of the Double Standard?, *Redbook,* October 1975, pg 40

2. *Right From Wrong*, Josh McDowell, Bob Hostetler, 1994 Word Publishing, Nashville TN, All rights reserved, pg 161

3. IBID, pg 162

4. Josh McDowell, Dick Day, *Why Wait*, Here's Life Publishers, 1987

5. IBID

6. *Right From Wrong*, Josh McDowell, Bob Hostetler, 1994 Word Publishing, Nashville TN, All rights reserved, pg 162

PRODUCTION

From the beginning there was work, for at the beginning there was creation - the work of God. When he rested on the seventh day, "he rested from all the work of creating he had done" and God pronounced his work very good.

God created human beings in his own image, and part of being "in his image" means that we are workers, like God himself. That's where that innate drive comes from. God called mankind to cultivate the world he had created and to exercise dominion over it. This was a call to work, to perform both physical labor (pruning the trees and tilling the fields) and intellectual labor (naming the animals). God vested both types of labor with dignity.

In order to live your life to the fullest, you must find your place in God's creation order. One of the ways God allows us to do this is that he gives us the tools and opportunities to produce. He gives us time, talents, and ambitions in order that we may produce fruit with our lives. God gives us the God-like capability to fill needs, solve problems, add value and create. Your vocation is a collaboration with God in the grand design of the universe, working for his glory, the common good, and your own fulfillment.

Production and the things that relate to it (education, work, time and money management) play a huge part in your quality of life. In this section, we will show you how to maximize your utility to God and yourself by living up to your capacity in this area. Potential is God's gift to you; what you do with it is your gift to him.

I love you,

CW

"No wind blows in favor of a ship with no destination."

"This is to my Father's glory, that you bear much fruit, showing yourselves to be my disciples."
John 15:8

"We all have different gifts according to the grace given to us."
Romans 12:6

WHO ARE YOU AND WHAT ARE YOU DOING?

You are a winner! No matter what you think about yourself, you need to understand that you are a born winner! Everyone is born a winner. People that lose choose to lose but they were born to win!

Let me show you. When your mother and father got together and decided to make a baby, God went to work. He culled over about 400,000 female eggs and hand picked one. Then, he chose one of about 300 million sperm cells to win the race to the egg. YOU are the result. YOU won! The odds of you even existing are about 120 TRILLION to one! But your reading this, so you must exist. Congratulations!

Not only are you a born winner, but God created you unique. No one else has your skills, talents, aptitudes and personality - no one.

In order to find your place in this world, you must find out who God made you to be. Waaaaaay to many young people float through life like a leaf on a river. They have no direction, no vision, no goals and no realistic dreams.

If you desire to pursue the best life has, you must not let life dictate your course. You must, with God's direction and wisdom, chart the best course for you. You must get a vision from heaven then make it your life's mission. In order to get a vision from heaven you must do four things.

- **Know God**. You must learn to know God. Know his likes and dislikes, learn to hear when he speaks to your insides. (John 10) Learn his value system and his priorities, this will shape your value system and your priorities.

- **Know yourself.** You must learn what God wired you up like. Learn what skills and aptitudes your have, your type of personality, your vocational interests and priorities.

- **Give the micro-visions back to God**. When you know God, and you begin to know yourself, God will birth micro-visions into your life. You will begin to think of things and say, "I wouldn't mind doing...." You must take these visions and give them back to God. Let him kill them if he so desires. Many times God will test you with adversity to see if you really have the mettle to accomplish what he has for you. If you don't, then he may give you more adversity to forge that drive and determination in you. If you have given them back to God and he resurrects these visions and hands them back to you, nothing on earth will stop you from this.

- **Lift your vision higher**. Don't shoot low, aim high. You will not accomplish everything all at once. But every year take time to evaluate your goals. If you attained your previous goals, aim higher this year.

Bon Voyage

Some of the most miserable people I know hate their jobs. Every day they have to work is a bad day. They have picked a job that mismatches their personality and skills. They have tried to stick the round peg of their life into the square hole of their job. I know too many people who have a job that does not suit them but they cannot leave it because life has them tied down. Don't let this happen to you. **Take this season of your life and learn what God has wired you to be.** Learn your strengths and weaknesses.

God has built you like a ship. The ship has sails, anchors and a compass. The sails represent strengths in the areas of skills and your personality. These sails, if unfurled (developed) will carry the ship of your life to great and marvelous lengths. The anchors represent weaker skills and personality imbalances. These anchors, if not brought out of the water, will keep your ship from moving very far or fast - no matter how many gifts and talents you have. The compass directs your decisions based on your vocational interests and work priorities.

Skills and Aptitudes

Aptitude tests measure different capabilities in people. Some of the better ones measure about 19 different aptitudes. There are more, but some are tough to measure, like kinesthetic awareness, of which you will have any combination of three to seven strong ones with any number of 'recessive' skills. As you read through them think to yourself, "Is that me or not?"

Graphoria identifies clerical ability in dealing with figures and symbols. You can handle paperwork at high levels of speed and efficiency. Graphoria is necessary for bookkeeping, editing, secretarial tasks, and so on. It is also a real indicator of how well a person will do in school, where many subjects require this ability.

Ideaphoria indicates creative imagination or expression of ideas. It is extremely useful in fields such as sales, advertising, teaching, public relations, and journalism.

Structural visualization is the ability to visualize solids and think in three dimensions. It is an aptitude possessed by concrete thinkers who don't do as well with abstract thinking. It is an absolute critical skill for engineers, mechanics, and architects.

Inductive reasoning helps an individual form logical conclusions from fragmented facts. This ability is important for lawyers, researchers, diagnostic physicians, writers, and critics - all of whom must be able to move quickly from the particular to the general pattern and see the big picture from all the details.

Analytical reasoning is useful for writers, editors, and computer programmers who need to organize concepts and ideas into sequences or classifications.

Finger dexterity is the ability to manipulate fingers skillfully. It is needed for any kind of manual or mechanical work. Secretaries need this skill for typing and for sorting papers.

Tweezer dexterity measures skill in handling small tools with precision. Surprisingly, there is little correlation between this skill and finger dexterity. Tweezer dexterity is vital for professionals such as surgeons and watch makers.

Observation is the ability to take careful notice. Observation is a useful skill for those engaged in research, particularly where noticing changes is important, for example, in the study of microscopic slides. It is also valuable for artists and painters.

Design memory tests how well someone can remember designs of all kinds. It is extremely helpful for anyone working with plans or blueprints.

Tonal memory is the ability to remember sounds and express an ear for music. **Pitch discrimination** differentiates musical tones. **Rhythm memory** maintains rhythmic timing. **Timbre discrimination** is the ability to distinguish the quality of sound of the same pitch and volumes.

Numerical reasoning is an aptitude for identifying relationships among sets of numbers. It is used in bookkeeping, computer programming, and actuarial work.

Silograms tests the ability to learn unfamiliar words and languages. This skill is extremely vital for translators, and international business people. It is also important for speech teachers, language teachers and persons doing Biblical translation work.

Foresight is the ability to keep the mind on a distant goal. A market research analyst, sales forecaster, political scientist, diplomat, or politician would all use this gift.

Color perception is the ability to distinguish colors. Fashion design, painting, interior decorating, advertising and any number of jobs requiring art and layout functions would be good for this skill.

All of these aptitudes fit together in a unique way in you. Depending on how you nurture them they will come out of in the form of certain skills. Here may be some. Circle the ones you are strongest in.

Perform athletically	Perform musically	Understand complex subjects
Handle complaints	Sell	Work with animals
Plan	Analyze data	Nurture people
Use hands skillfully	File records	Visualize things
Create	Calculate/compute	Handle heavy materials
Use imagination	Sketch	Work systematically
Paint buildings	Invent	Organize social functions
Work with tools	Teach	Work with children
Speak in public	Counsel People	Manage/direct others
Use tact	Type	Speak foreign language
Cut and style hair	Grow things	Build things
Repair things	Care for people	Provide customer service
Lift heavy things	Communicate	Write
Persuade others	Sensing beauty	Resist fatigue
Manage money	Lead people	Operate machinery
Schedule	Drive	Articulate ideas
Use a computer	Organize and plan	Program a computer

Personality

Along with the physical skill you may possess, God has given you sails in the area of your personality. Because of how you are 'wired,' you will fit better into some jobs than others. For instance, I would not enjoy accounting. I am primarily a big picture guy. To force me to balance every penny day after day would be torture, yet some people love being neat and detail oriented.

The human personality is a complex thing. What follows is a very simplified exercise to get you to think about what kind of person you are.

We all have some combination of specific personality types. Some people are dominant. They may be very prophetic or administrative in personality. They are motivated to control their work environment, usually assertive and direct and strong willed. They are bold and are not afraid to take strong action to get the desired results. They function best in a challenging environment.

> "SEE I HAVE CHOSEN BEZALEL...AND I HAVE FILLED HIM WITH THE SPIRIT OF GOD WITH SKILL, ABILITY AND KNOWLEDGE IN ALL KINDS OF CRAFTS TO MAKE ARTISTIC DESIGNS FOR WORK IN GOLD, SILVER AND BRONZE, TO CUT AND SET STONES, TO WORK IN WOOD, AND TO ENGAGE IN ALL KINDS OF CRAFTSMANSHIP."
> Exodus 31:2-5

Some people are highly influencing and are driven more to relate to others. Usually they are verbal, friendly, persuasive and optimistic. They may possess gifts of exhortation or teaching. They are typically enthusiastic motivators and will seek out others to help them accomplish results. They function best in a friendly environment.

Some people are conscientious. They focus on doing things right. Usually they are detail oriented and find it easy to follow directions. These people may be gifted administratively. Typically, they strive for accuracy and quality and therefore, set high standards for themselves and others. They function best in a structured environment.

Some people are steady and they are naturally motivated to cooperate with and support others. They may have the gift of helping or serving. They are usually patient, consistent and very dependable. Because they are pleasant and easygoing, they make great team players. They function best in a supportive, harmonious environment.

Your personality will contain a mix of the spectrum and it will come through in definite characteristics like these. Circle the ones you see as definitely you.

Calm	Compliant	Cooperative
Encouraging	Flexible	Steady
Motivated	Neat	Organized
Perfectionist	Prepared	Resourceful
Tactful	Sense of humor	Self - Motivated

God wants you to discover your sails (strengths) and unfurl them (develop them). Even though God has gifted you in a certain area does not mean it has reached its potential in you. You are a diamond in the rough. Take the time to develop your skills. Your sails do little good until you've done the work to place them in the wind.

Now along with your sails, you also have some anchors (weaknesses or personality imbalances). No matter how talented you are, if you have some large weaknesses, your sails can only take you so far. God does not ask that you turn your anchors into sails. He asks that you pull them out of the water - **bring them to a level of adequacy**. The world is full of talented losers. They lose because they did not bring their anchors out of the water. Work on your strengths, but don't let your weaknesses keep you from leaving the dock.

If anyone desires to become everything God has destined them to be they must either excel at the following skills or at least bring them to a level of adequacy:

- **People skills** - You must learn how to operate in the human environment. Learn how to meet and greet people, look them in the eye and present yourself. Develop a good handshake and a pleasant demeanor. Learn to love and honor people (see section on relationships). Maybe you hate crowds, and you would rather work with a machine than a person. That's cool, the world needs you to fix all the broken stuff and invent new and helpful things. Maybe you are very task oriented and you like to get things done. That's cool too, just don't let projects become more important than people. Nobody wants to go to visit or work with a cranky, rude, obnoxious, aloof doctor, mechanic, sales person or computer programmer. The sails of many people could not pull them to their destiny because the anchor of poor people skills held them back.

- Maybe you are not a real book learner type person - you must at least learn to **read, speak and write** clearly and effectively. In most organizations, communication is the key element to their success. Perhaps it's unfair, but it's true none the less. Not many things will brand you 'dumb' faster than lots of misspelled words and poor grammar. People who can read, speak and write clearly interview better, communicate their ideas better and they are not misunderstood as often. You may git entry level werk with poor literacee, but you will not reech the hights of God's best with out this ancer out of the water.

- Maybe you are laid back and easy going - you must still learn to **motivate yourself and manage your time well.** Too many talented people fail because of laziness, procrastination, late or no attendance. Everybody gets 168 hours per week. Pull this anchor out of the water and learn to use them well.

- Maybe you are messy and creative - you must still learn basic **organizational skills.** Losing things and time spent looking for things wastes your time and saps your productivity. That time would be better spent using your creative brain. Learn to keep your room and school stuff organized. I know it can be a pain, but it's more of a pain to work with someone who can't find anything when needed.

We are all different, and there are definite trends in human personalities. You need to find out what skills you have, what God wired you to do and identify your weaknesses. Too many people are in jobs they dislike because they push papers and God designed them to turn wrenches.

The Compass
Not only has God gifted you and wired you but he also put in you interests and priorities - things you like to do. (Philippians 2:13) What you

like to do should give you some clues as to the career you would enjoy. Most people that don't know what they like to do should spend less time watching T.V and more time trying different things. (Ecclesiastes 11:6) Examine the following experiences to see how God may be using them to shape your life.

- **Church:** What activities or ministries have you participated in point to a career choice? For example, working in the nursery may lead to a career in child care, or working with sound and lights many point you toward a technical career

- **School Subjects:** Which courses have excited your interests? Which bored you or frustrated you? Which involved special projects that you liked?

- **Employment:** What have you learned about yourself in summer or part time jobs? What aspects of these jobs have you liked or disliked?

- **Hobbies:** Do you have any hobbies that may have career implications? Many of the skills learned in hobbies transfer well into careers.

- **Clubs:** What club or activities may have given you insight into a career choice? How?

- **Leisure Time Activities:** What do you do when you have nothing to do? What interests do these reveal?

- **Careers of Other People:** Have you met anybody that did something that really interested you?

- **Unusual Experiences:** What unusual experiences have you had that may point to an interest of yours?

- **Reading:** What insights into your interests has reading developed in you? What do you like to read about?

Take your skills and interests and start praying for direction. Try different things while your young. Tell God, "I feel I need to go in this direction. Unless you change my direction, this is what I will do." Give him the freedom to change your mind and start doing stuff.

You may have skills and interests in an area but you also need one more thing. Someone must consider it valuable enough to pay you for it. You may be a skilled artist for example, but you may have to relegate your art to a part-time hobby or business while you earn money another way. You should still be able to find a job you enjoy that actually pays you. God has a plan for you. Get busy and discover it!

For a more extensive look into this topic, I highly recommend Larry Burkett's book *Finding the Career That Fits You*. Your high school and college career guidance offices will also have helpful info. The absolute best career guidance test is Christian Financial Concepts' *Career Direct*.

"ONE NIGHT I HAD THIS DREAM
ONE SET OF FOOTPRINTS THERE WAS SEEN

THE FOOT PRINTS OF MY PRECIOUS LORD
BUT MINE WERE NOT ALONG THE SHORE

BUT THEN SOME STRANGER PRINTS APPEARED
AND I ASKED THE LORD, "WHAT HAVE WE HERE?"

THOSE PRINTS ARE LARGE AND ROUND AND NEAT
"BUT LORD, THEY ARE TOO BIG FOR FEET."

"MY CHILD," HE SAID IN SOMBER TONES,
FOR MILES I CARRIED YOU ALONE"

"I CHALLENGED YOU TO WALK IN FAITH,
BUT YOU REFUSED AND MADE ME WAIT,"

"YOU DISOBEYED, YOU WOULD NOT GROW,
THE WALK OF FAITH, YOU WOULD NOT KNOW"

"SO I GOT TIRED, I GOT FED UP,
AND THERE I DROPPED YOU ON YOUR BUTT."

"BECAUSE IN LIFE, THERE COMES A TIME,
WHEN ONE MUST FIGHT, AND ONE MUST CLIMB"

"WHEN ONE MUST RISE AND TAKE A STAND,
OR LEAVE YOUR BUTT PRINTS IN THE SAND."

THE FRUIT-BEARING LIFE

God has blessed humanity with the opportunity to produce. We can create, manage, build, invent, paint, write, repair and add value to things. Those who do not produce up toward their potential God calls "wicked and lazy" (Matthew 25:26). Those who produce good fruit with their lives produce 30, 60 and 100 times more than they consume.

Producing fruit may include new levels of obedience to God, a more productive ministry or job, more money or developed talents. God expects us to bear fruit with what he has given us. As a general rule, the more productive your life, the more rewarding it becomes. What exactly do we mean by producing fruit?

Bearing fruit could mean new levels of obedience to God, bearing more of the fruit of the Spirit in your life - becoming more loving, patient, kind, joyful and self controlled. (Galatians 5)

It could mean working in a ministry, increased levels of prayer and work for the kingdom of God. You are expanding the kingdom of God through your efforts.

It could mean an increase in income, skills or talents developed.

We should all work to bear more good fruit in our lives.

Learn these secrets of increased production and apply them to your life. We will expound on them in the following chapters.

In industry and in life there exist four factors of production. These factors combined determine how productive any endeavor will end up. Miss any one of these and production will come hard to you.

- **Raw Materials**, these include iron ore, cotton, rubber, food, and so on. In personal lives, **talent, time, insight, energy and opportunity** are the primary raw materials.
- **Capital** - money used to finance production and the tools and developed talent used to produce.
- **Labor** - work, effort
- **Management** - intelligent direction

Do you want to be a 30, 60 and 100 fold-er? Do you want to produce lots of good fruit? Here are the secrets.

- **You must stay well connected to the source of all production -God himself.** What you produce is just a part of God's ultimate productive plan. Stay close to him; learn his ways. God and you can accomplish infinitely more than just you. (John 15, Psalms 1)

- **Everything must be worked for.** There is no free lunch. You will not get something for nothing. This is why you must find a job you enjoy (at least most of the time). Because of the fall of man, and the grip of the second law of thermodynamics (entropy), things tend toward decay and we must work harder to be productive. You live in a fallen world. You struggle with fallen flesh. You are surrounded by fallen people. Things fall down - but God wants us to grow up, rise up, stand up and work to produce good fruit in the midst of a dark world! Don't grow afraid of work; laziness will rob you of a productive, fruit bearing life.

- **Strive for efficiency** - work not only harder but **smarter.** Learn how to manage your time and talents well. Prune away dead or fruitless areas of you life. Learn to organize and continually ask yourself, "Is there a more efficient way to do this?" (We devote a whole chapter to this.)

- **Better tools mean increased production.** Practically, this means that when you increase your skills or get better tools like a computer, air wrenches, etc, your production will increase. Can you think of any skills you can improve upon? Can you think of any tools you could acquire that would increase your production?

- **Trade today's gain for tomorrow's increased capacity - less now for more later.** In order to get better tools or greater capital you must resist the temptation to use up what you have now. Learn to save in order to acquire better tools - which will increase your capacity for production. Invest time in a skill, save for more education, save for a computer, save for a bigger lawn mower or a faster printing press. When you trade today's gain for tomorrow's increased capacity, you usually produce more in the long run.

- **Harness the power of a team - specialize.** Synergy is when the total production of a group of people is greater than the sum of the individual parts. Henry Ford found this secret when he invented the assembly line. Find out what you are good at and then find people to compliment your weaknesses. Become part of a team or a body. The amoeba does everything itself, reproduces, eats, moves, and breathes. But one square inch can contain its entire world; it only sees differences in light and dark. When cells specialize and devote themselves to a greater whole, they all achieve greater heights! This is why people skills are important to increased personal production.

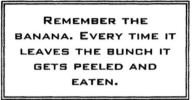

REMEMBER THE BANANA. EVERY TIME IT LEAVES THE BUNCH IT GETS PEELED AND EATEN.

As you grow, learn to enjoy activities that *produce* something or at least sow a seed (increase a skill) of production for the long term. When you watch T.V., movies, listen to music or go to the mall to hang out you are primarily consuming the fruit and labor of other people. Instead of watching a movie, get out your video camera and make one with your friends. Write a script, draw up some story boards and start filming.

Instead of listening to another CD, spend time practicing an instrument. If you are going to hang with your friends, *do* something. Play a sport or a game that challenges you. Talk about subjects that challenge the mind. Write letters of praise or protest to corporations and government leaders. Do things for people who can't do for themselves. Visit a nursing home or hospital.

All these projects need is a leader and organization. So if nobody is getting it done, *you* do it - organize and lead. Make a list of productive things to do when your bored. Here are some other suggestions:

- Read and memorize the Word of God
- Meditate on God and the Word of God
- Read: good fiction, non-fiction, memorize plays and

     poetry (Use Phil 4:8 as your guide)

- Write: fiction, non-fiction, plays and poetry
- Mathematics, Algebra, Geometry
- Learn an instrument, compose music
- Be involved in the arts; produce rather than consume, create rather than copy
- Work with your hands, conceptualize, build things, tear things apart, (hopefully) put them back together again.
- Learn a language
- Restore a car
- Paint someone's house or rake their leaves
- Plant a garden and preserve the vegetables

There exist thousands of things to do; get your mind out of the fog of non-productivity that consuming entertainment brings and you will see more clearly the opportunities to make a difference and have fun!

God bless you in your efforts at making your mark in today's world. When you get to be rich and influential because you followed these principles, don't forget all the little people who helped you along the way, especially this author. :) Next, we will look at education and the part it plays in leading a productive life.

> "IN EVERY MATTER OF WISDOM AND
> UNDERSTANDING ABOUT WHICH THE KING
> QUESTIONED THEM, HE FOUND THEM TEN TIMES
> BETTER THAN ALL THE MAGICIANS AND ENCHANTERS
> IN HIS WHOLE KINGDOM."
> DANIEL 1:20

> "...KNOWLEDGE IS HAPPINESS, BECAUSE TO HAVE
> KNOWLEDGE - BROAD DEEP KNOWLEDGE - IS TO
> KNOW TRUE ENDS FROM FALSE, AND LOFTY THINGS
> FROM LOW. TO KNOW THE THOUGHTS AND DEEDS
> THAT HAVE MARKED MAN'S PROGRESS IS TO FEEL
> THE GREAT HEARTTHROBS OF HUMANITY THROUGH
> THE CENTURIES; AND IF ONE DOES NOT FEEL IN
> THESE PULSATIONS A HEAVENWARD STRIVING, ONE
> MUST INDEED BE DEAF TO THE HARMONIES OF LIFE."
> HELEN KELLER

GET SMART

Ignorance is not of God. God expects to learn his truth in all areas of life, the knowledge of this truth will set us free. Ignorance is a type of slavery. Ineptitude keeps you locked up into a small world. God wishes to free you into an infinite universe that provides adventure and intimacy with the Creator of that universe.

The apostle Paul tells us that the way we are transformed is through the renewing of our mind. The mind is renewed by applying it to those things that will transform it. We are told to *think* on things that are pure, true, excellent, lovely and praiseworthy.

The man or woman of God should have a grasp on the truth of life and its secrets far more than anyone else. God is truth; those who know God should know truth. God is God in every scholastic discipline and he created mankind with scholastic dimensions.

In theology Christ is the fullness of God, in philosophy he is the Word of God, in ethics he is a sinless man, in biology he is The Life, in sociology he is The Son, in psychology he is the Savior who puts madmen in their right mind, in law he is the Lawgiver, in history he is the Fulness of Time, in economics he is the Owner of Everything, in politics he is the King of Kings!

We seem to have lost our edge in this area. Society has branded Christians as ignorant, unthinking people. We have lost the ancient tools of learning and we fail to love God with all our mind, in Spirit *and* in Truth.

Through "wisdom and understanding" God made the universe (Proverbs 3:19-20). Daniel and his friends were ten times smarter than anyone else in the kingdom (Daniel 1). Stephen, the first martyr, baffled his hearers with "his wisdom and the Spirit by which he spoke" (Acts 6:10), so much so, they killed him. Jesus himself was anointed with "wisdom and understanding" (Isaiah 11) - shouldn't we be?

We are terrible stewards of our mind. Compared with the children of history, we have slipped in our mental mastery. Yes, brilliant people still exist, but our educational system has "dumbed down" the average student. Like a socialist state, we now have an educated elite and a dumb middle class. One study found that American business loses nearly $40 billion in revenue a year because of the low level of their employees' literacy and the added time required to train and retrain workers for new technologies.[1]

Our nation, which used to lead the world in education, now trails in subjects like math and science.[2] What we call exceptional used to be called average.

In ancient times, they knew a way to train young people so that some of them could step into the role of kings, presidents and ambassadors *while they were still teenagers.* They not only knew what they needed to know to carry out great responsibilities; they knew how to find out what they didn't know, even if no one was there to show them.

A medieval child could - at 12 - study by himself a subject never seen before. He could sort out what it was and what it wasn't. Then clearly and simply he could present what he had found both written and orally.

Jonathan Edwards, a pastor God used greatly during the "Great Awakening," entered Yale at age 12 and graduated top of his class at age 17. George Washington's parents taught him at home. By the age of 12 he had mastered geometry and trigonometry. He started a successful surveying business by the time he was 15 and he was commander and chief of the Virginia militia at 21.

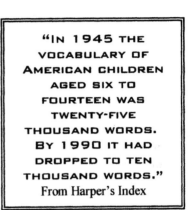

"IN 1945 THE VOCABULARY OF AMERICAN CHILDREN AGED SIX TO FOURTEEN WAS TWENTY-FIVE THOUSAND WORDS. BY 1990 IT HAD DROPPED TO TEN THOUSAND WORDS."
From Harper's Index

During the mid 1800's, Harriet Beecher Stowe wrote *Uncle Tom's Cabin*. But she started writing early. When she was 12 she won a writing contest with an essay entitled, "Can the immortality of the soul be proved by the light of nature." Can you imagine a twelve year old writing that today?

In high school, Hellen Keller, who was deaf and blind, took subjects like physics, algebra, geometry, Greek, Latin and German. During the summer before she entered Radcliffe College in 1900, she studied the writers Horace (a Latin poet) and Aeschylus (the father of Greek tragedy), and other subjects like, French, German, Rhetoric, English History, English Literature and Criticism, and English composition. [3]

In 1885, eighth graders who wished to win admission to Jersey City High School needed to pass a test that asked them, among other things, to:[4]

- Define Algebra, an algebraic expression, a polynomial. Make a literal trinomial.
- Write a homogeneous quadrinomial of the third degree...

- Find the sum and the difference of 3x-4y+7cd-4xy+16, and 10ay-3x-8xy+7cd-13...
- What is the axis of the earth? What is the equator? What is the distance from the equator to either pole in degree, in miles? Name the four principle mountain ranges in Asia, three in Europe, and three in Africa. Name the capitals of the following countries: Portugal, Greece, Egypt, Persia, Japan, China, Canada, Tibet and Cuba.
- Name four Spanish explorers and state what induced them to come to America.
- Name the thirteen colonies that declared their independence in 1776.

Would you have passed? God has given us much more brain power than we are using. I pray you would become a good steward of your mind. This chapter will clue you in on some of the lost tools of learning. Remember, no matter how smart you get, don't let pride enter in. Let love and humility propel your intellect.

But Why?

Have you ever sat in class and asked yourself, "Why do I have to learn...history, geography, math, language arts, or economics?" Why learn? Why go through the work and mental anguish just to know stuff?

Educating yourself allows you to produce more. Remember the principles of production, "Better tools mean more production." Education gives you better and sharper tools. It sharpens the mind and develops your skills.

Education allows you to enter in and contribute to a larger world. It allows you to understand and speak about the biggest questions of life, "Where have we come from," "What gives life meaning," "How should we live?" and "What is our destiny?" Your voice will enter in with our finest scientists and artists and it will span centuries and cross cultures. Doors will open up to a universal conversation about the nature of truth and beauty, knowledge and compassion, good and evil - ideas that form the foundation of our society. Ignorance will imprison you to a world of pop culture, sit-com's and talk shows.

Educated people know something about the various kinds of problems tackled in psychology, theology, philosophy and physics, literature and mathematics. They understand how people in all these fields arrive at conclusions and how these fields relate to each other.

We learn how to do things we get paid for and we discover things worth doing. Through studying, we raise our tastes. We learn ways to distinguish what is superficial and fleeting from what is lasting and profound.

Through the educational process you will learn about yourself, what you enjoy and what you do well. Jobs that involve responsibility and higher pay depend on self management skills. These include knowing how to manage time, resolve conflict, set goals, conquer stress and learn new skills. Education is a place to practice such skills.

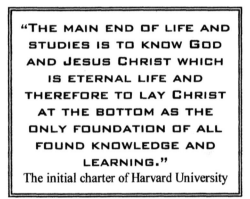

"THE MAIN END OF LIFE AND STUDIES IS TO KNOW GOD AND JESUS CHRIST WHICH IS ETERNAL LIFE AND THEREFORE TO LAY CHRIST AT THE BOTTOM AS THE ONLY FOUNDATION OF ALL FOUND KNOWLEDGE AND LEARNING."
The initial charter of Harvard University

When you know more, you *can* know more. Part of a quality education is having a reliable storehouse of information from which to draw upon. As you know more about more things, your brain finds it easier to absorb information because it associates information together.

Your brain relates your knowledge of great white sharks with the *geography* of their habitat with the *ecology* of their feeding habits, with the *physics* of their movement, with the *movie* Jaws. And all this information makes it easier to learn about the German U-boats of World War II, which makes it easier to learn about the merchant marine industry which makes it easier to learn about the world economy! Bits of information that you think of as useless, your brain makes useful.

In life, you will face problems. Not the carefully crafted and sanitized problems of the classroom, but the wild, untamed and unmerciful dilemma's of the real world. Because of how the areas of life interrelate, if you lack critical information in one area, say economics, your problem solving skills will be sorely hampered. Nothing will help you more than a large body of knowledge stored in your brain. All that stuff you thought you would never use becomes suddenly useful. If you base your decisions on falsehood, you're in trouble.

Learning is like lifting weights for your brain. Even apart from giving you a reliable storehouse of knowledge, learning will train your brain in critical thinking skills. When faced with real world problems, knowing how to solve a quadratic equation may not help you. But the critical thinking skills you learned while studying and solving these equations *will help you.* Professional athletes don't find themselves bench pressing or curling on the court or field. That does not mean, however, that the extra strength gained from weight conditioning is useless to them.

You will find each subject becomes useful in different ways and builds your brain in different ways. Learning different languages enables you to communicate better and obviously produces dividends as the world becomes a global village. Sciences will help train you to think clearly and test out what you believe. Scientists get the privilege of thinking and discovering the thoughts of God after him.

Classes in English, speech, and drama will show you how to speak and write so that people will listen to you. History gives your life a context. It teaches us what mankind is like, and what happens to nations that forget or ignore God. Biology will help you see what a wonderful creation God made and may give you opportunities to present a Biblical picture of creation.

Economics shows you the secrets of money and how people react to it. It gives you insight into raising your standard of living, running a business, saving and investing. Government shows you how our nation runs, and how they spend *your* money. You learn how America tries to walk the tightrope between liberty and law; and what part *you* play in the democratic process.

Lastly, a better education will most likely enable you to earn more money. People pay you to fill needs. You do this by solving problems or adding value to things. The more you know the better you can do this. The more you learn, the more you earn. In their book *Getting Rich in America*, economic guru's Dwight Lee and Richard McKenzie calculate the value of getting a high school diploma. Based on the extra earning power (problem solving power) high school graduates possess, invested from graduation to retirement, earning eight percent, the high school graduate's net worth would be about **$5.5 million dollars**.

Their book shows how education adds to income based on statistics from the late '90s.

Education	Median Household Income
Less than 9th Grade	$20,781
9th to 12th (no diploma)	$24,575
High School Graduate	$38,563
Some College (no degree)	$44,814
Associate Degree	$51,176
Bachelor's Degree	$64,293
Master's Degree	$76,065
Doctorate Degree	$92,316
Professional Degree	$102,557

Even though the more you learn, the more you earn, the total return on education is much more than money. The most valuable benefits from education have nothing to do with money. It is, however, a *nice* benefit. :)

"IT IS THE GLORY OF GOD TO CONCEAL A MATTER;
TO SEARCH OUT A MATTER IS THE GLORY OF
KINGS."
KING SOLOMON, PROVERBS 25:2

LEARNING TO LEARN

It wasn't until my junior year in college that I started to learn how I learned best. I wish I had learned this in the fifth grade. Knowing how you learn helps you learn. The brain absorbs and stores information a certain way, and everyone has a slightly different way of loading the information - we call them different learning styles. First, let's look at how your brain stores information.

The fundamental unit of the brain is the neuron. During the first nine months of life, God is wiring the brain at a rate of 25,000 neurons a minute. By the time a baby is born it possesses roughly a trillion neurons. If you covered half of the United States with a forest, the number of leaves on all of the trees of that forest would equal the number of neurons in your brain. These neurons are connected by a system of roads called neural pathways. These neural pathways are the key to learning and memory.

Each activity, sight, sound, smell, taste or touch causes activity along a set of neural pathways. The more you repeat an experience, the stronger the pathway becomes. If repeated often enough, the experience becomes a part of the permanent memory.

Imagine your brain as an empty field. Every day you walk across the field along the same route. A path begins to wear in the grass. Soon, the path grows larger and firmer. Then, you pave a road over the path and it becomes a part of your permanent landscape (memory).

Knowledge is merely the interconnection of these roads in your brain. The more interconnecting roads you have in your head, the easier information can get around. This is another reason you should be well educated in various areas.

Learning takes work just like paving roads takes work. We will discuss more about this when we show you how to study. Now let's briefly look at how *you* learn.

I Gotta Find My Style

Finding out how you best load information into your brain is critical to your academic success. Some students aren't cut out for the style of learning a classroom caters to. Many of them get labeled slow, ADD and so on. Don't let anyone put a label on you except God. Everyone is smart, just in different ways. Everyone can learn and everyone has something to contribute; we just learn in different ways and our contributions may seem valuable to some and worthless to others.

You may enjoy learning systematically, step by step; or you may like to work more randomly, on two or three projects at a time. You may need it quiet to study or you like a little music in the background. You may like to sit at a well lit desk or maybe you prefer to move around a little as you learn (like me). Maybe you are detail oriented or you see better the big picture. Maybe you remember better during a lecture, or maybe you like pictures to help you remember. Whatever the case, no one style is bad if you learn what you need to.

So how do you learn? Begin to watch yourself and your study habits. Try different techniques and remember what works. Here are some questions to aid in your discovery:

- What time of day do you seem most alert? Early morning? Late evening? Somewhere in between?

- When you are concentrating, do you need some kind of food or drink?

- Do you like to study using bright or dim light?

- When you are trying to memorize are you more successful when you: Repeat the information out loud or put it in a song or a rhyme? Visualize a picture of what is meant, draw or cut out pictures. Do you like to use colorful folders or stickers? Do you like to keep moving and take frequent breaks, shift positions?

- When listening to information or directions: Do you easily get the big picture or the main idea? Or do you more easily remember specific details and can repeat things word for word?

- Do you like to work in piles instead of files? Do you like to spread out materials?

- Do you work best with a structured schedule, need a clear efficient work space? Do you break large assignments into manageable parts?

- Are you more interested in facts than in hidden meanings and symbolism? Are you often interested in where the person got the facts? Do you like to know and do what will make everyone else happy? Do you like to do what the inspiration of the moment dictates?[5]

- Let's say you had the opportunity to take one test, and if you passed this test, you would receive a million dollars. You have one day to study for this test - how would you study? However you would study for this is a good indication of how you learn.

Tips on Studying

Learning how your brain stores information and how you go about collecting it is the first step in learning how to study efficiently.

When studying always work from **Broad to Specific**. First **collect information**, get the big picture, then **categorize** it, sort it out, find out what it is and what it isn't, find the main point or points. Then learn to **communicate** your findings by the written or spoken word.   When you can communicate what you have learned, you have truly learned.

Here are some more tips:

- Have a special place set aside for your studying. If you like to move around (like me), have a few places set aside. Have a good light source to avoid eye strain.

- Don't procrastinate, know when your assignments are due and set up a schedule to accomplish them at least one day early. Plan a study guide and pin it up where you can see it.

- Don't allow distractions (phone calls, radio, visitors). Teach yourself to CONCENTRATE. When your mind wanders, be aware of it and bring it back to the task at hand. Concentration is a learned skill. You can train your attention span by forcing yourself to concentrate. Over time, you become aware of daydreams and mind-wandering sooner and there is a greater time span between mental distractions. Take every opportunity to train your mind to pay attention in school, church, at home, etc. Remember, sugar and television will sabotage your concentration skills.

- If studying for an extended period, take a short break after achieving a goal. Take a **short** walk, play an instrument, make a phone call or do some push ups. Then get back at it. It is better to do a good hour of intense study and take a couple of hours off doing something else than to fritter away three hours fooling around half-heartedly at one subject.

- Discipline is something you must learn from the Holy Spirit. Commit each session to the Lord; ask for guidance. Don't wait for the mood to strike you, just begin anyway.

- When learning a new subject, learn the terms first. Take extra time at the beginning of the semester to learn the foundational terms of the course. If chemistry, learn what they mean by ion, element, valence, parts of the atom, mole and so on. If economics, learn what they mean by production, supply, demand, goods, services, etc. Use flash-cards; carry them around. If you get your books a day or two before class starts, begin learning the bold worded terms you don't already know before class. Get ahead and stay ahead.

Memorizing

Remember, when you remember something you are actually building a road in your brain; that takes work and repetition. These hints will help you:

- Never try to memorize things you don't understand. Understand it, then memorize it. **Broad to specific**. Put concepts into your own words. If you can't explain something in your own words, you probably can't understand it.

- Use your senses - as many as you can (sight, sound, smell, muscle memory). The best way to memorize is to write out and/or cartoon the material, and read it out loud, with emphasis. Use every input you can.

- In remembering whole lines and paragraphs such as in acting, always try to remember key words that will bring back the rest of the line. This will put you on the road; your brain will do the rest. If necessary, condense notes into single words or phrases. See if you can recite the concepts backwards.

- Recite material without notes after learning it. You will be able to see how much you have really learned. Repeat this often. Give yourself tests or have someone else quiz you. Try reciting it with feeling or imitate somebody when you do it.

- If you have any talent for drawing, or even if you don't, try to put things like history and time charts into line drawings and pictures. It's easier to remember pictures than words. For example, when trying to remember the physics equation for force - force = mass times acceleration, draw a picture of Darth Vader or Luke Skywalker using the 'force' against Jabba the Hut - the 'mass'- from the space ship jumping to light speed - the 'acceleration.'
    Another reason to draw pictures is that visual information

is stored in a different part of the brain than verbal. When you create a picture of the concept, you anchor the information in two parts of your brain. This increases your chances of recalling the information. Make the picture vivid and colorful, involve all your senses, imagine what it would be like 'accelerating' to light speed while fighting this 'mass.'

- Use mnemonic devices. Put letters together to make words that will help you remember bigger concepts. We already use a lot of these in our every day language like: NASA, LASER, RADAR. These all stand for something. Remember the colors of the rainbow? Roy G. Biv. Remember the Great Lakes? HOMES. How about the notes on a musical staff? Every Good Boy Deserves an F-16! (Yes, I know it's fudge.)

  Specialized industries like law enforcement, the military and aviation are full of these - because they work. When teaching students the procedures for landing a complex aircraft we do what is called a GUMP check. It stands for important things not to forget before you land. G stands for gas - make sure your fuel system is on. U stands for undercarriage - make sure your wheels are down. M stands for mixtures - make sure they are full rich. P stands for props - full for a go around. GUMP also stands for what you will feel like if you land without putting your gear down!

- Over learn. Carry on after you feel you have learned it perfectly just a few more times. When doing a musical piece, if you can do it perfectly three times in a row - you know it. Over learning makes results far more lasting. When you over learn, you make the path into a paved road, it becomes harder for the weeds of forgetfulness to grow over it. This technique is especially effective when learning problem solving. Do the assigned problems, then do more problems. Find another text and do more of the same type of problems. Make up your own problems. When you do this, you will gain speed, accuracy and greater confidence come exam time.

- Review. Put your summaries, cartoon charts on to flash cards.

Carry them with you during the day. At odd moments just thumb through them and test yourself. Reviewing an hour after studying will move information from your short term to long term memory faster.

- Recall - Don't be afraid you might forget or the worry might actually cause you to do just that. If you have studied, put your trust in the Lord and relax. If you can't remember, wait a while. Do something else and return to the problem later. Maybe something from another test question will jog your memory. If you can't remember the specific answer, try to remember a related one. Maybe the example used during the lecture or in the book. If your really stumped, just start a brain storm, go through answers to related questions and - pop! - the answer you may be looking for may come to you because you triggered a connecting road.

- Set traps for your memory. When you want to remind yourself to do something, link that activity to another event that you know will take place. Say your walking to class and suddenly you remember your accounting assignment is due tomorrow. Switch your watch from your left to your right wrist. Every time you look at your watch it becomes a reminder that you were supposed to remember something. You can do the same with a ring. If you empty your pockets every night, put an unusual item in your pocket to remind yourself to do something. The key is to pick events that are certain to occur. Rituals like looking for your car keys or looking at your watch or untying shoes are seldom forgotten. Tie a triple knot in your shoelace to remind you to set the alarm for your early study group meeting.[6]

Reading: How to Study Books Effectively

One man has said, "You are the same person you were last year except for the people you have met and the books you have read." Books are a wonderful source of information about the world. Books are so important, even God wrote one. God chose to express himself in print, the written Word. It will go well with you if you learn how to learn from books.

The first mistake people make when studying from books is that they think once they have read it one time, they know it. I have had students come to class and fail quizzes over reading material assigned from the previous day. They get frustrated and say, "I don't know why I failed, I read the material." They may have read it, but they haven't studied it and they certainly haven't *learned* it.

In order to read a book with the intent on learning from it (not pleasure reading) you must Power Read! Move from the broad to specific. Plan on reading the material three times, each with a different goal. Collect, categorize, then communicate.

The first time through, **collect** the information; find the big picture. No need to read every detail here, just get the general overview of the section. What is the main purpose of the chapter? To get you to know or understand what? Notice the headings, charts, diagrams and bold words. Start your garden - cultivate questions. Think of what your teacher could ask you. Make a question from any bold word. At the end of this procedure you should have good questions and a good grasp on the big picture.

The second time through, **categorize** the information into more specific details. Read each paragraph in detail. Look up any words you do not know; write the definition in the margin next to the word. Begin to harvest answers from your cultivated questions. Write them down in the margin of the book or a 3x5 card. The answers you cannot find write down in the book to ask your instructor.

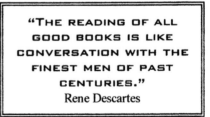

"THE READING OF ALL GOOD BOOKS IS LIKE CONVERSATION WITH THE FINEST MEN OF PAST CENTURIES."
Rene Descartes

If you notice your attention drifting, bring it back into focus. Make tick marks on a scrap piece of paper every time you notice your mind wandering. You might make a lot of tick marks at first, that's OK. Most students find that as they pay attention to their attention, the number of tick marks decreases. You can use the following techniques to help you stay focused while your read.

First, visualize the material. Form mental pictures of the concepts as the author presents them.

Second, read aloud, especially complicated material.

Third, get a feel for the subject, literally. For example, let's say you're reading about a micro-organism called the paramecium. Imagine what it would feel like if you ran your fingers around the perimeter of the cell membrane, feeling the cilia as they wiggle in your hand.

The third time through, **communicate** the information. Summarize it into your own words. You should be able to answer your cultivated questions in writing or in speech. Use your memory techniques to learn the information.

Be able to give examples of principles and concepts. If your science books says that one celled organisms move around by various means, be able to name them and describe them. If your economics book describes principles of command and market economies - be able to give examples of each. Try to think of scenarios where the concept works and where it doesn't work. Don't believe everything you read. Test everything and hold on to the good. Can you think of another source of information that corroborates or contradicts this concept? This third step is sooo critical to your success in all fields. *Think!*

Learn to summarize, in your own words, entire chapters into one paragraph and paragraphs into sentences. Jesus was a master at this. (Matthew 22:37-40, 7:12) If you can summarize a concept into your own words and give examples illustrating that concept, you know it.

After you have done your power reading, you are ready for the lecture. You are prepared and ahead of the game.

Improving Your Reading Speed

To learn to read faster, you must read faster. There are some good speed reading courses out there and they do work. Most of your time reading is spent between the letters as your eye moves in a jerky fashion across the page. (Watch someone's eyes as they read to see this.) To really speed read you must do two things. The first is easy, the second takes some work.

First you must train your eye to move faster. To do this, just move your finger under the line you are reading and your eye will follow it while soaking up the words. Doing this alone will increase your reading speed by at least 15%. Once you get up to speed with this technique you are ready for the next step.

Second, you must train your eye not to see one word at a time but groups of words. Practice 15 minutes a day reading two lines at once. Try it. Move your finger under two lines, follow them with your eyes then skip down two more lines and so on. Do this 15 minutes a day for a week then try three lines then four and so on. Some people have trained their eyes to read whole paragraphs at once! It's amazing what the human brain can do! I am only proficient enough to skim through reading material with this technique but it does work. Use it during the **collecting** stage of your study.

For more on this, check out a book from the library or go buy one My favorite is *Speed Reading the Easy Way*, published by Barron's. If you are a serious student and you have a lot of schooling ahead of you, this will be the best $20 dollar investment of your academic career.

Power Listening

Much of life's information is presented to us through lecture. Some instructors excel in this area and some bore your brains out. Either way, you can train yourself to absorb information like a sponge. All it takes is effort and training. Remember, you're building roads! Here are some tips:

- Your brain can process information three to four times faster than most people can present. So train your brain to run through the material just spoken during small pauses during the lecture.

- Sit near the front: less distractions, more eye contact from the professor and less temptation to wander off or nod off!

- Arrive a bit early to class and review the notes from the previous lecture or reading material. This will warm up your brain and get it in gear.

- Don't allow your mind to wander; bring it back on track. When class gets a little boring, give yourself more of a challenge; answer and ask more questions.

- Be alert to repetition; it's a signal that the instructor thinks the information is important.

- Watch the instructor's eyes. If she glances at her notes and then makes a point, that is a signal that the information is important.

If you don't get a concept, stop and ask the teacher to explain it again. If you still don't get it, ask *specific* questions and don't stop until you fully understand the concept - even if it means staying after or attending office hours.

Avoid this exchange: "Teacher, I don't get it." "Get what?" "I don't know, I just don't get it." You must learn to articulate what you don't understand. "Teacher, I don't see how the market economy allows workers to earn higher wages. Could you give another example?"

When you ask a question, your instructor is looking for a foundational concept you don't grasp. It may be something you covered three days ago but because you didn't understand it then, you will fail to understand all the concepts that build on it. If you don't know what a market economy is, you won't understand how it allows workers to earn higher wages.

Power Note Taking

Taking notes on a lecture is like all three steps in Power Reading - all at once. You are **collecting** - getting the big picture and cultivating questions. As you take notes, formulate questions and postulate answers. You must follow this with **categorizing** - getting a more detailed picture and harvesting answers. Ask specific questions if allowed. You must now **communicate** these concepts; summarize them into your own words to complete the learning experience. Follow these guidelines for taking better notes.

- Make your notebooks look cool. Messy notes are hard to study from. Use sharp pencils and ruled paper.

- Change your letter sizes for EMPHASIS. Try to color code different concepts. Red for formulas, black for terms and green for important fact or concept.

- Leave wide margins to summarize key material in a sentence or two.

- Use * to highlight important information for quick reference later.

- Use pictures and diagrams. Make relationships visual.

- Come up with your own shorthand system. Make sure you can understand it.

- After class, review your notes over lunch and make a note of things you don't understand. Quiz yourself. The next time you have the class, review the notes before the start of the lecture.

- Use your teacher's office hours! You paid for them!

God bless you in your pursuit of truth and wisdom. It is more precious than silver and more beneficial than gold.

Scripture Meditations: Proverbs chapters 1-4, James 1:5, John

14:26, Colossians 3:23-24, I Thessalonians 5:21. **For test tension:** Isaiah 26:3, 12:2, 33:6, Proverbs 3:5

1. Charles Sykes, Dumbing Down our Kids, St. Martin's Press, 1995

2. U.S. Department of Education, National Center for Educational Statistics, Pursuing Excellence: *A Study of U.S. Twelfth Grade Mathematics and Science Achievement in International Context*, NCES 98-049, U.S. Government Printing Office, 1998

3. Hellen Keller, *The Story of My Life*

4. Charles Sykes, Dumbing Down our Kids, St. Martin's Press, 1995

5. Cynthia Tobias at Applied Learning Styles, From the Learning Style Survey and Book: *The Way They Learn*. Apple Street, LLC Box 1450 Sumner, WA 98390

6. Many of these tips come from Winkey Pratney's, *The Daniel Files* found at www.moh.org and Dave Ellis's, *Becoming a Master Student,* Houghton Mifflin Co. The latter is an excellent book on learning. It contains a little bit of politically correct mumbo jumbo but all in all it is an excellent learning guide.

> "MAN IS MADE TO BE IN THE VISIBLE UNIVERSE AN
> IMAGE AND LIKENESS OF GOD HIMSELF, AND HE IS
> PLACED IN IT IN ORDER TO SUBDUE THE EARTH.
> FROM THE BEGINNING, THEREFORE, HE IS CALLED
> TO WORK."
> POPE JOHN PAUL II

> "AFTER A MAN BECOMES A CHRISTIAN, I WORK HIM
> DAY AND NIGHT. I BELIEVE THAT FOR ONE MAN
> KILLED BY OVERWORK IN THE CAUSE OF CHRIST TEN
> THOUSAND DIE FROM LAZINESS."
> D. L. MOODY

WORK

For better or for worse, work defines us. One of the first questions people ask is, "So what is it that you do?" Work is one of the few constants of our existence, one of our few commonalities. We spend about half our waking life doing it. But work is even more than this. Meaningful work is a fundamental dimension of human existence, an expression of our very nature.

Work is worship. God has invested in us talents and gifts so that we may have the privilege of collaborating with him in the grand design of the universe, working for his glory, the common good and our fulfillment.

Augustine said, *laborare est orare*, "to work is to pray." Johann Sebastian Bach inscribed the letters SDG on the bottom of his compositions, standing for *Sola Deo Gloria* - to the glory of God alone. With the same motivation, Albrecht Durer carved his woodcuts and engravings, and Michelangelo and Rembrandt sculpted and painted.

God placed such importance on labor and disdain upon laziness he said, "Unless a man work, he shall not eat" (II Thessalonians 3:10-12).

In an earlier chapter, we discussed the importance of finding the type of work that suits you. In this chapter we will tell you the secrets of finding the work you want and excelling in it.

From the Boss' Point of View

Contrary to what many must think, companies do not just exist to provide employment - the vast majority are in it for the money. If they don't make money, they don't stay in business. The foundation of your job search and your career must include the understanding that the employee is the most costly and complex asset of any company. A company must dip into company profits to pay for medical coverage, workers compensation insurance, social security taxes, payroll taxes, training programs, and salary.

To make matters worse, employees come as a complete package, with marital problems, alcohol problems, health problems and personal problems.

Employers take the risk to hire people for one simple reason: ROI - Return On Investment. The employer invests in the worker with the hope that the worker will give her a good return on her investment. Get this: **they hire you to make them money.** As a job candidate and employee, you must prove that you are a good return on the employers investment. (Proverbs 27:18)

> **"NO MAN BECOMES RICH UNLESS HE ENRICHES OTHERS."**
> Andrew Carnegie

Employee Greatness

The foundation of greatness is servant-hood. This foundation will lead you to greatness in the workplace. To achieve greatness as an employee or an entrepreneur you must do one thing: **find needs and fill them.** You do this by **solving problems** or **adding value.** The key to lifelong success in this arena is to get good at finding needs and filling them. All through history, people have exploited this simple Christian concept to bear a lot of fruit and make a lot of money.

To find needs, look for problems to solve or find ways to add value to things. Don't spend your early years looking to get out of problem solving. Don't run from problems, learn what it takes to solve them - it's what people will pay you for. The harder the problem to solve the more cash they will pay you to get it done. If all you can do is solve small problems - like getting the fries to the customer fresh - you will get small money. If, however, you have trained yourself to solve big, complex problems that few people can solve - like performing heart bypass surgery - you will get big money.

To recap: **small problems lead to small money, big problems lead to big money.**

You can also make big money by adding big value to low value items. Many people have the skill to improve cars, property, houses and people. When you improve something you make it worth more; you have added value. People will pay you for this extra value.

To gain opportunities for tremendous production, you must now understand that our economy has moved from a world in which the value of goods was locked up in the *materials* that were used to make the goods to a world in which the value of goods is locked up in the *ideas* that gave birth to the good. For example, only 2% of the value of a computer chip is in the material (basically sand) used to produce it. The rest of the value is in the idea, the logic and the know-how.

This means that to solve today's problems and to add value in today's economy, it helps to learn how to *think* critically and creatively. When you have problems at school, home and work - rejoice! - God has just given you opportunities for job training, job security and material prosperity!

When you stop adding value or solving problems you become a liability to your employer. They have just run out of reasons to keep you.

We dedicate an entire chapter on becoming a Right Hand Person.

The Hunt to Get Hired

Have you ever looked for a job? I used to hate it, walking humbly into place after place asking, "Do you have any applications?" Looking for work can be tiring and discouraging but only if you don't understand the secrets to finding employment. We have already shared with you the number one and number two most important pieces of information. People will hire you to solve problems or add value and this value must exceed the amount the employer will invest in you. Or put another way, you must fill needs the employer has while making them money in the process. Armed with these two facts, let us show you the in's and out's of how you really get hired.

Due to the scope of this book, I can only give you limited information on this subject. If you desire to learn more, I recommend, *How You Really Get Hired* by John LaFevre. Your library is full of job hunting books. Read them.

Job Availability

A good economy is usually marked by low unemployment. Good economies come and go. But good workers will have work, good economy or bad. *Do good work, always work; do bad work, look for work.* With the state of our educational system and family structure, two generations have grown up without knowing how to work. You now have the greatest opportunity to excel in your area of expertise than in the entire history of America simply because so much of the workforce is illiterate, incompetent, lazy and selfish. Managers are constantly looking for Right Hand People. If you become a Right Hand Person - Results oriented, Honest and you possess People skills, you will get hired even when no one is hiring.

Never let the excuse, "I can't find work because no one is hiring" come from your lips. Someone is *always* hiring and they will make room for Right Hand People.

When a job comes open, there is usually a long delay between its opening and when a company will publish an ad in a newspaper or campus job board. In fact, companies fill 80% of openings before they are ever listed in the classifieds or campus placement offices. This means when you look for employment, you must do it actively, from the street level. Don't send blind resumes if you can avoid it, find the people that make the decisions and talk to them. Show some initiative. Get hired before the classified hunters even know that a job existed.

Studies show that only one out of five jobs are listed in newspapers. If your Sunday paper has two pages of job listings, there are actually 10 pages of jobs out there. Life presents you with subtle hints that indicate "job opening here." Put yourself on a 24 hour alert for openings. Including the placement office and the want ads, these tips will point you in the right direction:

- Newspaper articles are 'job ads' if the article discusses an expansion program, new plant, personnel change or new product. A changing company is full of employment opportunities. When a manager gets promoted, write her a letter, I'm sure she will need to build a staff. When they build that new plant next year, get in on the ground floor. When they start a new product line, talk to the sales manager, I'm sure they will need a key person like you to help with the line. Train yourself to see the openings that haven't opened yet. Watch the evening news with the same eye.

- As you drive around town, look for signs of business change: construction, billboards, new buildings, "the future sight of..." signs all are good clues. Don't wait for the new hotel to be built; send corporate headquarters an application today. A new plant or business must have people hired before they open.

- New products on the shelves provide a direct link to growing companies. New products mean new supervisors, sales people clerks, marketing specialists and laborers.

- Network. Networking means using friends and contacts to learn about possible job openings. Sometimes it's not what you know but who you know. That tall guy that goes to your church knows his company is looking for someone in the shipping department; why not ask him about a job? If you have a friend that loves his job, investigate where they work. Get the inside scoop from people who are on the inside.

- Network with people you don't know but would like to know. Most students miss a golden opportunity to meet important people who work in their fields. If you want to work in the health care industry, for example, call or stop by a hospital and make appointments with doctors, nurses, food service managers or who-ever interests you. Tell them that you wish to discuss career opportunities within their field over lunch, and you will buy. Tell them you would appreciate their career guidance and expertise.

- Start early. When I taught flight school, I always gave my students an edge. Getting hired as a pilot is very competitive and relies a lot on *who* you know. All pilots know the same stuff, but they don't always know the same people. Those people will make all the difference. Even before they earned their private pilot certificate - at least two years before anyone would even think of hiring them - I had my students make up business cards that read "Steve Flymoore, Professional Pilot." Whenever we took trips to different airports we planned at least 15 to 30 minutes on the ground to network. If a pilot flew in from Atlanta, I sent my student over to introduce himself and hand him a card and get one in return. He would explain that he is working toward his commercial pilot certificate and would like to keep in touch. When we arrived home he would place the card in a neat file and send the pilot a letter saying that it was great to meet and talk with him. Then every new rating and accomplishment he would send another letter on personalized letterhead with the student's picture to that pilot or flight department head stating that he was one more step closer to employability.

  Soon we could have established relationships with hundreds of people already in the industry and files on hundreds of flight departments. We knew what they flew, and who flew them. When that flight department goes to hire somebody who do you think will come to mind? You better believe it: Steve Flymoore. Start networking early in the industry that interests you; that delivery boy you know now may be the department head when your ready to work for them.

What if you absolutely cannot find work?

Go to a company that suits your skill and talents. Find the person that hires people and ask if you can work part-time, free of charge just to keep your skills honed. Say something like, "Mr Bono, I am currently looking for work, but until I can find employment would it be OK for me to volunteer my skills here part time just to keep them sharp?"

Work part time for free, and fill the other time with job hunting. With this attitude you will not stay unemployed for long. You are on your way to becoming somebody's Right Hand Person.

What About Those Pesky Job Specifications?

When job hunting, don't let the specifications for the job weed you out. They may say minimum two years experience and a 3.5 GPA. Ignore them. Too many times specifications are biased, arbitrary, off- the -wall requirements generated by a business's pragmatic need to screen out a large portion of the job seekers pool. If you are really interested in a company, don't let them screen you out so easily. Be a fighter, persevere!

If you really want to interview with your dream company than implement the following plan of action given by former personnel director and hiring guru John Lafever in his book, *How You Really Get Hired*:

- Thoroughly investigate the company by reading the literature in a library or college placement office. Request an annual report or call the sales office or manufacturing facility to learn about future plans and products. Get the name and title of the person in charge of the department you would work for. Send a great cover letter and resume in application for the position.

- Call the company switchboard and ask for the department you desire. When the secretary answers, tell her you are sending something to her boss and you want to confirm the spelling of their name and their title. Then send a letter with attached resume describing your interest in the company, using specific information that only a person who has done extensive research would know.

Vice Presidents and managers are more impressed with business drive than GPA.

The Resume

Large companies typically receive over 8,000 resumes every year. Reviewers typically scan resumes in seconds looking for reasons to trash it. You must provide a resume that will not provide ammunition for a quick turndown. If you make the first cut, then the reviewer will put you on a smaller stack for a later, more thorough review. The goal of a resume is two fold:

- To avoid getting trashed in the first five to fifteen seconds
- To produce enough interest to generate a phone call or a written invitation for an interview.

After your resume accomplishes those two tasks for you, its value diminishes. Your interview skills will determine if they hire you or not.

There are a ton of good books on writing resumes out there. I just want to give you a few tips that will put you ahead of the Average Joe.

- Your resume should not exceed two full pages. If you cannot fill two pages, then just fill one - no half pages.

- After stating who you are and a brief statement of purpose, you should lead with your strengths. If your weak on job experience and strong on education, special awards and achievements, then place them ahead of work experience.

- Avoid selfish language in your statement of purpose. "My goal is to find a position where I can utilize my skills and be challenged." Emphasize what you can do for the company. Don't list your requirements, sell what you have to offer.

- In your work experience and accomplishment section never say the words 'responsible for.' Use short, powerful action verbs to highlight accomplishments, not duties or responsibilities. Look at these two examples:

> A. Counter person at McDonalds, 8-00 to present. Responsible for serving customers and working a register.

> B. Customer Service Representative, McDonalds Corporation, 8-00 to present. Effectively handled 450 business transactions per day; managed computerized check out station - $5000 per day. Perfect attendance award, installed promotional displays, handled customer complaints and is known by supervisor as innovative and dependable.

Who would you hire? Tell accomplishments, not responsibilities.

- Keep the education section brief, but make sure you include any special awards or honors. What about your educational experience would tell them you can solve problems and make them money?

- Spend the extra money to get it on nice paper. You should spend at least 30 hours on your resume. You should strategically place every word.

> Doug Berg, CEO of Techies.com favorite interview question: **"WHAT DOES OUR COMPANY NEED TO DO?"** Why he asks it: **"IF YOU WANT A JOB, START SOLVING PROBLEMS IN THE INTERVIEW. IF SOMEONE GIVES ME THE OLD "WELL, I NEED MORE INFORMATION," I DON'T LET THEM OFF THE HOOK. IF THEY CAN'T ANSWER ME HERE, THEY DON'T HAVE THE FAST-START MENTALITY A DOT-COM STARTUP NEEDS."**

The Interview

During your job hunt, everything you do should communicate, "Hire me, I will solve your problems and make you money." Nowhere is this more important than in the interview.

The difference between getting hired and getting turned down is usually fractions of a point on a rating system. The key to getting hired is out preparing your competition for the interview. You must work at showing *you* are the one who can solve problems or add value better than any of the other chumps interviewing.

Once invited to an interview, you should do your reconnaissance. Learn as much about a company as the job warrants. The more it pays, the more you should learn about the company. Learn what they do to make a profit. Learn their most profitable items. Do they have any new products or divisions? Did they make money last year? What do they need to do to improve their business?

You must find out the names and titles of those who will interview you; find out a little about what they do within the company. You can find a lot of this information by watching the business section of your newspaper, and other business periodicals, ordering an annual report, books in the library that track corporations or your network of people.

Learning about the company gives you a huge edge on anyone else that hasn't done their research. It also gives you the confidence you need to present the proper attitude.

The interviewing process has a way of intimidating people. *You* cannot be intimidated. You must approach the interview as a professional business meeting between two equals. Both have something to offer. You can solve their problems and add value and they can invest in you. You must approach the interview thinking (not saying), "These people are fools if they don't hire me." If you feel nervous, prepare more. Learn more about the company. Practice answering questions and get there early.

Hello, C'mon In

The first minute of an interview is the most important. How you meet and greet your interviewers must set you apart. You must have a firm and pleasant hand shake. (If they are sweaty, wipe them off before you go in) Look confident, but not cocky. You should say something to show them you did your homework.

"Good morning Mrs. Bensen, I understand you are the Vice President of Marketing, it's a pleasure to meet you."

Or, "Good afternoon Mr. Gooden, I'm pleased to meet you. After receiving your invitation for the interview I went ahead and ordered a copy of the annual report. I'm even more excited about the opportunities represented by Baker Industries. I was especially impressed with the new line of self-controlling heating elements you started last year."

Prepare yourself by rehearsing honest answers to common interview questions. Here are a few.

- Why should we hire you?
- What is your greatest strength/weakness?
- How can you contribute to our company?
- Tell me about your work experience?
- What motivates you?
- What was the biggest mistake you ever made?
- Why didn't you get better grades in school?

During most interviews, you are allowed to ask a few questions. Good interview preparation includes having a couple of key questions ready. These questions should point to your company research and zero in on the requirements for the position. Like, "How has the new product introduction improved your market share?" Or others like, "What does it take for an employee to become one of the top 10% of employees here at Baker Industries?" or "What characteristic would you say is most important for this position?" Never ask selfish questions about salary or benefits, discuss those after they make you an offer.

During your research, do your best to discern your company's needs - find the needs and tailor your interview answers toward filling them. Show them that *your strengths* fit the *company's needs*. Is the company noted for a family atmosphere? Be prepared to show you are a team player. Do they have a reputation for a high standard of quality? Let them know you can't stand mediocrity and you will work until it's done right.

The best way to show that your strengths fit the needs of the company is to use the SET principle. Say what your strength is, give an Example proving it, then Tell them again what your strength is.

If the position requires visionary leadership, show them your strength in this area by using SET.

Say what your strength is - "I feel one of my greatest strengths is providing visionary leadership." But don't stop there, you haven't proven anything. Continue with an Example: "During my senior year I led our forensics team to the state championship, and for the past year I have organized and lead service projects for our youth group to perform." Then tell your strength again, "If this job needs a visionary leader, I guarantee I can do it."

If they hone in on a weakness, like your lack of experience, then discern what they are really trying to say - you'll take too long to train and we need someone who can make an impact soon. Then use the SET method to prove them wrong. "Maybe you feel my lack of experience (or education or whatever) would hinder the impact I could make right away. I am a very fast learner and I can grasp big picture concepts with ease." Then prove it with an Example: "When I first hired on with my current employer they trained me to just do inventory. When two of the sales staff quit on short notice, I volunteered to help out on the floor and in two weeks time, I produced as much as all but their top salesman."

Then tell them your strength again: "There is no question in my mind I could step in and make the impact you *need* (there's that word again). I would come in early and study for as long as it took to become that impact player."

Where the Rubber Meets the Road

Find the needs and fill them with your talents and efforts. Look for needs in problems and ways to add value. Learn the tactics to find work then do good work. Next, we will show you what it takes to become a Right Hand Person.

"WHATEVER YOU DO, WORK AT IT WITH ALL YOUR
HEART, AS WORKING FOR THE LORD, NOT FOR MEN,
SINCE YOU KNOW YOU WILL RECEIVE AN
INHERITANCE FROM THE LORD AS A REWARD."
COLOSSIANS 3:23

"THERE ARE TWO TYPES OF PEOPLE WHO NEVER
ACHIEVE VERY MUCH IN THEIR LIFETIME. ONE IS
THE PERSON WHO WON'T DO WHAT HE OR SHE IS
TOLD TO DO, AND THE OTHER IS THE PERSON WHO
DOES NO MORE THAN HE OR SHE IS TOLD TO DO."
ANDREW CARNEGIE

"DO YOU SEE A MAN SKILLED IN HIS WORK? HE
WILL SERVE BEFORE KINGS; HE WILL NOT SERVE
BEFORE OBSCURE MEN."
KING SOLOMON

BECOMING AN IMPACT PLAYER

We have talked a bit about the importance of becoming a Right Hand Person. We will now share with you the traits you must develop within yourself to get there.

Labels

Like it or not, in the work environment (any environment for that matter), people will tend to label you. When your name comes up, certain traits and characteristics will come to mind. Like any company, you will live, die, prosper and perish by your reputation. When you first hire on to a new place, you must work hard to earn a good label.

Don't let people label you as "always late and leaving early" or "unorganized" or "unreliable." Don't let them brand you with, "she's nice but she talks way too much" or "she's always so crabby" or "she's a whiner." Work hard to have your fellow workers brand with good labels - '"He's the hardest worker on our team" or "If you need something done, ask Steve." If you become a Right Hand Person, the people that matter will give you good labels. The slackers in the company may resent you; love, honor and pray for them anyway. (See chapter on Friends)

Results Oriented

In school you get some credit for trying, In the real world you get credit for one thing - doing. Right Hand People are results oriented. People will not know how long you worked on something, they will only know that you got it done or you didn't. They won't know (or really care) that your boss gave you late notice to get it done and the project fell on the same week as your wife's family reunion. They won't care that you had to stay up until the wee hours of the morning. All they will know is that you came through or you didn't.

Learn to produce results by staying on projects until you have finished them with excellence. Most people underestimate the value of having household chores and school work to accomplish when they are young. God uses small tasks to prove you. He works on this principle - **faithful in little, faithful in much**. (Matthew 25:21, Luke 16:10) If you can sweep the garage and take out the garbage faithfully, God can trust you with larger and more rewarding tasks.

If, however, you can't even organize your school work, how can you expect anyone to pay you to organize a work schedule for 10 employees?

Show up on time. Do your work faithfully, with a smile and a good attitude. If you can handle more responsibility, you can expect more reward. Complete your tasks on time.

Results oriented people are **extra mile people**. They don't look for the bare minimum to do. They look for ways to take it to the next level. If it's due on Wednesday, it's ready by Tuesday. If the standard is 200 pieces per hour, why not set the bar a little higher? If they need you to stay past your scheduled time to help with the dinner rush, do it! Results oriented people look for ways to push the envelope in a positive direction. How much better or faster can I get? They will take the course, read the book or spend more time with the trainer to get better.

Results oriented people take **proprietory initiative**. There is a Biblical principle that states, "Until you can be faithful with someone else's property, how can you be trusted with property of your own?" (Luke 16:12, Genesis 39:2-6). More than likely you will start your working career as the steward of someone else's business. Learn to think like the owner; you may be the owner one day. Look to save money without compromising quality. Look to do things more efficiently; learn to work with and inspire your co-workers. Get the big picture; always try to solve problems and add value. When you run into a problem, seek to solve it. When you bring problems to your boss, bring two or three suggested solutions with you.

My sister worked for a travel agency for four and a half years. She learned the business and managed it faithfully for the owners. Then one day, the owners took her out to dinner and said they were retiring and they wanted to *give her the business!* Her **proprietory initiative** blessed her with proprietory ownership!

Pay your dues; some assignments given to you will challenge you and some will humble you. You may find yourself doing some demeaning task in obscurity for a year before anyone notices. So what? Nobody starts at the top. Memorize Colossians 3:23 and stay faithful! Work at increasing your production and soon you will have greater problems to solve.

Your first step to becoming a Right Hand Person is to become Results oriented. The next step - be Honest.

Honest

In today's society, employers can hardly find honest people. Most theft related losses in business occur from the inside - employees stealing from their employer! With 'values clarification' running rampant through our classrooms, a generation of workers don't realize the difference between *taking* money and *earning* it.

- A third of high school students and sixteen percent of college students said they have shoplifted in the last year. Nearly the same number said they have stolen from their parents or relatives at least once.

- A third of college students said they would lie to get a job. One in six said they have already done so.[1]

Your integrity will be your best friend as you grow. Integrity will guide you and provide you with peace of mind. It will give you boldness and confidence to do good work. Integrity and honesty may cost you something in the short run, but in the long term it will pay you handsomely! (Proverbs 11: 3, 14:11, 19:1, 22:1)

Don't steal from your employer; your taking value, not adding it. Don't lie to get accounts. If your supervisor asks you to lie to or cheat a customer, let him know gently that you cannot do that. If it costs you your job, God has a better one for

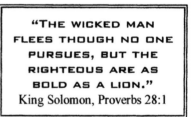

> "THE WICKED MAN FLEES THOUGH NO ONE PURSUES, BUT THE RIGHTEOUS ARE AS BOLD AS A LION."
> King Solomon, Proverbs 28:1

you. Right Hand People are **Honest!** Integrity is not lost all at once. Most people compromise their integrity with small things. Taking stamps, photocopies, long distance phone calls, punching in late and leaving early all compromise integrity.

It's better to be poor and honest, than rich and a cheater. A good name and reputation are better than riches. Keep your integrity; serve your employer with honesty. God sees your every move and motive.

People Skills

Right Hand People possess good **people skills.** Some people are naturally gifted in this area. Some have to work at it. But you will not reach your production potential without the aid of a team. You will not receive the benefit of a team without being on the team. A personality conflict in the initial months of your employment can hinder your advancement. Conflicts are fertile ground for bad labels. Do your best to avoid conflicts but *always* stand your ground on matters of honesty and integrity.

> WHAT DO ENTREPRENEURS LOOK FOR IN THEIR SUMMER INTERNS? NEARLY 50% OF 200 SMALL COMPANIES SURVEYED NAMED RELIABILITY AND HONESTY AS THE MOST IMPORTANT INGREDIENTS.

Work well with your co-workers. Take the advice of Paul the Apostle, "If it is possible, as far as it depends on you, live in peace with all men" (Romans 12:18).

Good people skills involve **good words.** Watch the things you say. Have the Holy Spirit put a guard on your tongue. Some workplaces are notorious for gossip, backbiting and slander. **Don't get involved with the gossip train; don't involve yourself in conversations that run down others.** Let your words build up and edify.

Become known as a person who says things of consequence. Too many people talk too much but they rarely *say* anything! Let your words be fitly spoken (Proverbs 25:11). Don't ramble, when you open your mouth; make it count and contribute to the betterment of the people around you and the company as a whole. You should reduce *quantity* input with *quality* input.

Be friendly - genuinely love and honor those around you. Smile more! Take an interest in what interests your co-workers. Ask about family and future plans; go out of your way to serve them.

Be flexible - learn to work well with all levels of labor and management. Labor is not the enemy, nor is management. You're all on the *same* team with *different* responsibilities and capabilities! Learn to feel comfortable in the king's palace or the king's fields.

Be teachable - nobody likes a know-it-all. Don't let pride or arrogance keep you from learning from the bottom of the company as well as the top. Try to learn something new each week.

Be an influence - use your personality to move those around you toward achieving the company's visions and goals. Understand that everywhere you go, you carry two buckets: one a bucket of gasoline and the other a bucket of water. Whenever you hear someone talking about something good, pour some gas on that conversation. "I agree, I think Tony is a great supervisor." Whenever someone downgrades the company or a person, pour some water on that conversation. "I don't know about that, it seems to be a pain now, but I think the new inventory reduction system will benefit us all in the long run."

Learn the company's vision and goals (proprietory initiative), then use your influence to push toward them.

It doesn't matter if you work with a computer or a machine all day long, you are part of a team - a team made of people, valuable, complex, moody, emotional people. Let love and honor rule your conduct with them. After all, *you're* one of them.

Where are you?

Where do you stand in your journey toward becoming a Right Hand Person? Do you need to become more results oriented? How is your integrity? Could you stand to work on your people skills a bit?

Regularly take time to reflect on where you stand in the process. Find what needs work and work at it. It doesn't matter where you are right now, it matters where you're going. Don't stagnate, move!

Charles Sykes, author of *Dumbing Down our Kids*, gives some sage advice to college and high school graduates just entering the workforce:

Rule 1: Life is not fair, get used to it.

Rule 2: The world won't care about your self-esteem. The world will expect you to accomplish something *before* you feel good about yourself.

Rule 3: If you think your teacher is tough, wait till you get a boss. He doesn't have tenure.

Rule 4: Flipping burgers is not beneath your dignity. Your grandparents had a different word for burger flipping; they called it *opportunity.*

Rule 5: If you mess up, it's not your parents fault, so don't whine about your mistakes. Learn from them.

Rule 6: Before you were born, your parents weren't as boring as they are now. They got that way from paying your bills, cleaning your clothes, and listening to you talk about how cool you are. So before you save the rain forest from the parasites of your parents' generation, try delousing your own room.

Rule 7: Life is not divided into semesters. You don't get summers off, and very few employers are interested in helping you find yourself. Do that on your own time.

Rule 8: Be nice to nerds. Chances are you'll end up working for one. :)

Where are you going? Producing More

The days of staying with the same company forever are over. It used to be that if you got a good job with a good company they employed you for life. Those days are gone. This means you must take control of your own destiny. You must look ahead and prepare for downsizing, layoffs, and mergers. Your skills, talents and reputation (label) are your greatest insurance against long term unemployment. The same techniques that prepare you for job changes also prepare you for advancement.

If you work as a Right Hand Person, your supervisors will notice and they may target you for advancement. They will see you faithful in the small things and they may wish to put you in a place where you could produce more fruit. They notice you solving problems and taking proprietory initiative. They may want to assign you to bigger problems with bigger pay.

If you want to produce more, take your work to the next level and develop an insurance policy against a layoff; *you* need to take control of your future.   Take PRIDE; **Personal Responsibility In Developing Excellence.** Remember the principles of production? Some come into play here.

- **Better tools mean increased production.** Continue to pursue your education. Don't wait for someone to send you to school. Take courses, read books (power read them), learn a new skill - better your personal tools. Can you think of any non-personal tools that would increase your production? I bought a laptop specifically to write this book. I didn't wait for my boss to buy it for me.

- **Harness the power of the team**. Develop your network. Get involved with your community. If your company doesn't do anything, you organize and lead the project.   If your working beneath your potential, one great way to get noticed is to organize and lead something - even if it's the company softball team.   Involve yourself socially with the company. Go to the picnic and the Christmas party.   Get involved in professional associations; what a great way to meet others who do similar work but not for your company. The man you have lunch with during the association meetings may be your next boss. The best way to improve your lot in life is through actions that improve the lot of others.

> "TWO ARE BETTER THAN ONE BECAUSE THEY HAVE GOOD RETURN FOR THEIR WORK."
> ECCLESIASTES 4:9

- **Everything must be worked for**. Set career goals and work towards them, even if your company doesn't have any. Ask for reviews; "Mr. Manager, do you see anything I can improve upon?" Subtly mention any interest you have in another position.

- **Strive for efficiency.** Get your work done as efficiently as possible then look to help others with their work. Learn other departments; fill in other places for lunches and shift changes.

My wife exemplifies all of these principles in her work. She worked part-time from our home for a large insurance company and she won the 'Employee of the Year - Customer Service Champion' award the first year they had it! Because of her results, honesty and people skills, she earned a great wage and incredible flexibility (work until 10:00 A.M. then to the beach!)

A friend of mine started working in the floor covering business when he was a teenager. Dan worked as their top salesman for five years. He made his employer a lot of money over that time. Other people within the industry knew of him and word spread that he was a Right Hand Person.

After five years, the owner of another carpet store wanted to sell his business to him. Because of his loyalty, Dan asked his current employer to make him a 25% partner and he would stay. His boss didn't seem too enthusiastic about the idea so Dan bought the other store.

He paid for the business in one year and in two years Dan went from making $25,000 to $200,000 per year.

As you remain faithful in little things, God desires to bless you with bigger things. If your company refuses to be the channel of that blessing, God will move you to someone who will. Besides, this is America; you can always start your own company and be a Right Hand Person on your own team.

History is full of people who started at the bottom; they worked in mail rooms, as shop boys, janitors and busboys. They learned business from the ground up. They worked hard to became Right Hand People. They began their success where most people left off and stopped trying. They refused to wear a poor label. They made the sacrifices and they traded today's gain for tomorrow's increased productivity. They invested in their talents and worked liked they owned the place - and sooner or later they did.

God's gift to you is your potential; your gift to him is what you do with it. I can't wait to hear how God will bless you as you honor him with your decisions and efforts.

Study Scriptures: Proverbs - 10:4, 10:26, 12:11, 12:24, 14:23, 16:3, 20:4, 27:18, 31:16, Ephesians 6: 5-9, Colossians 3:23-24

1. Charles Sykes, *Dumbing Down our Kids*, St. Martins Griffin, 1995, pg 158 - Charles was quoting a study done by the Josephson Institute for Ethics in 1992

TIME IS OF THE ESSENCE

Have you ever met somebody that had a place for everything and everything in its place? You walk into their room and the dressers are clear, the clothes are put away and they have their schoolwork neatly placed on a desk - they fold their underwear! I am not that kind of person.

I have become organized because I had to, not because I wanted to. Some would tell you that I haven't arrived there yet. I still have a bit to go but I have improved greatly in this area. This was one of my biggest anchors. I haven't made it into a sail but I keep it out of the water most of the time.

I grew up like a lot of kids, not really having to keep track of much. I developed bad habits of procrastination, laziness and I was chronically disorganized. Once I started college, these habits started to catch up to me. I had to change or fail at what I wanted to accomplish. I slowly changed.

Looking back, I see now how much time, talent, and money I wasted by not organizing and planning my life as a young man. I have lost potential that I may never regain. Don't be like me, be better.

Some people take the childish 'natural approach' to personal organization. They take things as they come and do what they feel like doing when they feel like it. It worked when they were kids so why not use it now? They played when they felt like playing with no need to schedule appointments to play with your friends. They had no deadlines. If your tree house or model airplane didn't get finished - no big deal! They didn't even own a calender. If they had a boy-scout meeting or dance recital, Mom or Dad made sure they didn't forget it and that they arrived on time.

As you grow, maturity brings with it responsibility and opportunity. Children *consume* more than they produce. The time comes when we must *produce* more than we consume. Children also are poor artists. Sure they create cute stick people and we ooh and ah over them but nobody would pay $1000 dollars for them. When they paint, they apply it however and wherever they wish - usually a muddy mess results.

As you grow, you get the chance to be the artist of your life. You get to join the ranks of the greatest painters, playwrights and sculptures. More than creating a work of art, you create your life. You will decide if you grow up as a masterpiece or just a piece.

Personal Organization

Bottom line: You need a system of personal organization. The sooner the better. I don't care how you work it, it just needs to work. Take some time and develop a system of organization that works for you. Try different systems; keep what works and scrap the rest. It must be simple enough so that you will use it and it must do three things for you.

- Organize important papers like receipts, transcripts, resumes, tax documents and birth documents.
- Provide a framework for prioritizing, goal setting and self management (time management).
- Provide organization for preserving the value and utility of your possessions.

Filing System

Have you ever needed to find a receipt for something and you couldn't? Have you ever lost homework? Do you know where your tax returns are from the last three years? Every person that lives in America past the age of 16 needs a filing system. You may not need a five drawer filing cabinet, but you need something. Most young, single people can get by with a small filing box purchased at an office supply store. Get one!

File your papers so that you can find what you need in a minute.

Try to handle papers just once. File it or throw it away. Avoid the pack rat syndrome. If you like to keep stuff, keep it in its place. Every year or so go through your files and thin them out.

Things you should have on file:

Birth Certificate	Passport
Tax documents	College transcripts
Financial aid forms	Insurance documents
Receipts	Car titles

Anything else you deem necessary

Time

Time is an unusual quantity. You can't really sense it; you can't touch it, smell it or taste it. Because time is so elusive it's easy to loose track of it.

Time is an equal opportunity resource. It doesn't care about your skin color or your heritage. It doesn't care if you're rich or poor. All of us get 168 hours per week.

Time is a non-renewable resource. Every day God allows us to live, he deposits 86,400 seconds in our bank account. You can't stockpile them or save them; once they are gone, they are gone.

As a child, time seemed to move too slow. We always had too much time. There was too many hours before school was over, too many weeks before summer vacation and too many days before Christmas.

As you mature, you will find time seems to move faster. You will find yourself trying to regain lost or mis-used time. The sooner you start using the most of your time, the fewer regrets you will have when you hit 30, 40, or 50.

The key to managing time is to **manage yourself**. We can't really manage time; it comes and goes without our permission or control. All we can do is manage what *we* do in the time we have. So any personal organization plan must include a framework to guide how you manage yourself, how you prioritize, set and accomplish goals and use the time given to you.

Priorities

Time (self) management is more than carrying around a calender or a Palm Pilot. It starts by **deciding what is important**. What takes priority in your life? Distinguishing between the important and trivial is one of life's greatest dilemmas. For those who discern it correctly, it harbors life's greatest rewards. The key to answering that question, (what is important and what isn't) is to **begin with the end in mind**. Start really living your life by deciding how you want the end to turn out - define your goals.

> TOMORROW BEGINS TODAY, TODAY HAD ITS ROOTS IN YESTERDAY, THE ROOTS OF YESTERDAY DETERMINE TOMORROW'S TREE.

With this in mind, **the best way to do this is by PRAYER** and **STUDY** of the Bible. To define your life backwards you must spend sufficient time with the One who knows ends from beginnings. Let God define the important things in life. One preacher said, "I am so busy I must spend three hours a day in prayer. If I have an especially busy day, I must spend four." God will show you what things are worth your time and which ones aren't. He will give you more time by pointing out unfruitful areas you should prune.

Let him show you what really matters in the end. You will spend about 80 years on this planet, but after you have spend 80 billion years off it, that's just the start. When planning your life - keep eternity in mind. You will spend it in one of two places. You get to choose what you love while here on earth. What you love now will determine what you will get later. Your choice, smoking or non. We have reliable records of a few people that speak from the dead; you would do well to read about them and listen to what they have to say. (Luke 16:19-31, Luke 23 and 24, John 14:1-7.)

Another way you can begin with the end in mind is to **talk to people who are near the end**. Spend time with some older folks and listen to their wisdom. Listen to what they did right and to what they regret. I have made this a habit since about the age of twenty.

I have never heard any of them regret making good use of their time, spending more time with their families, saving more money when they were younger or marrying as virgins. I have heard them say they regret wasting time, not spending enough of it with the people who matter, wasting money, and having sex before marriage. Listen to the wisdom in their words.

As you begin with the end in mind, divide your life into sections and prayerfully determine what goals you would like to accomplish. To the best of your knowledge right now, establish what you would like to accomplish in five to ten years. Then establish what you would like to accomplish this year, then this month, this week and this day.

You can divide your goals into life categories.

- What I would like to accomplish on a **spiritual level**. These goals may include time spent in prayer and study, a number of scriptures memorized, mission trips, church ministries and so on.

- What I would like to accomplish on a **personal level**. These goals may include getting married, having children, learning to play the guitar, competing in the Ironman Triathlon, getting out of debt or like me, learning to surf!

- What I would like to accomplish on an academic or **professional level**. These could include finishing a degree, starting a business, reaching a sales goal, making a million dollars or finally getting your dream job.

Your long term vision determines your short term decisions.
Your life is just an accumulation of choices. If you consistently make choices that take you away from the direction of your God-given vision you will never get there! At the end of each day, you should prayerfully examine if the

> THOSE WHO DO NOT CREATE THE FUTURE THEY WANT, MUST ENDURE THE FUTURE THEY GET.

choices you made took you towards your goals or away; make adjustments accordingly.

Take your plan to the next step by establishing a system where you **write it down** on a calender to get the big picture (yearly and monthly). Then establish a 'to do' list to keep track of the daily and weekly items that you must do.

It took me about two years to establish a plan that works for me. I have three calenders and a daily list: one small one that I carry with me that shows me two years in advance and month to month, a monthly calender on my desk and a family calender on which we put everything we do in order to avoid scheduling conflicts. I found that no matter what system I had, if I couldn't carry it in my back pocket, I wouldn't use it. If I didn't use it, even the greatest system failed.

Some friends of mine have gone digital with their Palm Pilots; they are small and can hold a ton of information. Go to an office supply store and look at all the calenders and systems. Get what works for you. If you try a system and it doesn't work, keep trying. You must **write it down!**

Establishing a calender establishes a plan. If you fail to plan, you plan to fail.

I wish I could tell you how many missed opportunities the kids I work with have experienced because they didn't have a written plan that they looked to frequently. They still relied on Mom and Dad to remind them over and over. That won't work any longer! They come in for tutoring and they don't even know when the assignment is due! They miss deadlines, have scheduling conflicts, turn in late and poorly done assignments and waste precious time because they have no written plan.

Soon the people around them label them as unreliable and poorly organized.

Simple Strategies for Planning

Try these time tested strategies:

- Want a recipe for academic success? Plan two hours of study time per one hour in class.

- As soon as you know about a project or term paper, make a project calender. Put it on a large calender, piece of paper or dry erase board on a blank wall. Break down the project into parts and schedule a time to work on each part. Assign a deadline for the completion of each part as well as the final project. The parts could break down like this:

Finalize topic	Check spelling and proofread
Initial library research (collect)	Get someone else to proofread
Prepare outline (categorize)	Type final draft (one week early)
Detailed library research	Proofread again
Write first draft (communicate)	Turn it in (three days early)

  You will continue to use project calenders as long as you live. I used one to write this book. It lets me know if I am behind or ahead of schedule.

- Schedule time for fun. Planning your life frees you to enjoy it. You don't have to worry that you should be doing something else. Some people see a plan as constricting; instead, it frees you. Remember, discipline brings freedom.

- Plan for the unplanned. Allow time for life to happen. Don't run such a tight schedule that when you get a flat tire, an unexpected phone call or a run in your panty hose that you miss your deadline. In the real world, cars break down, children get sick, and banks and the post office close for the most insignificant of holidays. Leave room for life to happen; plan to get it done early. If you always plan to finish at the last minute because 'you work better under pressure,' it will catch up to you sooner or later. It may be on a project that will determine a final grade or worse yet, a pay raise.

Getting More Out of a Day

  Ever wish you had more hours in a day? Follow these strategies and watch the hours come out of nowhere.

- Wake up! Stop bragging about how you slept in until 1 p.m. and get up and do something. Most people need about 7-9 hours of sleep.

- Do difficult or boring tasks first. Get them out of the way. Psyche yourself up for them and attack them early in the day.

- Prioritize what needs to be done today. Go through your list and label your responsibilities A, B, or C. A= must get done today, B = should get done today, C = could do today. Do the most important ones first. You can make this list just before bed and it will clear your head for better sleep.

- Find out how long it takes you to do routine tasks, then compete with yourself to do them faster without compromising excellence. How long does it take you to make your bed or get ready for the day? You can add minutes to each day by working faster.

- Use "nothing times" to do something. Often we have times where we wait in line, travel to and from work or school or wait for water to boil. Find ways to use this time. Use 3x5 cards to help you study, pray for five minutes or read something from the Bible.

- Catch the time stealers - T.V., video games, phone calls and procrastination. Most kids growing up today will spend over fourteen years of their life in front of a T.V., computer or movie screen. Phone calls can take an hour from you without you noticing. Tell them you'll call them back, unplug your phone or use dead silence; it kills conversations. I usually pick a dead spot in the conversation and say something like, "Well, thanks for calling, I'll see you later." If you want to watch a show or play a video game, schedule it in and then stick to it. When the show ends or your allotted time runs out, **shut it off!**

- The number one word in time management is: **no.** Many people over-commit themselves because they hate to say no. The more results oriented you become the more people will ask you to do things. Make a commitment to praying over any new time commitment. If you don't like to say no, then do like I do, say, "Yes, I would love to, but I have previous commitments."

Protecting your Assets

A personal organization system should give you the framework to protect and find the things you own. When you're young, you accumulate things through the generosity of other people. If you take care of them, you won't have to buy them when your older. Too many people allow their possessions to deteriorate because they don't take care of them or they lose them through carelessness. Your system of organization should include a place to put your sports equipment, outdoor gear, hobby supplies and music gear.

Find a place and a container for your stuff. Go and buy some containers if you don't have any. Use your habit forming nature to your advantage; put your things in the same place every time. I used to lose my keys quite often. I would waste about thirty minutes a week looking for them. I solved the problem by buying little hooks that I placed by the door. As soon as I walk in the door, I hang the keys on the hooks. I've had no problem since then.

Killing the Killer

Procrastination kills. It kills projects, mission trips, relationships and productivity. Don't let procrastination get a hold of your life. The procrastinators favorite hiding place is 'someday isle.' They always think, "Someday I'll do this or that." Procrastination has its roots in fear, lies and laziness.

Some people procrastinate because they fear they will fail or not attain perfection. Perfectionists are great procrastinators.

> THE BEST TIME TO START STUDYING FOR FINALS IS THE WEEK AFTER THE SEMESTER STARTS.

Some people think they will have more time later. No, you won't!

Time is passing by right now. You won't have more time to finish it, you will have less.

Some underestimate how long projects will take. When I estimate how long a project will take, I give it my best guess and then double it to allow for things to go wrong and unplanned problems to appear as they most certainly will.

Some people mistakenly believe that they must 'feel like' doing a project before they will start it. Actually, if you start a project, you will feel like doing it.

How I Beat Procrastination

Procrastination used to have a tight hold on my life. Sometimes it still rears its ugly head. I realized a number of things and took some concrete steps to over come it.

First, as I grew I kept getting burned by procrastination. Procrastination stole from me lots of money through lost financial aid, lost work, late fees and poor last minute decisions. It also took from me opportunities to do some really cool things and get better grades due to missed deadlines and poor last minute work. I hate getting ripped off. Once I realized that procrastination stole from me rather than gave to me I made up my mind to kill it.

I took some time and mental effort to realize why I did it. For me, I did it because I was lazy. I rationalized why I could do what I wanted and still get the project done and sometimes I feared rejection and failure.

I saw my laziness for what it was: sinful. I began to overcome it like any other sin. Since lies are the basis for every sin, I learned and memorized the truth. I found scriptures that spoke the truth about the battles going on in my mind and memorized them. Whenever my flesh wanted to be lazy, the scripture would come to my mind and I would act on it instead of the lie.

I learned that discipline brings freedom. I forced myself to get ahead of projects and I became addicted to the freedom and reward accomplishment brings. The thought of the reward of accomplishment began to win over the temporary satisfaction of procrastination.

I learned that when you start a project, even when you don't feel like it, the feelings will follow.

I learned physics; an object at rest tends to stay at rest and an object in motion tends to stay in motion. When I started a project I created **a positive momentum**. It then became easier to keep going rather than stop. The trick is to just start! **I prayed and asked God for more courage.**

As I grew older, I realized three things: **that life happens, that you will never have more time than you do this second and that it takes me longer to do good work than I thought.** Procrastination forced me to run projects right to the edge of available time. When unforseen things happened, I lost out or turned in poor work. Proverbs says, "A prudent man sees trouble ahead and prepares for it, but the simple keep going and suffer for it" (22:3).

Where the Rubber Meets the Road

If I want to get the most out of life, I need to manage myself to maximize my potential. To do that I need to get organized and work more efficiently. You are no different. Don't let a childish outlook on life rob you of your maximized potential. Pursue the best, and you will not regret it!

MONEY

Have you ever played games in your head with money? I used to sit with catalogues and dream I could spend a thousand dollars at the store. I would go through books and pick out everything I wanted. Have you ever planned out what you would do if you won the lottery? What if I explained how you could become a millionaire; would you read on? Well, read on.

Does money interest you? Do you wish you had more? God cares about money, not because he worries about it or wishes he had more but because he cares about us. He knows that money matters to us so money matters to him. Just like every other important area of life he has given us some eternal financial principles to help us live life to the fullest.

God uses money to demonstrate his faithfulness, stimulate your prayer life, cultivate your self control, clarify your values, provide for you and give you opportunities to bless others and further his kingdom.

Money matters to most people. But most people don't understand the principles behind sound money management, so money (or lack of it) holds them in bondage. As of this writing, America rides high on the longest period of economic growth in its history - yet bankruptcies are at all time highs. While the middle class shrinks, the rich get richer and the poor get poorer. During America's economic boom, the top five percent of earners gained an average of $50,760 per family while the bottom twenty percent gained only an average of $100 per family.[1]

The richest 225 people in the world have a net worth that equals the annual income of the poorest 2.5 billion people in the world. Don't get me wrong; I am not for taking money from the rich and giving it to the poor. I'm for teaching people how to work with their talents and manage their money using sound wisdom.

The number one cause of poverty in America is teenage pregnancy. The number one cause of poverty around the world is war. Speaking economically, the long term cause of poverty is ignorance, laziness and lack of opportunity. In America, no one should be impoverished because we have a free education system, and no lack of opportunity if you're willing to make some tradeoff's (ie: move, go back to school). If you're lazy, you deserve to live lowly.

Poverty is not the only symptom of financial bondage. Many more suffer from overdue bills, worry, debt, greed, covetousness, dishonesty and self - indulgence.

Money Myths

Do you remember losing your baby teeth then sticking them under your pillow? How much did you get? I used to get a quarter. I used to yank the loose ones out a little prematurely so the tooth fairy could pay me a visit. Later, I realized my parents actually gave me the money! Not to burst your bubble but there really is no tooth fairy. It's a myth. That's just one of a few money myths we will dispel.

Myth: **That money stuff doesn't matter until I'm older**.
Fact: **That money stuff does matter.** By the time the average person in America reaches 20 years old, they will have received over $33,000 in income and gifts.[2] Ask the average 20 year old to tell you what they did with it. The younger a person learns the principles of sound money management the better.

Myth: **I don't have enough money to worry about it.**
Fact: **American young people have more money than ever.** They spend $108 billion dollars yearly: $36.7 billion on clothing, $23.4 billion on entertainment, $6.7 billion on sporting goods. The average teenager spends $68 per week.[3] Take care of the

pennies and the dollars will take care of themselves.

Myth: **It's my money**
Fact: **It's God's money.** He owns it all. (Psalms 24:1) He even owns you. (I Corinthians 6:20) He chooses to let you manage some of his resources while you tread this planet and he will hold you accountable for your stewardship. (Luke 12:48, 16:2 Romans 14:12, Matthew 12:36, 25:14-30)

Myth: **I don't need to know about money, it will take care of itself.**
Fact: **Your ignorance about money is making other people rich and keeping you from living life to the fullest.** Young people have a lot of spending power but they lack the knowledge to use it wisely. Forty percent of teenagers do not know that you pay interest on a loan. Twenty-eight percent of 12-year-olds did not know that credit cards are a form of borrowing. So pay attention and put God's principles of money management to work.

Money problems are like a raging case of herpes. Herpes has symptoms like burning blisters and irritating cold sores. But the symptoms come from an underlying problem - a virus. And the virus came from an underlying choice - to have sex with an infected partner. Just as cold sores and blisters show up because of a virus, all money difficulties are symptoms of greater underlying problems. If you treat the symptoms, the problems will not go away - they may hide for a while - but they will come back because you did nothing to eliminate the root problem. Here are some typical root issues:

> "YOU DO NOT HAVE BECAUSE YOU DO NOT ASK GOD. WHEN YOU ASK, YOU DO NOT RECEIVE BECAUSE YOU ASK WITH WRONG MOTIVES THAT YOU MAY SPEND WHAT YOU GET ON YOUR PLEASURES."
> James 4:3

- **Get-me-itis** - a desire to own more and more stuff. This disease has its roots in 'me.' One must crucify pride and the approval of men in order to conquer this disease. Symptoms include - impulse buying, credit card balances, jammed closets and garages.

- **Ungratefulness** - not thankful or content for what you have. (See chapter on Attitude) This condition is marked by cases of depression, whining, griping and complaining because you don't have _____. Also, it may include large amounts of debt owed on assets that are going down in value. Contentment, contrary to popular opinion, is not being satisfied with where you are. It is knowing God's plan for your life, having the conviction to live it, and believing that God's peace is greater than the world's problems.

- **Greed and Selfishness** - putting yourself and possessions above God and others. Symptoms include not paying God his tithes, rarely giving to missions or other causes, spending on himself, gambles with God's money including lottery or speculative investments, getting caught in "get rich quick" schemes.

- **Impatience and Faithlessness** - not willing to wait on God's timing, will often move ahead of God with borrowed money. Symptoms include impulse buying, heavy debt load, and not believing God can provide what they need.

Money Management Made Easy

Money management is *not* complicated. People sometimes make it complicated but they don't have to. Here it is; money management made easy in one sentence. Blow the horns and sound the trumpets!

Income must meet or exceed expenses. Simple. The hard part is planning for expenses and having the discipline to carry out your plan.

The second principle of money management is that there are only two ways to manage a deficit: **increase income or cut expenses. You will always find it easier to trim expenses than to increase income**.

There are only eight legal things you can do with money - receive it as a gift, earn it, borrow it, give it, lend it, spend it, save it and invest it. Breaking this down into two groups; ways you can get money: gift, earn it, borrow it; and ways you can use it: give it, lend it, spend it, save it and invest it. Your financial freedom depends on how you balance these eight things. Like all balancing acts, they become easier when you have a plan.

Just before I turned five, my parents took us to Florida. I remember walking on the beach in front of our rented cottage. I met a nice older man and we started walking down the beach together looking at seashells without my parents noticing. I didn't care. I just walked and talked, walked and talked. After a while, I looked up and the man was gone. Nothing looked familiar to me. I was lost. I had no way of getting back. Some nice people took care of me until my parents found me.

People manage money much the same way. As they grow up, money takes care of itself; they have food, clothes, allowances, jobs, and birthdays. Then they start to walk on their own down the beach of life and everything goes well for a while but they look up and they're lost. They have mounds of credit card debt, a car payment, a mortgage and student loans. Many file bankruptcy, default on their bills, and suffer serious trauma and depression because they failed to plan. When you fail to plan, you really plan to fail. Without a vision, the people perish.

Allow me to help you find your way out or to keep you from getting lost in the first place.

Your Plan

Where are you going? Do you want to go to college? Do you want to own a nice car or house? Do you want to be a millionaire and give it to needy charities?

Whatever you do, your future will require a lot of money. Our culture has made the transition into adulthood very expensive. You will need money for cars, rent and living expenses, college, a house, a wedding and on and on. When you graduate from high school, you could easily need $5000 for a car and $10,000 for your first year of school. Where will you get this money? **Because most people fail to plan on these expenses**, they live off borrowed money. As we will learn, borrowed money will *cost* you hundreds of thousands of dollars over your lifetime if you fail to plan. If you plan for, and avoid it, you will gain hundreds of thousands of dollars over the course of your lifetime. (This is no exaggeration, as you will see)

A large part of maturing is seeing past the end of your nose. You must think beyond your next meal into next year or better yet, into the next 10.

Just like any plan, you must begin with the end in mind then work toward the goal day by day. Every financial plan should at least include these basic goals:

- Know where your money goes. Track every penny for at least two months. This may seem like a pain but it will reveal a lot *to* you and a lot *about* you.
- Establish a habit of tithing and giving.
- Get out of debt. Pay off the highest interest loans first. We will discuss the villainies of debt later.
- Build a cash surplus for near term needs and wants such as a car, car repairs, clothes, food, education, housing. (Saving)
- Put your money to work. (Investing)

Once you establish your plan - follow it! Create a map toward financial freedom then have the discipline to follow it.

Your plan will tell the world and God a lot about you. We really could call money management - self management. Because how you handle your money tells us more about you than anything else. It tells us if you're selfish or cooperative, if you're prideful or humble, if you have self control or if you're impulsive. It lets us know if you trust God or not, if you're greedy or generous and if you're organized. It points to everything you consider important. Where your heart is, your treasures will be also. (Matthew 6:19-24)

Putting the Plan Into Action

Let's say you earn $100 per week for simplicity. You have five categories to choose from - give it, lend it, spend it, save it or invest it. When you receive your pay, divide up your money into the different categories by percentages according to your plan.

Your current priorities, goals and life circumstances will dictate how you divide up your money. (Your current life circumstances for the most part are dictated by your past life choices.) If you live at home, you will not have to allocate money for housing, food, laundry and so on (unless your parents ask for rent). If you need to pay phone bills, electric bills, car payments and others you will need to include that in your plan.

The best time to get ahead for your future is when you still live at home. You can make some good cash with part-time jobs or businesses (babysitting or lawn-mowing) but a large percentage of your money is not already spoken for.

Let's go through the eight things you can do with money and expound on each. This will help you formulate and follow your plan.

Tithing & Giving

God established a financial principle for his people called the tithe. It means for every dollar you earn or receive, you give back to God his dime. Not after you pay for taxes, rent, food, phone bill, and flea dip - but off the top. (Proverbs 3:9-10) Simple, every dollar God let's you have, you give God back a dime - the dime is his, not yours. He really gives you ninety cents and he give you the extra dime to see if you will rob him or thank him for the ninety cents and trust him so that he may bless you. (Malachi 3:8-12)

God's Word describes the tithe as a testimony to God's ownership. The amount of the tithe (it literally means a 'tenth part') is not for God's benefit because he owns it all. It is for *our* benefit.

For a dime out of every dollar tithing keeps our greed in check, promotes personal discipline, testifies to God's ownership and to our faith in him, promotes God's work in the world and alleviates human need. It also opens the windows of heaven above our homes to provides a channel through which God can bless us. (Genesis 14:20, Leviticus 27:30, Luke 11:42, I Corinthians 16:2)

God never lies. In a society driven by deceit, it's hard to realize that under no circumstance will God lie. With that in mind, he gives us these promises to those who give above and beyond their tithe. (I don't consider tithing giving because it is not ours to give; giving means above and beyond our tithe, what the Bible calls - offerings.)

"Give and it shall be given to you. A good measure, pressed down, shaken together and running over, will be poured out into your lap. For with the measure you use, it will be measured to you" (Luke 6:38).

"Whoever sows sparingly will also reap sparingly, and whoever sows generously will also reap generously. Each man should give what he has decided in his heart to give, not reluctantly or under compulsion, for God loves a cheerful giver. And God is able to make all grace abound to you, so that in all things at all times, having all that you need, you will abound in every good work" (II Corinthians 9:6-8).

Some people really have a hard time giving back to God his tithe and giving offerings. Some have said that a man must go through two conversions, one for his heart and another for his wallet. Money has become an idol in their lives. They have lost a true picture of reality. They don't see God as the owner of it all and the ultimate provider of everything; they see him as a taker - when in reality, *they* are the thief.

> "NO MAN CAN SERVE TWO MASTERS. EITHER HE WILL HATE THE ONE AND LOVE THE OTHER, OR HE WILL BE DEVOTED TO THE ONE AND DESPISE THE OTHER. YOU CANNOT SERVE BOTH GOD AND MONEY."
> Jesus Christ, Luke 16:13

The Bible records the fate of a few people who placed material wealth over true riches. You would do well to learn from their examples. (Luke 12:13-21, 16:19-31, 18:18-30)

So in your financial plan, take out 10% ($10 dollars in our example) to give back to God his tithe, then you decide in your heart what percentage to give above and beyond that. For the most part, I think your tithe should go to your local church body. I believe there are exceptions to that rule that you can discern with prayer and study. Your offerings come with a little more autonomy. Give when and where God leads you to give. He may lead you by making a need known to you or by an impression on your heart to give or you may have a dream or a vision or whatever; just be obedient to God.

One word of caution: Don't let your sensitivity before God turn into gullibility. Generous people can fall for many schemes. If it seems to good to be true, it is. Use discernment; when in doubt, get counsel from a respected, mature brother or sister.

Interesting Interest

Before we move on to the other categories it is essential that you learn about interest. If someone would have told me what I'm about to tell you when I was 13, I would be independently wealthy right now; so listen up.

Interest can work for you or against you. You can receive it or pay it. You receive it when you save or invest; you pay it when you borrow.

Let's say you help a little old lady across the street one day and she smiles, thanks you and says, "Your such a nice boy. Here, please take this $10,000 as a token of my appreciation." Then she hands you $10,000 in cash. When you regain consciousness, you run to the bank and open an account. You deposit it into an account at 6% annual percentage rate (APR), *compounded monthly*. The bank keeps your money and your off to tell your friends (they will now want you to buy lunch, *for the next year)*.

On the first day of the next month the bank's computer multiplies your money by .005. Why that number? It's 1/12 of 6% - one month's worth of your interest rate. When the computer multiplies your 10 grand by .005 it shows that the bank owes you $50 in interest for the first month. They apply it to your account; you now have $10,050. Lucky you.

The banks computer does this again next month. It now multiplies your $10,050 by .005 and adds $50.25. The extra .25 cents came from multiplying your original money with what interest you earned last month ($50); we call that *compounding*.   At the end of the year, you will have $10,616.78. Your money earned you 616.78 in interest. You must learn the magic of compounding. This is how the rich get richer.

Compound interest works best **over time**. In 10 years your $10,616.78 would equal $19,320. In 20 years, it would equal $35,158 and in 30 years it would be $63,980!

The interest *rate* also determines how much money you make (we call this your *rate of return*). When you're receiving interest, you want a high rate; when you're paying interest, you want a low rate. Figure one shows how different interest rates affect the growth of $1000 over time. One thousand dollars over 30 years at 3.7% would earn you $2,974. At 5.1% over the same time, your thousand dollars would earn you $4,447, while if you could earn 10.7% or 12.6% on your money you would have $21,107 or $35,168 in 30 years, respectively. I'll tell you why I picked those rates later.

If you borrow money, the bank charges you to use that money. They charge you a certain percentage depending on the type of loan. In this case, interest costs you money instead of making you money. It can cost you a lot of money over time. We will show you in the section on borrowing.

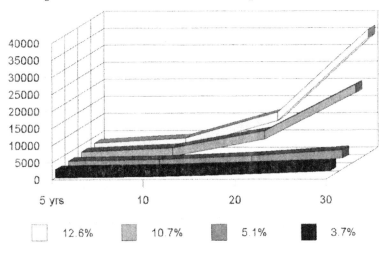

Fig. 1: Different Rates of Interest Working on $1000 Over Time

1. Center on Budget and Policy Priorities, Economic Policy Institute 1998

2. ABCNEWS.com, *Cash Course for Teens.*

3. Teenage Research Unlimited

MO' MONEY

Oseola McCarty dropped out of school in the sixth grade to help care for a sick aunt. She made her living by doing other people's laundry. She never made over minimum wage. She had to work around the maze of racial prejudices in the South, given that she was a Black American. She stunned the world when at age 87 she made a gift of $150,000 to the University of Southern Mississippi. When she made her gift, she had almost $250,000 in the bank - two and a half times the average net worth of American retirees, most of whom probably earned several times more than what she did.

How did she do it? In this chapter I will show you that including giving, the secret to building wealth rests in how you handle borrowing, saving and investing.

Borrowing: Debt is a Four Letter Word.

Many people pay for their expenses the American way; they get loans! It's hard to believe a generation ago people rarely borrowed for a car, to go to school or to get a new outfit. Now many couples find themselves thousands of dollars into debt only a few years into marriage. Most people fail to realize - perhaps because they are scared to know - how much money they throw out the window in interest on their loans.

When you borrow money, the lender charges you a fee for giving you the money. I am going to share with you the naked truth about paying interest. We will look at four common loans: home mortgages, car loans, student loans, and credit cards.

Let's say you get married and buy a house. Now you really can't afford a house but you've wanted one so you finance almost all of it with a hundred thousand dollar loan. The bank gives you an interest rate of 10% over 30 years. If you make the payment every month, you will pay **$215,929** in interest over the life of the loan! So you will pay a whopping $315,929 for your $100,000 house. Can you think of anything you could do with $215,929?

Most people cannot afford to pay cash for a house; they can, however, refuse to pay the entire amount of interest. To save yourself money on interest, you should pay more than the minimum payment which would also pay it off early. On your house, you would pay $877 per month (not including taxes and insurance). If you made just one extra payment per year instead of paying the full amount you would save $79,111 in interest and pay it off nine years early! You would, however, still pay $136,818 in interest. If you paid just $100 per month extra you would save $90,511 and pay it off 11 years early.

You just graduated from college and you want to reward yourself with that nice new car. You really can't afford that nice new car but you can afford the payments of only $290 a month for five years, so you buy it. If the car cost $15,000 with an interest rate of only six percent you would really pay $17,399 for your car - $2,399 in interest. If you paid an extra $35 dollars per month you would save $303 in interest and pay it off seven months early.

Just before your senior year in college, you run plumb out of cash. You take out a $5000 student loan to get you through. Once you graduate, the loan comes due at eight percent for 10 years. At the end of 10 years, you actually paid back $7,279 and as usual, if you paid more than the monthly payment, you would pay it off sooner and save money in interest.

Finally, your out of school and you get a pretty good job. You get an apartment but you need some furnishings. You buy some with your newly minted credit card. One week later, your car needs new brakes. You really don't have enough in your savings to cover it, so you charge it. Over time, you find you have run up about $2500 on your credit card. No problem, with your new job you can easily make the minimum payment of $65 per month. Providing you don't buy anything else with your credit card and you make the minimum payment, it would take you almost five years to pay it off and you would pay an extra $1,255 for the use of that money.

People often borrow money for the same predictable reasons: a house, car, school, impulse buys and unexpected expenses. As you will see, a good savings plan could conceivably keep you from borrowing for anything. If your thinking about borrowing money, keep in mind the total cost of borrowing. If you don't borrow, the interest becomes yours!

Some people make the distinction between *good* debt and *bad* debt. I prefer to call it *bad* debt and *really bad* debt. Bad debt is borrowing to buy something that doesn't go down in value (depreciate). Money managers place your house and your education in this category. Most houses hold their value or even go up in value and education makes you more productive. Really bad debt is borrowing to buy something that depreciates. If you wish to make the most out of your finances, *never* borrow money to buy something that depreciates - cars, electronics, music, clothes, furniture and so on. It's much better to save and pay cash for these things; better to earn interest than to pay interest.

If you have debt, make one of your financial goals to pay it off. Start with the highest interest rate first (usually your credit cards) then work your way down. Pay extra on your monthly payment and they will fade away more quickly. Some money managers recommend that you start paying off the smallest debt first and then work your way up the food chain. This gives you a certain momentum as you pay each one off. You also see results faster when you pay each one off.

Saving

In order for you to avoid debt, you must make saving an integral part of your financial strategy. Your savings plan should build up a one to three month cash surplus. Most people fail in their financial plan because they fail to build a simple surplus of cash. Whenever they get money, they spend it. When they need money, they borrow it. Their financial life begins in the hole because they failed to save. Pay yourself first, not the banker!

Plan for your future expenses and save for them. If you know you will need a car in two years, start saving. If you know you will start college next year, save. Plan for things to go wrong. Your car will need fixing, your pet will need de-worming and your clarinet will need new pads before your next concert. Saving requires you get a vision for the future and save accordingly. Read Genesis chapter 41.

One of the smartest financial moves I ever made was to open another savings account just for our cars. After Kim and I payed off both of our cars, we kept making a car payment - to ourselves. Every month we put in $300 towards our next car or the upkeep of our current ones. Whenever one of our cars needed some maintenance, we just pulled it from our car account. Over time, we built up enough money to pay large down-payments for our cars. We payed off our loans early and kept paying ourselves the $300 per month. In four years, we built up enough money to pay cash for our next vehicle. Now we would never get a loan to buy a car. We don't drive Ferrari's, but we have nice cars and we don't pay the thousands of dollars in interest for a loan. Instead, we earn the interest and use it for other things. We are living proof that you don't have to have a car payment! You can do it, even on a modest income.

The keys to building a cash surplus are **planning ahead and delaying your gratification. Remember - less now for more later**.

My wife and I could live in a larger house, drive nicer cars, wear nicer clothes, have more toys than we do right now. We don't for two reasons. First, I don't believe Christians should live to the edge of their means. This enables us to give more. As we give, God's kingdom increases and he blesses us.

Secondly, we decided to make the tradeoff - less now for more later. We don't want to owe on a house, a car and a boat when we get older. We want to gain financial independence, and we will. By delaying our gratification, we enable our money to work *for* us not *against* us. Over time, our money increases to the point where we could buy whatever we want, as we will show you in the investing section.

Before we move on, I want to let you know that banks have a few different vehicles to help you with your savings goals.

Savings Accounts give you access to your money at any time but they give you a pitiful return - usually less than two percent. Only hiding the money in your mattress will give you a worse return. This interest rate will barely keep you even with inflation. In fact, over time, you will *lose* money in a savings account because of inflation. On the positive side, the federal government guarantees your money will be there no matter what - so you take no risk.

Money Market Accounts act just like savings accounts except they give you better interest rates - usually between five and six percent. The government guarantees the money so you take no risk but the bank usually requires a minimum amount to open a money market account - usually around one to five thousand dollars.

Certificates of Deposits give you an even greater rate of return - between six and seven percent. They require a minimum amount (usually $500) and they make you give the bank access to that money for a specified period of time. You can't withdraw it before it matures or else you pay a hefty penalty. CD's have no risk other than you may need the money before they mature.

The interest rates on all these will vary slightly with economic fluctuations too complicated to discuss here. Pay attention in economics class!

Investing

Wise people save primarily for short term spending. If you plan on needing the money for the car, the school, the wedding or retirement within *one day to four years,* keep it in some type of guaranteed savings vehicle (savings account, money market or CD). Remember to always have some cash available for emergencies. Once you have those bases covered, and you have payed off your debts, (at least your *really bad* debts), you are now in a position to take a few risks for potentially greater rewards. You're ready to put your money to work for the long term - *five to one hundred years.*

Investing is not just for those people who actually *read* the Wall Street Journal. **You** can and should learn about it just like anyone else. If you plan on living financially free, you must either win the lottery, get a huge inheritance or learn how to put your money to work. Most of us do the latter.

Like any subject, investing works on simple principles that can get more complicated depending on how much you desire to learn. I will tell you about the basics and will trust you to learn more from other sources as your hunger develops.

The first principle is this: **For increased return, one must take greater risks.** Because you will not need your investment money for at least five years, you can afford to take more risk with it. You need to decide how much risk is enough for you. No amount of money is worth losing your peace of mind. The realm of investing offers plenty of products that will enable you to gain a healthy return without taking too much risk. All you need to do is learn how the investment vehicles work and decide how much money you desire to invest. We will discuss the three most common - stocks, bonds and mutual funds. Think of them as cars. They all have different characteristics; you pick the one that suits you.

Stocks. When you own a share of stock, you actually own a part of the company. If the company does well, the stock price usually goes up over time. Then you can sell it for a *capital gain.* If the company has healthy profits, they may distribute a portion of them to all the shareholders in *dividends.* Those are the two main ways of making money with stocks.

Whenever you buy or sell a stock, you must go through a broker who charges you a commission for his work. Commissions range from $5 online to over $40 (depending on how much you buy) for a full service broker (he gives you advice). As a rule, small investments in stocks are expensive. Buying a single stock is also risky. If you tie up all your investment money in one company and the value of the stock goes down, the value of your investment goes down. You do not lose the money, however, unless you sell the stock lower than when you bought it. Stock mutual funds give you good returns and automatic diversification. **Diversification** is when you divide up your money to protect it from a down time in any one company or section of the economy.

Money managers advise not having over 4 - 14% of your money in any one stock or sector (like retail, technology, auto).

Bonds. Bonds are loans to companies and governments. When you buy bonds, you become the lender. With most bonds, you lend the issuer money for a certain amount of time - up to 30 years. They send you the interest every year. Some bonds don't pay you every year; they wait until the term expires and then pay you your interest and principle at the end of the term.

Bonds are a lower risk than stocks so they give you a lower return. Bonds are good for people who need to earn a regular income from their investments.

Mutual Funds. Mutual funds are like a club for your money. People get together and pool their money together into a fund. Then they pay a professional money manager a percentage of their money to buy stocks and/or bonds for them.

Mutual funds are probably the best investment for young people. They do a number of good things for you. First, they give you automatic diversification without needing a boatload of cash. For your thousand dollars you may own a part of over 300 companies.

Secondly, they don't require you to become a Wall Street guru. You pay a professional to worry about what stocks to buy and when to sell them. You can even buy funds that just buy the stocks in certain indexes like the S&P 500 or the NASDAQ. (An index is formed by people who take certain companies and group them together for easier tracking purposes. The S&P 500 are America's largest 500 companies, the Dow is an index made up of only 30 large companies like General Motors and WalMart) These funds don't have managers and they charge lower fees - we call these index funds and they are great investments.

Thirdly, they allow you to begin investing with small amounts. You can buy into some mutual funds with as little as $100, although most require a minimum of over $1000.

Investing for Returns

Deciding where to invest your money can seem daunting. History gives us some good information to help guide you.

Since 1925...

        stocks in small companies returned 12.6%

        stocks in larger companies returned 10.7%

        long terms government bonds returned 5.1%

As you can see, stocks have provided the best returns over time. Smaller companies have better growth potential but they tend to go up and down more. Larger companies like WalMart, IBM and General Electric don't fluctuate as much but they have smaller upside potential.

If you want to save up a large chunk of change, here's what I would do. I would save up a cash surplus for my short term needs and emergencies. Then I would save another thousand dollars. As I saved I would begin my research into what fund I wanted to buy into. Morningstar is a company that researches and rates the thousands of mutual funds out there. They give

> **MARRIED MEN CAN'T UNDERSTAND WHY EVERY BACHELOR ISN'T A MILLIONAIRE.**

each a 'star rating' much like movie critics. You can do your own research on the web or buy magazines like *Money* or *Smart Money*. Funds belong to different families. These families are really companies that make money managing the money of others. Some of the more popular families include Fidelity and Vanguard. You can find them both on the net.

You could buy a fund that buys large companies, small companies, bonds or a mix of all of them. You can also buy sector funds that just invest in one sector like the internet or new technology. Each fund has a written description called a prospectus. The prospectus tells you the fund's investment strategy.

Once I picked my fund, I would send them my money. Then I would send them a certain amount each month. Money managers call this **dollar cost averaging.** No matter what the economy or stock market does, you send in your money. Over time, you ride out the lows and the highs without trying to time ups and downs. Let me show you how your money would grow over time.

Figure one below shows your return if you invested your initial $1000 and then just $28 (about a dollar a day) for up to 40 years. Assuming historical returns, after 10 years, you would have $10,174 had you invested in smaller companies, $8,872 if you had invested in larger companies and $6,034 had you invested in bonds. Now watch the magic. If you continue investing a dollar per day, after 30 years (assuming historical returns) you would have $154,857 if you put your money in smaller companies, $98,000 if in larger and $28,330 if in bonds. The longer you keep your money invested the more you will have. After 40 years you would have $549,034, $290,328 or $51,517.

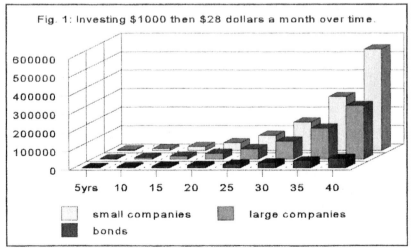

Fig. 1: Investing $1000 then $28 dollars a month over time.

The other tables show the returns from investing your initial thousand plus adding two dollars per day ($56 per month) or $100 per month.

Remember, past returns are no guarantee of future performance but they give us a good guide to use in our examples.

Table 1
Results of investing $1000 then dollar cost averaging $56 per month.

	Bonds (5.1%)	Larger companies (10.7%)	Small companies (12.6%)
10yrs	$10,405	$14,843	$16,847
20yrs	$26,052	$55,014	$72,353
30yrs	$52,080	$171,572	$266,753
40yrs	$95,378	$509,774	$947,605

Table 2
Results of investing $1000 then dollar cost averaging $100 per month.

	Bonds (5.1%)	Larger companies (10.7%)	Small companies(12.6%)
10yrs	$17,274	$24,227	$27,333
20yrs	$44,348	$91,625	$119,564
30yrs	$89,384	$287,184	$442,589
40yrs	$164,302	$854,617	$1,573,930

The second principle of investing is: **Time is your biggest ally; investing a little early is better than investing more later.** The later you start, the less (much less) you will have in the future.

Notice how the money grows exponentially over time (pay attention in algebra). This only happens if you continue to re-invest your gains. When you do this, the money compounds just like interest. The minute you pull money out, it stops working for you. For a quick guide as to how fast your money will double, divide the number 72 by your rate of return. If you gained a return of 10%, your money would double in 7.2 years. If you earned 20%, your money would double every 3.6 years. Money guru's call this the rule of 72 - cool!

Most people start investing through a company retirement fund like a 401K plan. Retirement plans allow your money to grow tax free but they penalize you if you pull them out before your 59.5 years old. Most retirement plans allow you to choose what kind of mutual fund you want your money invested in. If your company has a retirement plan, use it! Take the time to learn about it and take out as much as you can afford.

I Want, Therefore I Must Have: Spending vs. Saving

Americans are spending crazy. We save less than four percent of our incomes. The marketing industry has catered to our selfishness and pride to create a society that consumes, wastes and obsesses about possessions.

Some people have real trouble keeping any money available. I have had teenagers in my youth group make over $10,000 per year and have nothing to show for it but a few shirts and a rusted out car. You may be thinking, "I would like to invest some money but I don't have any to spare." Most people have little extra money because they simply spend too much. They blow their money on dumb stuff. They think that if they could only make more money they would have more money. Sadly, this is rarely true. People

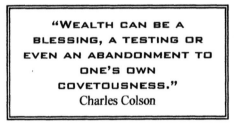

"WEALTH CAN BE A BLESSING, A TESTING OR EVEN AN ABANDONMENT TO ONE'S OWN COVETOUSNESS."
Charles Colson

have a nasty habit of spending more as they make more.

Saving requires you to have a vision for the future (complete with a plan) and delay your gratification. Remember - less now for more later.

Allow me to show you the secrets behind spending. Think of every dollar you spend as an investment. What you buy with that dollar can go up in value or down. The moment you buy a stereo or a video game system, clothes or a pair of shoes, you start losing money because you can never sell the used item for the price you paid for it. That's called *depreciation*. That's bad.

But wait, it gets worse! When an item depreciates, you not only lose money in the value of the thing, you also lose the money you would have gained had you invested it instead of spent it. That's called *opportunity cost.* It could be worse if you bought something on credit. You now lose more money by *paying interest.* This is how the poor get poorer. Every time they spend money, they lose it three different ways without even knowing it. Let me show you how this works.

Matilda loves her music. She drives an older car with only a mediocre stereo system. She desperately wants the new ninety watt super bass blaster box system for her car. She likes the way it tickles her tummy on the low notes. She really can't afford it though, so she takes the stereo shop's finance plan (18% interest) and pays for it ($500) over one year. "The payments are only $45 per month," she reasons. Now pay attention; Matilda loses money in *three* fabulous ways.

First, the stereo depreciates the moment she installs it in her car and continues to depreciate over time. In five years, she could barely sell it because nobody wants to buy an old broken down bass box. She unloads it at a garage sale for $50. She loses $450

Secondly, she pays an extra $50 dollars in interest over the year.

Thirdly, she could have invested the original $500 in a safe, large company mutual fund earning 10% over the five years and gained $300!

Matilda's $500 investment over 5 years		
	Cool stereo	Large cap mutual fund
Original investment:	$500	$500
Interest income	- 50	+$300
Depreciation	-$450	$0
Opportunity cost	-$300	$0
Total profit/loss	-$800	+300
Five year return:	-160%	+60%

Matilda loses her $500 through depreciation and interest. Then she loses an opportunity to gain $300 through investing (the opportunity cost). She also loses her hearing and she doesn't enjoy the tickle in her tummy as much any more.

When your realize how much your spending actually costs you, you can more wisely determine the value of your purchases.

Remember, every purchase is an investment. You make a trade off between having more now and less later or less now and more later. If you can make wise tradeoffs you will be financially successful. Let's look at some tradeoffs worth making and their value over time assuming a 12.6% rate of return.

- If you quit smoking and invest the amount you spend on cigarettes, over 15 years you would have $56,453. After 30 years you would have $403,924 and two pink lungs!

- If you bought an $8,000 used car as opposed to a $15,000 new one and you invested the difference over 15 years you would earn $41,512 and $246,178 in 30 years. New cars depreciate 20-25% the instant you drive them off the lot. In two years they depreciate 35-45% depending on the make and model.

- If you rented videos half the time instead of going to the movies and invested the difference ($21/month) you would earn $11,245 over 15 years and $84,824 over 30 years.

- If you ate two less meals out per month ($240/yr)and invested the money, at 15 years you would earn $10,710. In 30 years a whopping $80,784.

- If you bought one less CD per month and invested the money, you would earn $9,638 in 15 years and $72,706 in 30 years.

- If you just played your friends new video game system and invested the $400 instead, you would have $2,372 in 15 years and

$14,067 in 30.

If you don't learn to save now, you will have a hard time saving later. If you take the advertiser's advice, you'll abandon your savings goals and spend all of your money on piles of stuff - stuff that gives momentary pleasure, some laughs and a few thrills, and maybe an occasion of silly pride as you parade your possessions in front of your friends. Spending money is the best way to get into debt, the best way to let others take advantage of you, and the best way to forfeit your financial future. Most people have no trouble spending money. Money guru Todd Temple gives us some tips for *not* spending money in his book, *Money, How to make it, spend it, and keep lots of it:*

- Ask why. Sometimes the reasons we want something are simply foolish or prideful.

- Live by the 7 over 7 rule: Anytime you want to buy something that costs over $7 dollars, wait seven days. This will blow a big hole in your impulse buying. Retailers plan for you to buy on impulse anything priced under $20.

- Don't save money by spending it. Don't buy something just because it's "on sale." Walk away when someone says a deal is "too good to be true" or "This won't last for long!"

- Hang around people who spend less. If the central pastime of your friends is shopping, you will spend more money. Learn to have fun producing instead of consuming.

- Write it down. Track every penny you spend; don't spend money you don't have allocated in your spending plan. When the money in your clothing budget is spent, stop buying clothes!

- Buy off a bad habit. Quit eating junk food, smoking or drinking pop. Figure out how much you spend on your habit, then put the money to work for you instead.

- Look for real deals in re-sale shops and end of season closeouts.

Sales Techniques Your Not Supposed to Know About

The world has tons of people wanting your money. They do a good job of getting it from you most of the time. It helps if you know some of their techniques.

- Discounts. Stores use that word a lot. They want you to think your saving money. 'Discount' or '50%' off could mean anything. Sometimes stores mark up an item only to mark it down. Shop around and find the lowest price. If you buy something just because it's 'on sale,' you lose.

- Buy now! Many stores use an emotional ploy to create a sense of urgency. They know that the moment you walk out of the store, they lose their best chance at a sale.

- Bait and Switch. They bait you with an advertised low price on an item but when you get to the store, they're out of that item but they will try to sell you a higher priced version it.

- Up-selling. Up-selling is probably the most common sales technique. How many times have you heard, "Would like fries with that?" You're already spending money so a little more won't hurt. When you buy an outfit, they sell you accessories. When you buy electronics, they sell you a warrantee. Make sure you know exactly what you want, then pay for just that.

- Package deals. Stores often package more than one item together, then tell you that you're getting a lower price than if you bought each item separately. But if you don't want everything in the package, why spend more money for it?

Where the Rubber Meets the Road

Money can do a lot of things for you - good and bad. If you operate according to God's principles in this area, blessings will follow. Get a vision from God, write it down and follow your financial plan accordingly. Every time you get paid or receive a gift, divide it up by percentages according to your goals. Track your money and adjust your plan according to your goals.

For more on this topic I recommend anything by Larry Burkett, or Austin Pryor and Todd Temple's *Money*. Mutual fund companies will give you lots of free investment information. Also check out *www.Money.com* for lots of cool strategies and calculators for calculating investment income. Get these books from your library or better yet, buy them: *Getting Rich in America* and *Rich Dad Poor Dad*. A book called *The Tightwad Gazette* will show you strategies for saving copious amounts of cash. You can also search 'Frugal' or 'Tightwad' on the internet for cool sights on saving. God bless you!

Study Scriptures: Psalms 1: 1-3, 24:1, Proverbs 13:11, 21:13, 27:23-27,3:27-28, 22:7, Ecclesiastes 11:1-2, Malachi 3:8-12, Haggai 1:1-11, Matthew 6: 19-24, 25:14-30

> "THE WAY TO WEALTH, IF YOU DESIRE IT, IS AS PLAIN AS THE WAY TO MARKET. IT DEPENDS CHIEFLY ON TWO WORDS, INDUSTRY AND FRUGALITY; THAT IS WASTE NEITHER TIME NOR MONEY, BUT MAKE THE BEST USE OF BOTH."
> BENJAMIN FRANKLIN

AN APPLE A DAY

Just one page here to tell you to take care of your body. Many older people regret not taking care of the body God gave them while they were young. When you're young you don't think about hearing loss, vision loss, heart problems, and arthritis. Time passes and as the Lord wills, you too will grow old. So here are some tips older people give looking back on their health.

- Keep weight off. As you get older, it is easier to keep it off then to get it off. Most people gain an extra pound or two per year. How much would you weigh in 30 years? Your metabolism slows as you get older and less active so you can't eat like you used to without gaining weight.

- Find an activity you enjoy, then do it regularly. I have gone from running to triathalons to raquetball to martial arts to wrestling over the years. God created your body to stay active. You will rust out before you wear out!

- As you age, weight lifting and stretching become more important. Weight lifting keeps up your strength and bone mass, stretching helps maintain your flexibility.

- Simple formula for weight loss: Eat less calories than you burn each day. It works! Try and stay away from up and down fad diets. Just get the discipline to stop eating so much and stay active. Eat lots of natural food, fruits and veggies and such.

- Use ear protection while operating noisy things.

ADVERSITY

There are few things that are common to all of us; adversity is one of them. Even Jesus said, "In this world you will have trouble...," and "It rains on the just and the unjust." Temptation, distress and persecution come to us all. Many times, the difference between those who live life to the fullest and those who just live can be traced to how they handled adversity.

During times of trouble, we often ask ourselves one of life's toughest questions. Why? If God is so good then why did this happen? How can there even be a God with all this evil and suffering in the world?

In this section, we will explore the origins of evil. We will try to explain why bad things happen to people and how you should best handle adversity.

So get ready. You will face trials and hardships during this life. To pursue the best, you must learn how to walk in the valleys on your way to life's peaks.

I love you,
cw

"MY DEAR WIFE, THIS IS MY GOOD BYE TO YOU AND TO MY TREASURE LOLUNIA AND MY MOTHER, I LEAVE THIS WORLD ON THE 30TH AT 7 PM TO THE OVENS CONDEMNED TO DEATH LIKE A BANDIT. BRONIA, MY TREASURE, I AM SORRY THAT I DEPARTED YOU BELIEVE ME THAT I JUST CAN'T WRITE YOU ANY MORE, MY HAND SHAKES TEARS FLOODING MY EYES TO KNOW I AM DYING LIKE THIS AND NOT GUILTY 58 OF US ARE GOING AND 10 WOMEN. I KISS YOU COUNTLESS TIMES AND LOLUNIA. IN THE NIGHT REMEMBER THE 30TH OF OCTOBER AND PRAY. SAY A PRAYER, TELL LOLI THAT DADDY IS GONE. I CAN'T WRITE, I CAN'T. GOOD BYE TO YOU ALL, GOD BE WITH YOU."
THE LAST LETTER OF A POLE, WRITTEN SECRETLY BEFORE HE WAS SHOT AT THE NAZI CONCENTRATION CAMP OF AUSCHWITZ

EVIL & SUFFERING

The twentieth century was the bloodiest century in history. It was a century marked by empires of tyranny and evil. Names like Hitler, Stalin, Mao and Pol Pot mar the historical landscape like bomb craters.

We hear of poverty, famine, sickness and disease around the world. Even on a local level, it seems evil triumphs over good. Our newscasters tell us of sexual abuse, abductions, murders, rapes and burglaries on a nightly basis.

This often causes us to ask 'why?' Many people look at the evil around them and conclude that there must not be a God. Or if there is, they question his power or character.

Every system of belief must answer these tough questions. The atheist, pantheist, and agnostic must all give their answer. As you will see, the Christian system answers the question of evil and suffering better than all others. It also provides us with a framework and a strategy for avoiding and persevering through adversity.

The Validity of the Question

When someone looks at the injustice and cruelty of the world and concludes, "There must not be a God," they come to a faulty verdict. God must be in the picture for their question to have any validity. Without God, their question self destructs. I'll tell you why.

In order for humans to have the slightest concept of evil, we must admit there is a corresponding good. If good and evil exist, then a moral law must also exist by which we differentiate between the good and the evil. If there is a moral law, it follows then that there must be a moral law giver. This law giver must be above humanity - we call him God.

If no God existed, then no good would exist. If no good existed, then no evil would exist and we couldn't legitimately raise any question about it. Actions would merely be actions, not good or bad. A rape would seem just as legitimate as sex between married, consenting adults.

The fact that we see evil and raise questions about it tells us there must be a God to give us the moral law by which we can question and condemn evil. When God created life, he created a moral law to protect its purity and vitality. Evil is a violation of this purity and spirit.

Some may contend that men and societies invented the moral law, and that we don't need God to tell us right from wrong. This thinking has formed the basis for much of the bloodshed of the twentieth century. If men determine our morality, our next question becomes which men? Hitler or Mother Teresa? There must be a moral law above our laws to guide the human race. We have proven our inability to guide ourselves.

The Definitions and Origins of Evil

In the defining of evil, we find the starting point for answering the tough questions about evil and suffering. We can define evil as two things - a loss of something we were meant to have or a corrupted relationship. Many times, they occur simultaneously.

Blindness is a loss of sight. Somebody paralyzed has lost ability in their lower limbs. Poverty and famine are the result of a loss of basic needs. Birth defects and disease are a loss of wholeness. Natural disasters are only disasters because they cause great loss.

Murder, rape, and abuse are examples of corrupted relationships. Lying and stealing are examples of both of these - a loss of honesty and a corrupted relationship.

I want you to notice something about evil - that it is totally dependant upon the good. Without the good, evil cannot exist. In other words, good can exist on its own while evil can't.

For instance, when we see a baby born blind we sense something wrong only because we know what sight is. When we see a diseased person we know this is tragic because we know what health is. When someone takes advantage of another person in one way or another something inside tells us that people ought not to act that way because we know what good relationships are.

In order for evil to exist, good must first exist. In fact, evil is just a portion of the good - something less than the good. Therefore, good must exist before evil can. In order for us to say a line is crooked, we must first know what a straight one is.

The Bible plainly describes the good of the universe existing before evil entered the scene. Logic cannot support any system that explains good and evil as equal, opposing and eternally existing forces. Opposing maybe, but certainly not equal and eternally existing. Only the good eternally existed in the character of God. Therefore, the Biblical view of evil at least starts logically, whereas others - namely pantheistic and new age philosophies - fall flat here.

C.S. Lewis puts it brilliantly in his book *Mere Christianity*:

"Goodness is, so to speak, itself: badness is only spoiled goodness. And there must be something good first before it can be spoiled. We call sadism a sexual perversion; but you must first have an idea of a normal sexuality before you can talk of its being perverted... It follows that this Bad Power, who is supposed to be on an equal footing with the Good Power, and to love badness in the same way the Good Power loves goodness is a mere bogy. In order to be bad he must have good things to want then to pursue them in a wrong way: he must have impulses which were originally good in order to be able to pervert them. But if he is bad, he cannot supply himself either with good things to desire or with good impulses to pervert. He must be getting both from the Good Power. And if so, then he is not independent. He is part of the Good Power's world: He was made either by the Good Power or by some Power above them both.

To put it more simply still. To be bad, he must exist and have intelligence and will. But existence, intelligence and will are in themselves good. Therefore, he must be getting them from the Good Power: even to be bad he must borrow or steal from his opponent. And do you now begin to see why Christianity has said the devil is a fallen angel? That is not a mere story for children. It is a real recognition that evil is a parasite, not an original thing."

If God is Good Then Why is There Evil?

We have seen that God must exist in order for us to recognize good or bad. So if he exists, what kind of God is it that allows so much evil? Why would he do that? What kind of Creator would make such a creation?

If you think about it, God could have only made four kinds of universes.

- No creation at all. Would it have been better for God not to create anything rather than to have created this one where good and evil are possibilities?

- A world where only good can be chosen, a sort of robotic world.

- A world where there is no such thing as good or evil.

- The world we live in, where good and evil exist along with the possibility of choosing either.

Now understand this: *Our world system, the one God chose, is the only way love is genuinely possible.* The love of a man for a woman, a mother for her child, a friend for a friend, and a human for God are only possible in a world where its inhabitants are free to choose good or evil.

In order for God to create us with the capacity for love - the supreme ethic - he needed to create us with the capacity to freely love *or* reject him. For God to force us to love him would not be love at all but coercion.

So, God took a risk. He risked that people would misuse their freedom to choose evil so that they would have the ability to experience the jewel of our existence: love. And where love is possible, pain is also possible. Rejecting God is the greatest evil one can do, while loving him, is the greatest good (Matthew 22:36-37).

God does not cause evil, but people freely choose to reject his love and his laws. God doesn't always stop it, thus violating our autonomy, in hopes that one day we would choose the supreme choice - to love him. (II Peter 3:9) Let's face it, if God were to eliminate all evil, who would be left standing?

Dr. Ravi Zacharias puts it this way in his book *Cries of the Heart*,

"God alone is the absolute expression of love that is never separated from holiness. God cannot be at the same time holy and unloving or loving and unholy. In turning our back on Him, we lose the source of defining love, live with the pain of unholiness, and suffering remains an enigma - leaving our blemished characters in search of a moral law and our finite minds crying for an answer... Our hearts reveal a hunger for a love that is pure, and in this world we have lost both definitions because we have denied their source."

What has God Done About It?

We understand the risk God has taken to allow us our free will. If he hasn't eliminated all evil (and us in the process), what has he done about suffering and evil?

First, God did not sit back and watch as sin and selfishness victimized the human race. He left his place in heaven to be a victim himself. The God of the universe allowed himself to be subject to the most heinous of cruelty - the Roman cross. Jesus Christ was truly the only innocent man to suffer.

We have a God that can sympathize with our sufferings. When a house burns to the ground, God understands. He knew what it meant to live homeless. When a person is abused by another, God understands. He endured physical, verbal and sexual abuse at the hands of corrupt men. When a family loses a child, who can fathom the tragedy and heartache? God can, he understands what it means to lose a son.

Jesus went to the cross in order do be our substitute for the curse of sin. He took our place at the gallows so we wouldn't have to. The cross lets us know that sometimes pain has a higher purpose. Before the cross, we knew God was big and powerful; he kicked Satan out of heaven. But a question still lingered like smoke from a forest fire over the universe - God was big, but was he good?

The cross eliminated any doubts regarding the character of God. But it didn't end at the cross. We don't serve a dead man on a stick but a living, risen savior.

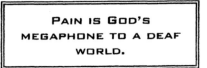

PAIN IS GOD'S MEGAPHONE TO A DEAF WORLD.

If the cross shows us that pain sometimes has a purpose, the resurrection shows us that God can redeem suffering. The author of life can restore it; he guarantees that those who believe in Christ will not see death. (John 3:16, John 11:25)

Those that have lost loved ones who knew Christ have an opportunity to meet them again, provided they have repented and trusted Christ also. God has redeemed death and suffering (John 16:20, Romans 8:18, I Thessalonians 4:13-14).

Not only has God identified with pain, shown us pain sometimes has a purpose and redeemed it, he has given us an agency to alleviate human suffering - his church. God has set up a fellowship of believers and he has charged them with a number of missions. One of them is to alleviate human suffering. He tells us to bear one another's burdens, feed the hungry, heal the sick, clothe the naked, set free the captives and fight against injustice. (I Peter 4:9-10)

The true church of Christ is responsible for more hospitals, orphanages, feeding programs, schools and ministries than any other organization in the history of the world.

God has also done one more thing about evil - he has brought it to justice. Dr. Josef Mengele was one of history's most evil people. He helped run the death camp of Auschwitz. Auschwitz was a gruesome kingdom of human misery. Mengele's stated goal was to perform genetic research on the inmates at the camp. The goal of Mengele's work was to unlock the secrets of genetic engineering and to devise methods for eradicating inferior gene strands so as to create a super race. Despite the scientific premise for his work, Mengele's accomplishments added volumes to the annals of human cruelty while contributing nothing of value to science.

Mengele once caught a woman in her sixth attempt to escape from a truck transporting victims to the gas chamber. He grabbed her by the neck and proceeded to beat her head to a bloody pulp. He hit her, slapped her, and boxed her, screaming, "You want to escape, don't you? You can't escape now. You are going to burn like the others, you are going to croak, you dirty Jew." Her two beautiful, intelligent eyes disappeared under a layer of blood. In a few seconds her straight pointed nose was a flat, broken, bleeding mass.

On one occasion, when the crematoria became too full to accommodate the thousands of Jews streaming into the camp, he had trenches dug which were then filled with gasoline and set ablaze. Both the dead and the living, adults as well as children and infants, were thrown bodily into these pits. After a while, dump trucks with children inside arrived and backed up to the fire. They started throwing the children into the fire. The children started to scream; some of them managed to crawl out, but an officer walked around the pit and pushed them backed into the fire with sticks.

Mengele occupied his time with numerous other acts of cruelty, including dissection of live infants, the castration of boys and men without using anesthesia and the administration of high-voltage electric shocks to women under the auspices of testing their endurance. He performed experiments with twins. He would take blood from one twin and inject it into another even though it was of a different type. Experimenting with eye color, he would inject die into the eyes of some twins. This would sometimes result in infection or blindness. If one of the twins died he would harvest the eyes and pin them to the wall in his office. He would perform operations without anesthesia, removing the limbs and organs of prisoners.

Just before the allies liberated the camp, Mengele escaped to his hometown. He hid there until he fled to Argentina in 1949. Mengele was never captured. In 1979, he died on a beach in Argentina. He escaped earthly justice. He did not however, escape justice.

God has a place prepared for Satan and his allies - Hell. Hell is real. Hell is forever. Hell is God bringing justice to an evil world. All who break God's law deserve God's justice. Have you ever broken the law of God? Have you ever lied? Stolen anything? Dishonored your parents? Have you ever dragged God's name in the gutter like a curse word? Have you ever worshiped anything besides the one true God? Have you ever committed sexual sin; have you ever lusted in your heart? If you have ever violated one of these laws you deserve God's justice.

Instead of asking God to do something about the evil in the world, we might be better off asking ourselves, "What have we done about the evil in *our* hearts and lives?" Unless you have repented of sin and believed in Christ you will pay for your crimes against heaven and humanity.

The good news is, God has paid the price for you. If you will just accept his conditions, he will redeem the evil in *you* and restore innocence to your soul. (See section on "How to know God" pg 67)

What does the atheist have to say to those experiencing suffering and tragedy? Tough break? Better luck next time? It looks like you're on the short side of the evolutionary totem pole? What does the pantheist and new-age guru have to say to the abuse victim? You're just working out your bad karma? The evil you have experienced is just an illusion?

In April of 1999, two teenage gunmen ripped through the halls of Columbine High School killing 13 and then themselves. Out of this tragedy, two brothers penned a song that helped a nation deal with its grief. They tapped into the core of what we all should tap into during times of unfathomable hurt. They didn't sing songs about the United Nations or pull some comforting words out of the Humanist Manifesto; they pointed us in the direction of the God who can truly understand pain.

> "Columbine, flower blue, tenderly I sing to you
> Columbine, roses are red, heartbreak overflows my head
> Columbine, flower blue, Columbine there's hope for you
> Columbine, friend of mine
>
> Turn our pain into your gain
> Keep our hearts on the mark
> Comfort us with your love again
>
> Comfort peace and sweet release
> Come from you
> Where it's true, I hide myself in you
>
> Can you still hear the raging guns
> Ending dreams of precious ones
> In God's son, hope will come
> His red stain will take our pain
>
> Christ of grace, oh turn this place
> To look to you, honor you
> Fix you in our view......Columbine, friend of mine,
> peace will come to you in time

Only the Christian has a God that can identify with suffering. The Christian can rest in knowing that sometimes God has a purpose for pain and that he can redeem suffering and bring justice to an evil world.

Why do We Suffer?

It's one thing to talk about the suffering in the world around us and it's another to talk about *our* suffering. People go through adversity for different reasons, and sometimes it helps to know 'why' when you're in the midst of it, trying to find your way out.

Reason #1: I don't know. Sometimes suffering and adversity are beyond our comprehension. With our limited knowledge of the big picture, we can't always understand the purposes of pain. (Job 38-42, Isaiah 40, 55:8-9)

Reason #2: We have neglected the principles of God. When we think we know better than God and we violate his principles, we will suffer the consequences. God gives us the power of choice, but once the choice is made, that choice now has power over us. Most of our suffering we bring upon ourselves. The top three causes of premature death in America are all self inflicted - Tobacco use (37.7%), Obesity and Inactivity (28.3%) and Alcohol Abuse (9.4%).[1] Solomon told us that keeping the commands of God would prolong our years and bring blessing to our homes. Disregarding the principles of God would bring calamity and disaster to our lives. (Galatians 6:7-8, Proverbs chapters 1-4)

Reason #3: Our world suffers from the curse of sin. Because people sin and act selfishly, others will be hurt. Jesus came to free us from this curse. (I Peter 2: 23-25)

Reason #4: Spiritual Warfare. Humanity has an enemy. Satan goes around like a roaring lion looking for someone to devour. He and his demons hate God and they hate you. They can't get to God but they can get to you. They have one motive - to kill, steal and destroy everything good. God has come to give us life, and he gives Christians authority over the dominion of darkness. (John 10:10, I Peter 5:8-9, Job 1-2)

Reason #5: To bring us to maturity. God allows some suffering and trials to enter our lives to purify us and cause us to grow. He places us in the fire to burn the impurities out of our lives. God has a great concern that we grow in character. Nothing provides character producing growth quite like adversity. James said, "Consider it pure joy, my brothers whenever you face trials of many kinds, because you know that the testing of your faith develops perseverance. Perseverance must finish its work so that you may be mature and complete, not lacking anything" (James 1:2-4).

Reason #6: The discipline of God. God is the perfect father. Just like any good father, he disciplines his children out of an all consuming desire to see their lives lived fruitfully and joyfully. Sometimes when we persist in behaviors that will bring us harm, he must bring his loving correction into our lives in order to shape us into fruit bearing children. (Hebrews 12:3-13)

We have answered the tough questions about suffering and evil. In our next chapter, we will show you how to walk through the valleys of life without getting stuck.

1. Data from: Partnership For Prevention, published in *Business Week* April 17, 2000, pg 8

OVERCOMING ADVERSITY

During the mid 1700's, England and France nursed an uneasy peace. Both countries busied themselves by colonizing territories and they carried out a spirited rivalry in America's Ohio valley. In May of 1754, Lieutenant Colonel George Washington commanded the Virginia militia on behalf of Mother England. He led a small band of 150 men about 200 miles into the wilderness to garrison, a strategic point at the site of modern Pittsburg, thereby preventing the French from placing troops there. On the way there, however, Washington learned that the French had already occupied the area with a force much larger than his and had built a fort, Fort Duquesne, to defend it.

Washington continued to advance, cutting a primitive road through the forest toward the Ohio Company storehouse that he could fortify while awaiting further orders and, he hoped, reinforcements.

He never made it to the storehouse. Friendly Indians reported that a French party was advancing toward him. He decided to set up a makeshift fort in a large field about 40 miles south of Fort Duquesne. His fort consisted of nothing more than a square formed by trenches and wagons. He called it 'Fort Necessity.' The Indian chiefs described the fort as 'that little thing in the meadow' and he urged Washington to move to a site with better natural defenses. But the young colonel refused.

During the making of Fort Necessity, Washington received word that a band of about 30 Frenchmen were not far away. He set out with about 40 men to join the dozen warriors who had given him the report. The next morning, he discovered the French encamped in a hollow but he unexpectedly found himself and his party exposed on a ridge in full view of the French. Seeing the French running for their muskets, he gave the fateful order to commence firing. The French surrendered not long after the battle begun. With the help of three or four interpreters, Washington had learned that 10 of the French had been killed and 22 had surrendered; among the dead was their captain. One of the Frenchmen furiously pulled papers from his pouch and presented them to Washington.

These papers identified the Frenchman as a diplomat, *not* a soldier. He was an ambassador under instructions to find the English and offer to maintain the existing peace, but to warn them not to trespass on French territory.

After Washington mistakenly killed the french diplomat, the French paid Washington's little fort a visit. They pinned down Washington's men for hours, when finally, the firing let up and Washington sent an interpreter under a white flag to talk with the French.

The French made an offer to allow Washington and his men to return home if they just surrendered the fort. Unbeknownst to Washington, the French included in the document of surrender statements saying Washington 'assassinated' the French diplomat who was seeking peaceful ends. When Washington unknowingly signed the document, it was as though he admitted that this was the official view of the incident. On the way home, Washington spoke not a single word.

When the document reached Paris, Washington was ruined. Paris accused London of deliberately breaching the faith. London, through the actions of their colonel, violated the uneasy trust between the two nations.

Washington desperately tried to defend his tattered reputation but he was stripped of his command and offered a demotion. He declined the offer as humiliating and resigned the military altogether. Cheerless, dishonored and hopelessly depressed, Washington retired to a life of farming - at the age of *twenty-two*.

Most people don't know this part of Washington's life. They know him as the brave leader of America's War for Independence, the father of our country - but a defeated, dejected, beat up loser?

As we know, his story didn't end there. And what we can learn from the rest of his life and the lives of countless other heroes will separate us from the mediocre life that awaits those who are too cowardly, lazy or ignorant to learn how to face and conquer adversity.

All great people have one thing in common: They triumphed through adversity. If you show me a hero, I will show you a tragedy. This chapter outlines seven general principles of overcoming adversity that you can apply to your specific circumstances.

Principle # 1: Prepare Proverbs 22:3, 27:12

Some think that the best way to handle adversity is to take it as it comes. They express a kind of fatalistic "Whatever will be will be" attitude. This type of attitude will leave you like a boat tossed in a storm. The best way is to maintain a long term vision then anticipate trouble and prepare for it. If the ship's captain sees the storm ahead, he can avoid it all together or sail the best route through it.

There are several ways to prepare for adversity. First, **know the principles of God.** When captaining your ship, know the principles of seamanship. Learn navigation, learn emergency procedures and learn the laws of the water. **Most people face unnecessary and prolonged suffering simply because they don't know the principles of living put forth by God!** The prophet Hosea faced intense adversity and he said, "My people are destroyed from lack of knowledge" (4:6).

If you know the principles of God, you will avoid much suffering. Take the time to study his book (and this book) for eternal principles that will guide you out of troubled waters. Many of your troubles will come from neglecting the principles covered by this book (Faith, Attitude, Authority, Pleasure, Relationships and Sex, Production and Adversity).

Have you ever had transportation troubles? If so, you know what it means to try and cast a demon out of your car. Our car just recently lost its transmission - it cost us $1400 to fix it. We were able to pay cash for the expense because we planned for adversity and followed God's principles of money management which allowed us to maintain our car without going into debt. (Proverbs 21:20) God has since restored the lost $1400 and he is blessing us with more. This brings us to the next way to prepare for adversity.

Learn God's promises. God cannot lie. He gives promises to those who love him, promises of healing, provision, and deliverance. He promises to never leave you, to guide you through valleys and to give you peace in the midst of life's storms. When you know the promises of God, faith rises up within you, and God responds favorably to faith. (Hebrews 11, Romans 1:17)

Check out these promises:

- **Provision**...Phil. 4:19, Psalms 37:25, 111:5, 1:1-3, Malachi 3:8-13
- **Deliverance from affliction**....Psalms 34:19, 91, 20, 23, 18:2
- **Healing**...Mt. 8:16-17, Isaiah 53:4-5, I Peter 2:24, James 5:14-16
- **Worry and Fear**...Isaiah 26:3, 41:10, I Peter 5:7, Phil. 4:6-7
- **Hope**... Proverbs 23:18, Jeremiah 29:11
- **God's love and acceptance of you**...Zephaniah 3:17, John 3:16 Lamentations 3:22-23

God has given us thousands of promises to cling to during times of adversity. Take care to follow the conditions of his promises. God does not give us a credit card without any terms and conditions - most of his promises are conditional. There are two promises that are unconditional; however, he will always love you and he will never leave you no matter what you do.

The third and best way to prepare for adversity is to get to know **his Person**. People that have gone through hell on earth and come out of it with their faith still in tact have said that when nothing made sense, when they couldn't follow the hand or reason of God, they could still *trust his* *heart.* They *knew* God; they knew his character and his love for them, and that made all the difference.

Get to know God and what he has done about evil on your behalf. Get to know a God who took a risk and gave everything with the hope that mankind would turn to him again. Get to know a God that

> **"GREATER LOVE HAS NO ONE THAN THIS; THAT ONE LAYS DOWN HIS LIFE FOR A FRIEND."**
> Jesus Christ

always has your best interest in mind. (Romans 8:28) Get to know a God who loves you; he didn't just say it, he proved it.

Principle #2: Pray Matthew 7:7-8, I Timothy 2:1-4, Daniel 9:3, James 5:13-18

Adversity seems to naturally bring out the prayer in people. But the secret to prayers that accomplish something during adversity is a prayer-life that flourishes even when things are going well. (Luke 5:16)

Prayer is a means to an end, not an end. The ends to prayer are first to develop an intimate relationship with God, second to move the hand of God, thirdly, to change us into the image of God and fourthly, to give us marching orders.

Don't allow your prayer-life to become a legalistic exercise. If your not developing intimacy with God, your wasting your time. The Pharisees prayed, but they didn't know God. If you find yourself praying just to say you have prayed, you should re-evaluate your prayer-life.

God tells us to pray; "Ask and it will be given to you; seek and you will find; knock and the door will be opened to you. For everyone who seeks, finds; and to him who knocks, the door will be opened" (Matthew 7:7-8). The tense of the Greek verbs in verse eight actually designates continued action. This means we must keep asking, keep seeking and knocking.

Prayer is the tender nerve that moves the muscle of omnipotence. Nothing is beyond the reach of prayer only because nothing is beyond the reach of God. Kingdoms rise and fall all on the wind of prayer because God causes kingdoms to rise and fall.

You can do more *after* you have prayed but you cannot do more *until* you have prayed.

Even medical science is beginning to realize the power of God through prayer. In 1988, cardiologist Randolph Byrd at San Francisco General Hospital tested 393 patients from the coronary-care unit. He randomly assigned half to be prayed for by Christians and the other half would not receive any prayer. To eliminate the placebo effect, the patients were not told of the experiment. Remarkably, Byrd found that the group that didn't get prayed for were *five times* more likely to need antibiotics and *three times* more likely to develop complications as those who were prayed for.

A 1995 study at Dartmouth-Hitchcock Medical Center found that one of the best predictors of survival among 232 heart-surgery patients was the degree to which the patients said they drew comfort and strength from religious faith. Those who did not had *more than three times* the death rate of those who did.

If your prayer life is dead and boring, you're going about it the wrong way! Prayer is a dialogue between the God of the universe and you; how can that be boring?

Here are some tips to spicing up your prayer life:

- Get clean before God. Repent of any known or unknown sin; forgive others that have hurt you. Make amends with anyone you hold something against. (Psalms 139:23-24)

- Rearrange your schedule to give your best time to God. Everything else at that time must be second priority. Decide to pray even when you don't feel like it. It's when you need it most. (Matthew 6:33)

- Keep focused. This comes with practice. Have a paper and pencil handy; make and keep a prayer journal or diary. Use lists to help keep you on track. Treat a stray thought or daydream like a child wandering on to a basketball court; gently remove him and move on.

- Pray out loud.

- Change activities. Read the Bible, worship, stand, kneel, write a letter to God in your journal, change location, take a prayer walk.

- Realize that the results of prayer occur first in the invisible spiritual world. Something is happening or Satan wouldn't fight you so hard.

- Pray the Scriptures. Use the promises of God as your prayers. Pray in the footsteps of the great people of God throughout history.

- Read great books on prayer. Start with - *The Hour That Changes the World* by Dick Eastman. This is a great starter book on prayer.

Here are more great scriptures on prayer: Psalms 105:4, Ephesians 6:18-20, Mark 11:24, John 14:13-14, Matthew 6:9-15

Principle #3: Praise Habakkuk, Acts 5:41, 16:16-40

Adversity provides us with one of the few opportunities to worship God because he is God and not because he gives us stuff. One of the most powerful things you can do to conquer through adversity is to continue to praise and worship God throughout your circumstance. Nobody can understand the magnitude of good this will do.

The book of Acts records an incident of trouble for Paul and Silas. The authorities flogged and jailed them for casting a spirit out of a slave girl. The warden thought them to be dangerous prisoners so he assigned them a guard who tossed them into the inner cell and shackled their hands and feet. At about midnight, the other inmates could hear praise and worship coming from Paul and Silas's cell. In the midst of their trouble they could have moaned and groaned about their circumstances; "Lord, what's the deal? We're trying to do good work and build the kingdom and look where it's landed us." Instead of getting a good case of PLOM disease (See section on Attitude), Paul and Silas continued with the fab five attitudes and praised the Lord in the midst of their circumstance.

Just then an earthquake hit the city that shook the foundations of the prison. The prison doors shook open and everybody's chains came loose. Coincidence? I don't think so.

Praise and worship elevates God over your circumstances. It makes God bigger in your eyes and builds your faith. Nothing aggravates the enemy of your soul more than when you still praise God even after he has attacked you.

The prophet Habakkuk expressed dismay and questioned God about his dealings with the nation of Judah.

"How long, O Lord, must I call for help, but you do not listen? Or cry out to you, "Violence!" but you do not save?

He carries out a dialogue with God and comes to this conclusion: "Though the fig tree does bud and there are no grapes on the vines, though the olive crop fails and the fields produce no food, though there are no sheep in the pen and no cattle in the stalls, *yet I will rejoice in the Lord, I will be joyful in God my Savior."*

Bryon Sparks was born with a tragic, debilitating disease called Epidermolyses Bullosa. This disease is a genetic disorder which causes a person to be born without collagen. Collagen is that substance that holds the upper layer of skin to the lower. His skin was as fragile as a butterfly's wing. It would blister with the slightest touch. When he was born, the doctors said he wouldn't last a day.

He often had burn-like sores over his body. The scarring of his body caused his fingers to fuse together.

Bryon lived a lot longer than one day. He graduated from high school and taught junior age Sunday school. He planned contests, birthday parties and memorization for his students. He lived for the field trips to the go-kart track, mini-golf course and ice cream shop. Bryon lived his life to the fullest. He studied to become a teacher, led worship in his youth group and sang in the choir even on the days his skin would stick to the back of his pants as he walked down the halls of his church.

Bryon had every reason to complain and grow bitter. He started his days by eating a special diet of tea, wheat bread and fruits and vegetables. After breakfast came an hour long session of breaking blisters, changing bandages and putting cream on open sores.

How did Bryon overcome his adversity? Instead of feeling sorry for himself, he lived a life of praise.

When he was young he tragically lost all the skin off his right arm. His parents took him to the hospital and after his treatment he rode a little red wagon through the hospital corridors singing, "God is so good!" The doctors and nurses will never forget it.

He later learned that a small lump on his hand was cancerous. Surgeons had to amputate his arm to the elbow. Two hours after the surgery he was cheering up his grandmother over the telephone saying, "Nanny, don't cry for me, I still have a lot more to do for God!" Twenty one years after the doctors pronounced that he wouldn't last the day, God called Bryon to praise him up close and personal. If Bryon can praise God through his circumstances, can't we?

Purpose in your heart to praise God not only through the easy times, but also times of adversity.

Principle #4: Hold on to the Promises of God Hebrews 10:23

In your preparation for adversity, you learned the promises of God for your life. Now is the time to include them in your prayer life and your everyday attitude.

As I prepared myself for fatherhood, I knew that God did not want my children to be raised in America's day care system. I knew that when he gave us children he expected us to care for them, nurture and train them. After our first child was born, the church I worked for could not afford to put me on full time. My wife had a good job but our financial situation forced us make some decisions - provide for ourselves and put Cal in day care or allow God to provide for us while one of us stayed home.

We decided to hold on to God's promises of provision and guidance. My job allowed me to work from home in the mornings while my wife left every morning for the office. I couldn't tell you how hard it was for my wife to have to leave her first baby and go to work each morning. After she arrived home in the afternoon I would have to run out the door to work a second job as a flight instructor at our local college. Some days we had to leave Cal with a friend from church. We weren't having the best life at the time.

I spend many long nights in prayer with my Bible opened to the promises of God. We prayed together as a family that God would provide us a way to work in his field of ministry and allow my children to grow up with a mom at home. Some nights I would get pretty frustrated at the Lord.

We did what we could do in the natural and believed God to move whatever mountains he needed to in order that we could live how we believed he wanted us to live.

Three months passed and we decided to have Kim ask her employer if she could go part time. People just didn't do that where she worked. God worked in their hearts and she went part-time working thirty hours a week. Her medical coverage would no longer cover me but God did. For two years I barely even caught a cold!

God gave us a second child - Madison. With two children, and a youth pastor for a husband, 30 hours a week was too much. She worked one month and she couldn't take it. We decided to take a leap of faith onto God's promises and have her quit. My job still wasn't enough to pay the bills but we had made some wise money decisions that would open up channels for God to bless us.

She nervously went in to quit and her boss offered to set up an office in our home complete with a computer, phone line and a raise so that she could be with her children, working only 20 hours a week! Her employer had never done that before! God moved in the heart of her boss. She worked four hours a day in the morning and the rest of the day she could tend to her duties and pleasures.

God provided for us according to his promises. My children have never seen the inside of a day-care center. We have lacked for nothing; God has provided for our needs and many of our wants - *according to his promises.*

Through that process of adversity, God stretched us and taught us many things. We had to do our part and God did the rest. This brings us to principle number five.

Principle #5: Paddle Nehemiah 2:18

When adversity comes, you can't just pray and praise your way out of it. You must do your part; you must paddle. God will always seek to partner with you.

Let's say you and your friend took a canoe trip down a beautiful river in the middle of a magnificent canyon. The sun is bright, the birds are singing and the trout practically jump into your boat. You brought along your CD player and your favorite tune echoes softly through the canyon. Suddenly a noise comes from ahead in the river. A dull roar comes from around the bend. As you round the bend, you see a 15 foot waterfall straight ahead of you. The current catches you and it

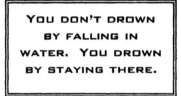

YOU DON'T DROWN BY FALLING IN WATER. YOU DROWN BY STAYING THERE.

propels you toward the falls. You look at your friend and ask, "What do you think we should do, pray or paddle?" Your friend astutely answers, "Both!"

When life presents you with hard times, you must do both - pray and paddle. During your prayer times, God will speak to you about certain things. He will give you direction and ask you to obey him. Do it!

Noah and his family built the ark. God didn't do it for them, he just gave them the instructions.

Plow ahead, do what *you* can do, enlist the help of others, improvise and overcome. God will open doors for you but *you* must walk through them.

Why does God want you personally involved with overcoming adversity? Principle #6 tells us.

Principle #6: Progress Hebrews 12:11, James 1:2-4

Remember that we undergo much of our adversity for the purpose of growing and maturing. God wants grown up children. Nothing causes us to grow more than adversity and testing. The more you act like a child, the more adversity will come your way.

When a baby eagle is about ready to leave the nest, the mother will begin to take out the soft feathers she used to line it. Why would she do such a thing? Because the baby bird begins to get a little too comfortable in the nest. The baby thinks, "It's soft, warm, comfy and mother delivers food every day right to my doorstep. What more could I ask? I think I will stay here forever." The baby eagle becomes content to live like a chicken when God destined him to fly like an eagle.

The mother knows the magnificent potential of the bird so she brings a little adversity into its life in order to bring it out of him. As she slowly rids the nest of the featherbed, it becomes picky and uncomfortable and soon the baby doesn't want to stay there forever so he learns to fly and hunt on his own - like an eagle should.

As we grow, God sees all of the tremendous potential he gave us. But many times, we get comfortable and complacent with our station in life. We have just enough of the comforts of this world to keep us satisfied with our relationship with God and our degree of production. If you get to this place, God may take a few feathers out of your nest to bring you to where you ought to be. He may prune you a little in order that you may bear more fruit.

> THERE ARE TWO TIMES IN LIFE WHEN PEOPLE QUIT: AFTER GREAT FAILURES AND AFTER GREAT SUCCESSES.

When this happens, you must go to God in prayer and ask him to point out the areas in your life that need work - then work on them! If you are violating any of God's principles, then you must stop and align your life with his standards. Allow God to bring out the character and potential he has placed in you.

You can do two things with a wall in front of you. You can stare at it and eventually you will grow used to it blocking your way or you can climb it and enjoy the view on the other side.

In 1904, St. Louis hosted the Louisiana Purchase Exposition in conjunction with the Olympic games. Forty two states and fifty three nations took part in the great celebration.

Among the vendors were two men, one with an ice cream booth and the other sold hot waffles. As the crowds grew, both men did tremendous business. After a few days, the waffle vendor ran out of the cardboard plates upon which he had been serving his waffles, with three different kinds of topping. He went to the different vendors but no one would sell him any plates. All the other vendors jealously guarded their supplies.

The ice cream vendor with great sympathy said to the waffle man, "That's the way the old waffle crumbles. It looks like you would be better off selling ice cream for me."

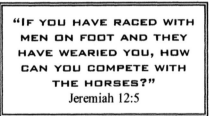

"IF YOU HAVE RACED WITH MEN ON FOOT AND THEY HAVE WEARIED YOU, HOW CAN YOU COMPETE WITH THE HORSES?"
Jeremiah 12:5

The waffle vendor considered his alternative, which was attempting to serve his waffles without plates and watching the syrup run down the sleeves of his irate customers. He agreed to buy the ice cream at a discount and resell it at his booth near the arcade.

The waffle vendor tried to recoup his losses by selling the ice cream at small profit margin. In the back of his mind he thought about the waffle ingredients going to waste. He had spent his life savings trying to capitalize on the huge crowds this fair would bring.

Suddenly, an idea struck him like a bolt of lightening. He wondered why he hadn't thought of it before. He was sure it would work. At home the next day, the waffle vendor made a batch of one thousand waffles and pressed them thin with an iron. He then rolled them in to a circular pattern with a point at the bottom.

The next morning he sold all of his ice cream before noon and all one thousand waffles with three different toppings as well! As a result of the adversity posed by the running out of plates, he progressed all of civilization by inventing the ice cream cone!

Don't stagnate, grow! We will all wait to see what God brings from your trials!

Principle # 7: Persevere Hebrews 10:36-39, Galatians 6:9

I've known too many people who have used a tragedy as a reason to terminate their faith. They say things like, "I used to believe in God, but then my Father walked out on us when we were young and so I couldn't believe in a God anymore." Yes, a father leaving is a tragedy of immense proportions, and nobody knows why every calamity happens. But why perpetuate another tragedy of even greater proportions by walking out on your Heavenly Father?

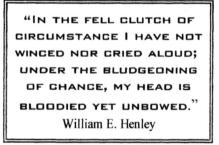

"IN THE FELL CLUTCH OF CIRCUMSTANCE I HAVE NOT WINCED NOR CRIED ALOUD; UNDER THE BLUDGEONING OF CHANCE, MY HEAD IS BLOODIED YET UNBOWED."
William E. Henley

During the middle ages, there was an Arab king who would take certain prisoners of war and offer them a choice. They could choose between a firing squad or what was behind a black door. The king would never tell them what was behind the black door. The prisoners of war would deliberate, then nine out of ten would choose the firing squad. They didn't realize that had they possessed the courage to choose the black door, they would have chosen *freedom.* But because of their fear of the unknown, most chose to be executed.

Too many people, when faced with a tragedy of unknown origin or reason, or an adversity of unknown magnitude or length, choose to let go of the hand of God. They abort their faith, because it's easier to choose the firing squad than face the unknown through the black door. They fail to realize that if they would just hold onto the hand of God into the unknown *and persevere through it,* he will guide them through the black door, and they will gain their freedom.

Hananiah, Mishael and Azariah faced a great obstacle in the form of a giant furnace. Their boss forced them to decide between worshiping an idol and living or refusing to bow and dying. Their words echo the determination all people should possess; "Our God is able to deliver us, but even if he doesn't, we will not bow." They refused to let go of the hand of God even though they didn't know why this was happening (they were good people who loved God and served their boss well) or what the end would be. (Daniel 3)

Job echoed this same sentiment in the midst of his trial with the great declaration, "Even though he slay me, yet will I hope in him." (Job 13:15)

Every great person has faced adversity and they have persevered through it! They all had a never-say-die attitude. Perseverance is a habit, and so is quitting. Be a finisher, not just a starter. Anyone can put the armor on; be the one that takes it off! (I Kings 20:11)

It is said of Winston Churchill, "Never have so many owed so much to so few." After World War II broke out, he succeeded the hapless Neville Chamberlin as England's prime minister. He addressed the parliament which was preparing for a long battle with Hitler's Germany. He said,

> "I say to the House as I said to ministers who have joined this government, I have nothing to offer but blood, toil, tears, and sweat. We have before us an ordeal of the most grievous kind. We have before us many, many months of struggle and suffering.

You ask what is our policy? I say it is to wage war
by land, sea and air. War with all our might and with all the
strength God has given us, to wage war against a monstrous
tyranny never surpassed in the dark and lamentable catalogue
of human crime. That is our policy.

As Hitler's war machine mowed across Europe, the British army
suffered a terrible defeat during the Battle of France. They returned home
with their tails between their legs and the island of Britain cowered in fear.
Winston Churchill galvanized a nation with his famous speech over the
airwaves of England:

"The Battle of France is over. I suspect the Battle of
Britain is about to begin. Upon this battle rests the survival
of Christian civilization. The full might and fury of our
enemy must soon be upon us, for Hitler knows that if he is to
win the war, he must break us on this island.

So let us therefore brace ourselves to our duties, and
so bear ourselves so that if the British empire were to last
1000 years men will say, "This was our finest hour."

Where did Winston Churchill learn this resolve? He learned it
from persevering through challenge after challenge. His military career
was spotted with defeat, demotion and discouragement. After a retreat in
Belgium during WWI, he was made the brunt of jokes and stinging
criticism. As the Admiral of the British fleet during WWI he orchestrated
the Gallipoli campaign in Turkey which failed miserably three times.
People blamed him as the author of the navy's losses, the army's setbacks,
the failures in communication, the shortages of ammunition, the
inadequacy of command, and the thousands of casualties. Whatever had
gone wrong was Churchill's fault.

Members of the House demanded Churchill be fired from his post.
On May 26th, the former First Lord of the Admiralty became unemployed.
Despite numerous applications, he could not get a job in government at any
respectable level, so he decided to join the army. He didn't stay there long,

however, in 1917, a friend brought him back to the Cabinet as munitions minister, giving him the opportunity to introduce thousands of tanks to help break the stalemate on the Western front.

After the war, political exile and impotent frustration marked his government career. But with the outbreak of war in September of 1939 he found himself once again the Admiral of the Navy and by May of 1940 he succeeded Neville Chamberlin as prime minister.

With years in the furnace, purified and strengthened by adversity, Hitler now had a worthy adversary. Had he given up anywhere along the way, the world would look entirely different today.

Persevere!

History is full of people who turned their stumbling blocks into stepping stones. Your failures can cause you to stumble or you can learn from them to see farther and stand higher.

Beethoven went deaf as a child. Did he quit? No, he persevered! He overcame his deafness by cutting the legs off his pianos so he could play them on the floor and feel the music through his legs!

Press on! Nothing in the world can take the place of perseverance. Talent will not; nothing is more common than unsuccessful people with talent. Genius will not; unrewarded genius is almost a proverb. Education will not; the world is full of educated derelicts. In the hands of God, persistence and determination are alone invincible.

I love you,
cw

EPILOGUE

As I sit and write this last page, two full years after beginning this project, I have come to realize the great lack of people willing to live their life abandoned to the principles of God.

I have found many who want to live by a mongrel mix of self serving principles with Biblical wisdom thrown in so that many will admire them for their spiritual guru like status. When they encounter a circumstance that challenges their selfishness, they abandon what God would have them do for what they want to do.

When I find myself becoming comfortable in living life to the fullest, God seems to place a flame of purification upon me. When that happens, a new layer of selfishness is revealed. It is then I must renew my efforts to pursue God and His wisdom continually.

My cry, my plea to you is summed up by an anonymous writer who said:

"Do not follow where the path may lead. Follow God, instead, where there is no path and leave a trail."

I love you so very much,
cw

ABOUT THE AUTHOR

Carey Waldie is a husband of one wife (Kim) and a father of two children. He founded Freedom Youth Ministries and served as its director for seven years. He specialized in training and inspiring those who will lead the world into the next millenium. He now pastors a great church, Living Hope Assembly of God in Traverse City, Michigan.

He has a bachelor of Science from Western Michigan University and has served on the faculty of two colleges.

He founded a small business called Fun Science which consults with public elementary schools providing them with laboratory experiments and school assemblies.

He spends his spare time loving his wife, playing with his children, writing, speaking, fishing, playing his guitars and flying airplanes.

For lots more about living life to the fullest, don't miss the website...

PursuingtheBest.com

To Order More Copies of...

Please write clearly

Name: _____

Address:_____

City: _____ **State:**____ **Zip:**_____-____

e-mail_____

Sales tax: Please add 6% for products shipped to Michigan addresses.

Send $14.95 plus $4 shipping to:
Daniel Communications
1242 E M-113
Kingsley, MI 49649

If you are interested in other products from Daniel Communications or having Carey speak at your event write to the above address or see the website:
PursuingtheBest.com